Cambridge Topics in Geography: second series

Editors   Alan R.H. Baker, Emmanuel College, Cambridge
Colin Evans, King's College School, Wimbledon

Weather systems

Leslie F. Musk
School of Geography, University of Manchester

CAMBRIDGE
UNIVERSITY PRESS

Published by the Press Syndicate of the University of Cambridge
The Pitt Building, Trumpington Street, Cambridge CB2 1RP
40 West 20th Street, New York, NY 10011–4211, USA
10 Stamford Road, Oakleigh, Melbourne 3166, Australia

First published 1988
Fifth printing 1994

Printed in Great Britain at the University Press, Cambridge

British Library cataloguing in Publication Data

Musk, Leslie F.
    Weather systems.—(Cambridge topics in
    geography, second series).
    1. Weather
    I. Title
551.5   QC981

ISBN 0 521 26240 2 hardback
ISBN 0 521 27874 0 paperback

Library of Congress catalogue card number: 87–12801

Acknowledgements
The author is grateful for the use of the facilities of the Geography Department at the
University of Manchester, without which this book would not have been written. I
would also like to thank the staff and students of the Department for their advice and
encouragement (both intentional and unintentional) during its preparation. I thank the
staff of the Drawing Office for their assistance, especially Graham Bowden who drew
the majority of the figures.
    I would particularly like to acknowledge the support, encouragement and good
humour of my wife Linda, and son Martin, during the preparation of the book, and
would like to express my gratitude and love to my mother and father, to whom I owe
everything.

Leslie F. Musk
Manchester

SE

Front cover

A METEOSAT image of
Europe, Africa, the
Middle East, the Atlantic
Ocean and eastern
South America, on 15
June 1979 (visible
wavelengths). Note the
shallow depth of the
troposphere on the edge
of the visible disc of the
earth – the depth of the
clouds is hardly
perceptible. The poor
illumination of features
at the bottom of the
image is due to the low
angle of the sun in the
southern hemisphere
winter. *Kindly supplied
by the European Space
Agency*

Contents

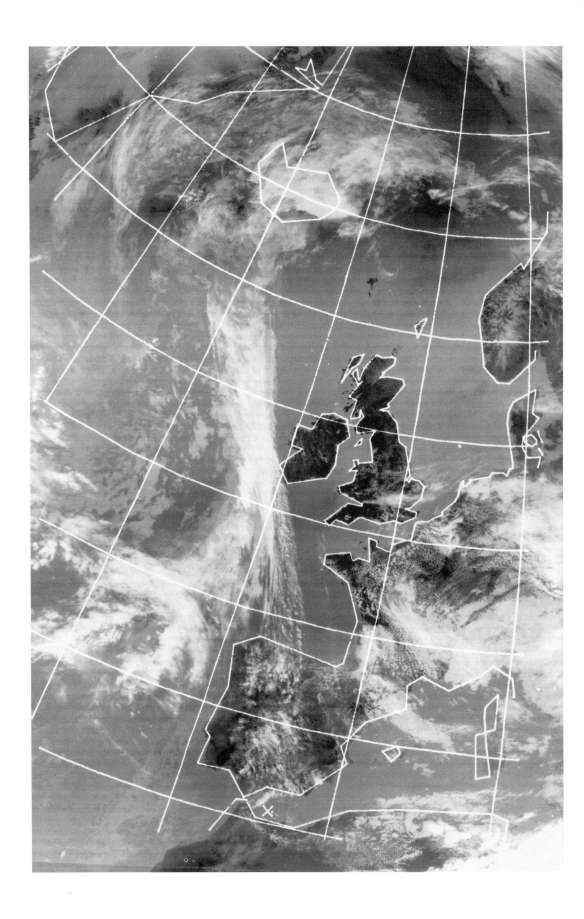

1 Introduction

An understanding of weather systems and of how they develop over time is an important prerequisite for a full understanding of the climate of a particular locality and its inherent variability.

The study of the atmospheric sciences has conventionally been divided into two main subject areas: meteorology and climatology. Definitions are never all-embracing, but meteorology seeks to analyse, explain and ultimately to predict atmospheric processes and their behaviour over *time*. It is perhaps the science of the atmosphere, and thus the science of the weather. Climatology, which is closely dependent on its parent science of meteorology, endeavours to document, analyse and explain the *spatial* variation of meteorological processes on a number of time-scales, as related to the human environment.

The climate of a particular place is a concept; it is a statistical generalisation for the place rather than an actual reality, for it is misleading in most cases to assume that the climate of a place is simply its 'average weather'. For many locations, particularly in temperate latitudes, the average weather is rarely the weather that is experienced at any given time. The weather systems which determine the climate of a locality are governed by many interactions and complex feedback processes involving the underlying surface, whether land, sea, snow, ice, mountains, forest or cities, and the overlying atmosphere with its variable winds and clouds. All of these elements and their interactions are variable over time; climatic variability about the average state is therefore only to be expected. It has been said that in Britain, for example, there is no climate, only weather, implying that the variability is the very esssence of the climate. It is thus perhaps preferable to consider a climate as being the integration of the spectrum of weather likely to be experienced over time at a particular place.

A TIROS-N infrared image of the British Isles and western Europe, 1518 GMT, 17 May 1980. The white tones indicate cold surfaces (e.g. cloud tops), while dark tones indicate warm surfaces (e.g. the land surface of the British Isles). Note the largely clear skies in the area dominated by the blocking high over Scandinavia, the frontal depression cloudiness around the periphery of the high and the relatively cool sea surface temperatures of the North Sea. Compare with Fig. 11.6. *Kindly supplied by the University of Dundee*

Traditionally, almost by historical accident, meteorology has tended to be taught and studied in university departments of physics and mathematics, where students are familiar with the laws of radiation, thermodynamics and hydrodynamics. Because of the spatial and environmental aspects of climatology, the subject has tended to be taught in university departments of geography, where it is studied as a component of the physical environment. Climatology may well have lost more than it has gained from this division, and it is good that the division between the two branches of the atmospheric sciences is now fading. A climate can only be understood in terms of meteorological mechanisms, no matter what the spatial scale. Climatology in its modern form can be looked upon perhaps as *spatial meteorology*.

The science of climatology has undergone a metamorphosis within the last quarter of a century. It has come of age and is one of the growth sciences of the 1980s, receiving increased scientific attention, increased attention from national governments (and the EEC) and increased investment of funds for research. In the first half of the twentieth century it was a strongly geographical subject, concerned with the study of regional climates in terms of the documentation, analysis and classification of climatic statistics. These climatic statistics were often treated as an end in themselves rather than the means to understanding the atmospheric conditions and meteorological processes which produced them. Some valuable documentary work, valuable analysis and valuable research were produced at the time, but the subject was in danger of becoming sterile.

The subject has evolved from this formative stage in its development in two directions. Modern climatology is firstly a dynamic discipline concerned with the problems of analysing and differentiating climates on a variety of spatial scales (global, regional and local) by understanding the underlying meteorological mechanisms involved, and how these are modified by the underlying environment. It is *these* processes which produce the climatic statistics. To take an analogy from the world of soccer, although the classifications of soccer teams into a number of divisions, the tabulations of the football results and their statistical summaries in terms of league tables are of interest and are important, it is even more interesting to study and watch the processes at work on the soccer field which give rise to the results and the statistics.

A second development in the subject is the growing interest in the applied and applicable aspects of climatology, concerned with the interaction of man and his climatic environment. Particular recent attention has been given to the human and economic consequences of climate. Climatic extremes such as droughts, floods, storms, frosts, fogs and blizzards have economic repercussions for industry, transport, agriculture, tourism and even health. Increases in global carbon dioxide concentrations, decreases in stratospheric ozone levels and the regional problems of acid rain may also have serious consequences for Man's well-being, while the nightmare possibility of the 'nuclear winter' is the one scientific experiment which must never be tested.

Linked to these two developments is the study of climatic change (Fig. 1.1). This change may operate on a variety of spatial and temporal scales, and the problems of understanding and modelling the meteorological processes and the complex feedback processes in the earth-atmosphere system, together with the documentation of past climatic change represent some of the most important areas of climatological research today.

One of the main reasons for this evolutionary development of modern climatology has been its ability to use some of the more

Fig. 1.1 The fields of study of modern climatology. Climatology can be studied on a number of scales ranging from the global scale (via the general circulation) through the synoptic scale (via the weather systems portrayed on the synoptic chart) to the meso- and micro-scale where local features (such as urban areas, forests or topography) may distort the prevailing circulation. Each scale generates its own particular form of data, each may influence man and his economic and social well-being (applied climatology), and the climates may themselves change over time.

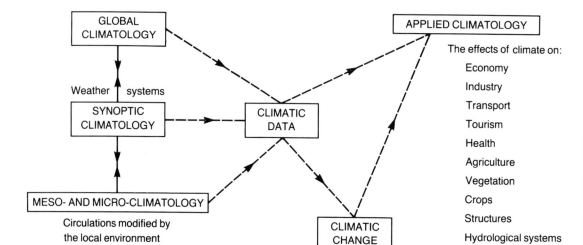

General circulation

GLOBAL CLIMATOLOGY

Weather ↑ systems

SYNOPTIC CLIMATOLOGY

MESO- AND MICRO-CLIMATOLOGY

Circulations modified by the local environment

CLIMATIC DATA

CLIMATIC CHANGE

APPLIED CLIMATOLOGY

The effects of climate on:

Economy

Industry

Transport

Tourism

Health

Agriculture

Vegetation

Crops

Structures

Hydrological systems

notable fruits of twentieth century technology to monitor the global atmosphere. In particular, data derived from the radiosonde, weather radar, aircraft and weather satellites have provided valuable new information on world weather at a variety of spatial scales. The analysis of this and more conventional data has been facilitated and considerably improved with the use of high-speed computers.

In the 1930s the development of the radiosonde balloon allowed the three-dimensional structure of the atmosphere to be monitored on a regular basis in terms of temperature, pressure, wind and humidity. Reconnaissance aircraft flights through and around weather systems (particularly frontal depressions, tropical cyclones and thunderstorms) have provided new information on their three-dimensional structure.

The first weather satellite, TIROS I, was launched on 1 April 1960, marking the beginning of a new era for the subject. Since February 1966, when the first of the ESSA polar-orbiting satellites was launched, climatologists have had the exciting facility of complete global cover of the world's weather by satellite imagery at least once a day, offering new insights into circulations, particularly in areas where conventional meteorological data are either scarce or absent (such as the oceanic areas of the world – where many significant weather systems are spawned). Since December 1966 when the first geostationary satellite was placed in orbit 'hovering' over the equatorial Pacific Ocean, imagery for large sectors of the planet have been available every 30 minutes or so (such as that currently produced by the European Meteosat). In the last decade the observational capabilities of the satellites (particularly in terms of direct and indirect measurement of radiation, vertical temperature profiles, wind and precipitation), the quality of the imagery (in terms of resolution and frequency), and the processing of the satellite imagery, have all improved dramatically. Weather satellite data have provided climatologists with a more complete and detailed view of global weather systems and circulations over both land and sea than has ever before been possible.

Finally, the development of modern, high-speed electronic computer technology permits large quantities of meteorological data to be analysed and mapped both accurately and speedily; it can rectify and grid weather satellite imagery on an operational basis; but above all it can be used to test and develop new models and theories of atmospheric circulations, and to produce short- and long-range weather forecasts.

These new tools have allowed many new fundamental advances to be made in the understanding of the global atmosphere and its operation in recent decades. They have revolutionised the atmospheric sciences. Much new information has been obtained; some questions have been answered, while many new questions have been posed. It is hoped that this book will indicate some of these recent advances in our knowledge of weather systems. It is intended to provide A-level Geography students and those in first-year courses in higher education with a basic knowledge of the structure of weather systems, the processes operating within the systems, and how they evolve over time – the 'bread and butter' of the modern climatologist.

The next six chapters (Part One) should provide the necessary meteorological background for a full understanding of the material on weather systems and the general circulation of the atmosphere contained in Chapters 8 to 15 (Part Two) of the book.

2 The structure and composition of the atmosphere

The earth is not quite a sphere; it is technically an oblate spheroid, with a radius which varies from 6,356.9 km at the poles to 6,378.4 km at the equator. The slight difference is due to the centrifugal effect of the spinning of the planet which causes the equatorial bulge. However, the earth is approximately spherical; the highest mountains are less than 10 km high, which is less than 0.2% of the mean radius of the earth, and are therefore relatively insignificant in global terms. These mountains are of significance in their influence on the atmosphere, however, for the troposphere – the region of the atmosphere which contains the clouds and the weather – is only some 8–16 km deep.

The atmosphere is a mixture of transparent, odourless gases held to the earth by gravity as a shallow envelope. It provides oxygen, the vital support system for human existence; it allows temperature conditions which are far less extreme than those on, say, the moon (on average the same distance from the sun, but lacking an atmosphere) and thus is suitable for life as we know it; it allows us to communicate by sound; but it is only a thin veneer over the planet and is a finite, non-renewable resource that we must conserve and treat with care.

By international convention, the extreme fringe of the earth's atmosphere is assumed to be at 1,000 km above sea-level, but this statement does not emphasise the extremely rarified nature of the gases which exist at such heights. Air compresses easily (unlike the other major fluid on the earth's surface, water), and the effect of gravity is to concentrate the atmosphere near to the surface of the earth so that there is a rapid fall in both air density and pressure in the lowest few kilometres, while at greater heights the decrease gradually slackens. As a result of this compression, about one-half of the atmosphere's mass lies in the 5.6 km nearest the earth, and more than 99% within 40 km. At a height of 100 km the air is so rarified that it is almost a vacuum, and has only one ten-millionth the pressure that it had at ground level. Higher still, weather satellites which orbit the earth at altitudes of some 700 km upwards are almost free from atmospheric drag and heating.

Meteorologists measure atmospheric pressure in units called *millibars* (mb). The normal pressure of the atmosphere at sea-level is about 1013.2 mb; this pressure, caused by the weight of the atmosphere above, is sufficient to support a column of mercury some 30 cm high. Typical pressure values at selected heights in the atmosphere are shown in Fig. 2.1.

While atmospheric pressure and density decrease rapidly with height, the vertical temperature structure of the atmosphere is not as simple as was once believed. At the end of the nineteenth century it seemed reasonable that a decrease in temperature should accompany the lowering of pressure at the outer limits of the atmosphere. The lower temperatures recorded on mountain summits confirmed this assumption. It was not until the very last years of the nineteenth

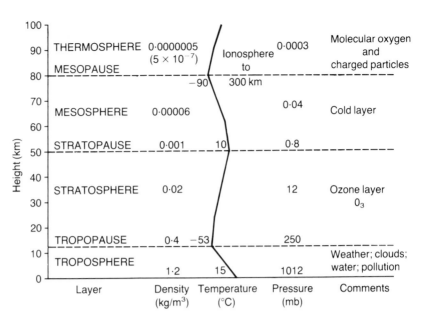

Fig. 2.1 The structure of the atmosphere, indicating the main features of each layer.

Layer	Density (kg/m³)	Temperature (°C)	Pressure (mb)	Comments
THERMOSPHERE	0·0000005 (5 × 10⁻⁷)		0·0003	Molecular oxygen and charged particles
		Ionosphere to 300 km		
MESOPAUSE		−90		
MESOSPHERE	0·00006		0·04	Cold layer
STRATOPAUSE	0·001	10	0·8	
STRATOSPHERE	0·02		12	Ozone layer O₃
TROPOPAUSE	0·4	−53	250	
TROPOSPHERE	1·2	15	1012	Weather; clouds; water; pollution

century that a pioneering French meteorologist, Teisserenc de Bort, made one of the most surprising discoveries in the whole history of meteorology: that temperature does not just continue to decrease to the outer edges of the atmosphere. De Bort worked from an observatory near Versailles and explored the structure of the atmosphere using ballonsondes, which were balloons carrying recording thermometers. On 8 June 1898 he obtained his first significant record, when the temperatures showed the normal decrease to a height of 11.8 km after which they remained constant to 13 km. So ingrained was the assumption that the air temperature should always decrease with height that the data were written off as instrumental errors. He continued his work, however, and by 1902 he had records from 206 balloon ascents, 74 of which attained a height of 14 km, which was a remarkable achievement. From these he was able to show that above a height of about 11 km over Europe, temperatures cease to fall and may even increase with height. He had in fact discovered the stratosphere, a name which he gave to this region of the atmosphere in 1908. Today it is normal to divide the lower part of the atmosphere into two layers: a lower layer called the *troposphere* in which, on average, temperature decreases with height, and a layer above this called the *stratosphere*, where it does not.

Detailed information about the structure of the upper atmosphere has been obtained from balloon and rocket ascents, and more recently from meteorological satellites. This information is summarised in Fig. 2.1. The divisions or layers of the atmosphere are based on changes in the vertical temperature structure of the atmosphere; such changes are largely determined by the ability of each layer to absorb radiation.

Troposphere

The term 'troposphere' stems from the Greek 'tropos' meaning 'turn', which is descriptive of the layer's convective and mixing characteristics. This, the lowest layer of the atmosphere, contains 75% of the total atmospheric mass, and is the most important in terms of our weather, exhibiting the following characteristics:

(1) It has a more or less uniform decrease in temperature with height, averaging some 6.5°C per km, except near the winter pole where a temperature inversion (where the normal decrease in temperature with height is inverted, i.e. temperature increases with height) normally persists above the ice-covered surface.

(2) Except near the surface, where topography greatly influences wind speeds and circulations, it has generally increasing wind speeds with height to a level just beneath the tropopause at the level of the main tropospheric jet streams.

(3) It contains virtually all the water vapour and clouds.

(4) It contains all the convective activity (associated with cloud formation), and has an appreciable vertical component of air motion.

(5) It contains the weather.

(6) It contains nearly all the major atmospheric pollution.

The top of the troposphere is marked by the *tropopause*, an extremely important meteorological phenomenon. It occurs either as a temperature inversion or as an isothermal layer (where temperature remains constant with height), and forms an effective lid on any convection within the troposphere and an upper ceiling for the weather. The height of the tropopause is neither constant in time nor space, and there are especially marked latitudinal and seasonal variations in its altitude. At the equator it usually occurs at about 16–17 km, but only at about 8–9 km in polar regions. Linked to this altitude difference, the temperature at the tropopause falls to as low as −80°C over the equator, while in the polar regions the temperature is on average only −60°C. Thus there is rather a surprising paradox that in the upper troposphere colder temperatures are found over the equator than over the poles; the thicker the depth of the troposphere through which the temperature is decreasing, the colder are the temperatures at the tropopause.

Breaks and distortions in the tropopause occur in the vicinity of the major jet streams and above tropical cyclones. These are areas where interaction occurs between the troposphere and the dry stratosphere above.

Stratosphere

The word 'stratosphere' is derived from the Latin 'stratum' meaning 'a layer' which is descriptive of its stratified, non-convective nature. It extends from the tropopause up to about 50 km (the stratopause), and its main characteristics may be summarised as follows:

(1) In the lower stratosphere (up to about 25 km) temperatures either increase gradually with height or are isothermal; above this level temperatures increase with height to near-surface values.

(2) Winds tend to decrease with height in the lower stratosphere, and then increase with height in the upper stratosphere, being mainly easterly in summer and westerly in winter.

(3) The layer is extremely dry, with no clouds or weather.

(4) It contains a very important gas called ozone (triatomic oxygen, O_3), which although only present in very small amounts (it has a

maximum mixing ratio of ten parts per million) is vital for the existence of life on earth, for it has the important property of absorbing and filtering out ultraviolet radiation of wavelengths 0.23 to 0.32 microns (one micron = one-thousandth of a millimetre or one-millionth of a metre). Ninety per cent of the ozone occurs at levels below 35 km, and it has a maximum concentration at a height of 25 km. The absorption of the ultraviolet radiation leads to a warming of the stratosphere (hence the temperature inversion at the tropopause), with maximum temperatures occurring at the more exposed upper levels at 50 km.

A further protection afforded to humankind by the stratosphere is that this is the layer in which the majority of meteorites burn themselves out as they enter the earth's gravitational field.

One curious feature of the stratosphere occurs above the polar regions. It has been observed that the cold polar night stratosphere can undergo sudden and very dramatic warmings in late winter or early spring, when temperatures may jump from −80°C to −40°C in periods of only two days or so. This is still largely unexplained, but may be caused by subsidence connected with major circulation changes in the high atmosphere at this time of year.

Mesosphere

The mesosphere (from the Greek word 'meso' meaning 'middle') occurs above the stratosphere up to a height of about 80 km. In this layer temperatures again decrease with height to a minimum of about −90°C at the mesopause, the top of the layer. Some of the lowest temperatures observed anywhere in the atmosphere occur at the mesopause, where temperatures are often as low as −100°C. The winter westerlies increase in the lower mesosphere to a maximum strength of 80 metres per second at a height of some 70 km.

Thermosphere

In the thermosphere the temperature again increases with height. In this layer the density of the atmosphere is extremely low, the lower part of the layer being largely composed of nitrogen and oxygen in molecular form, but above 200 km, atomic oxygen predominates. The high temperatures (up to 1200°C) are due to the ability of the atomic oxygen (O) to absorb ultraviolet solar radiation with wavelengths less than 0.2 microns. This is important, for such radiation would cause skin cancer in human beings if it were not filtered out at these levels.

The composition of the atmosphere

Although the atmosphere behaves in a complex manner and its vertical structure is somewhat complex, measurements of its chemical make-up such as those first made by Regnault in 1852 have shown that the composition of clean dry air (air from which water and unnatural pollutants have been removed) is remarkably uniform and constant. If any sample of dry, unpolluted air is taken from any region within 80 km of the earth's surface and analysed, the relative proportions of its major constituent gases are found to vary by no more than a few thousandths of 1%. Such uniformity implies that up to 80 km there must be sufficiently large-scale vertical interaction and mixing to counter the natural tendency of the constituent gases to separate out owing to gravity. Above 80 km the mixing is weak enough to allow molecular diffusion to begin to effect a redistribution of the individual gases, there being progressively greater proportions of the lighter constituents with increasing height.

The air is a mixture of gases rather than one chemical compound; all the components are diffused to give dry air a set of fixed chemical properties as if it were one gas. The composition of this mixture is shown in Table 2.1.

Table 2.1 The composition of dry air.

		% by volume	% by mass
Nitrogen	N_2	78.09	75.51
Oxygen	O_2	20.95	23.15
Argon	Ar	0.93	1.23
Carbon dioxide	CO_2	0.03	0.05

Plus traces of hydrogen, neon, helium, krypton, xenon, ozone, methane and radon

The natural atmosphere is made up of three types of constituents:

1 Permanent gases

Of these, nitrogen and oxygen make up over 99% of the volume. These are mostly passive in meteorological processes, although oxygen is highly active chemically and readily combines with other substances. Argon is an inert gas and does not react chemically with other gases or compounds.

2 Variable gases

Some of these occur naturally and others are the result of local processes such as combustion. There are three main types of variable gases, and these are the most important components in terms of meteorological processes:

(a) Water vapour   This is important in terms of its response to solar radiation, and because it can change phase, naturally occurring in the form of a gas (water vapour), liquid (water) or solid (ice). It contributes up to a maximum of 4% of the volume of atmosphere near the surface, but is virtually absent above 10–12 km. It is of course a very important component of all weather systems.

(b) Carbon dioxide   This gas absorbs long-wave radiation from the earth, and is also important in the photosynthesis process in plants whereby the carbon dioxide we exhale is converted into oxygen by plants. The oceans contain a large store of dissolved carbon dioxide.

(c) Ozone   This is an important constituent of the stratosphere, absorbing ultraviolet radiation and thus raising the temperature of the layer.

3 Non-gaseous constituents

These include dust, smoke, salt particles from the evaporation of sea spray and condensed water. They are present in a wide range of concentrations, from a few to millions of particles per cubic metre of air, and all affect the transmission of radiation through the atmosphere.

One way in which the composition of the atmosphere does change is with time rather than with space. Opinion is largely divided on the nature and extent of changes in the composition of the atmosphere in the last thousand million years. Geological processes such as volcanic action and the deposition of limestone and coal must have had some effect. There is growing evidence, however, to suggest that the actions of human beings have had a significant influence on the atmosphere's delicate chemical balance in recent years in two areas.

Increasing carbon dioxide concentrations

It is generally accepted that the atmospheric concentration of carbon dioxide in the late-nineteenth century was probably about 290 parts per million (ppm). Careful measurements at remote observatories away from industrial pollution, such as that on Mauna Loa in the Pacific, indicate that the annual average concentration of CO_2 had increased to 341 ppm in 1982 (see Fig. 2.2), an increase of 15%. Observations at the South Pole and elsewhere confirm these levels, and the increase in CO_2 concentrations is now considered to be approximately 0.3% per annum.

One of the main reasons for this is the burning of carbon-based fuels such as coal, natural gas and oil; large-scale deforestation (as in the Amazon Basin) has been a further contributory factor. The consumption of carbon-based fuels has doubled every decade since 1900, and Man now adds some 18 billion tonnes of CO_2 per year to the atmosphere from the use of these fuels. This amount is not large compared to the huge natural fluxes of CO_2 within forests and the

Fig. 2.2 Changes in atmospheric carbon dioxide concentrations at Mauna Loa, Hawaii, 1958–82. The overall change from 315 ppm in 1958 to 341 ppm in 1982 is clearly evident. The strong seasonal variation is due to the removal of the CO_2 from the atmosphere in the northern hemisphere's spring and summer, during the growing season, producing an annual minimum; decay of the biomass leads to an annual maximum in autumn and winter.

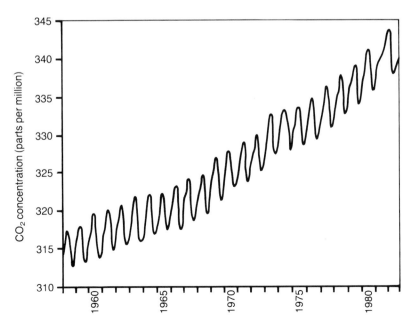

absorption within the world oceans (a major store of carbon), but about 50% of the artificial input remains there. If the current rate of increase continues, by the year 2000 the increase in the CO_2 content of the atmosphere will be nearly 25%, and by 2030–2080 CO_2 levels will have doubled. The critical problem is that such an increase has the capacity to alter the global climate.

Carbon dioxide is transparent to incoming short-wave solar radiation, but absorbs some of the long-wave infrared radiation emitted from the earth to space (in the region of 13.8 to 15.4 microns) which would otherwise be lost. This warms the atmosphere, producing the so-called 'greenhouse effect'. The overall effect of this is that the mean temperature at the surface of the earth is about 15°C; the moon, at the same mean distance from the sun, but lacking an atmosphere, has a mean surface temperature of -16°C.

Climatologists are in general agreement that increased CO_2 concentrations will lead to an increase in surface temperatures, but it is presently impossible to predict the timing and the amount of increase with certainty because of the many feedback mechanisms which operate in the earth-atmosphere system; the amounts vary according to the predictive model chosen. It is generally felt, however, that a doubling of CO_2 levels from 300 to 600 ppm would cause an average surface temperature rise of 2°–3°C, with more warming at high latitudes (up to 7°–8°C at 80°N) due to the decrease in areas of snow and ice which would result. Such a change would have serious repercussions for low-lying areas which might become flooded. It is certain that we are currently changing CO_2 levels as a by-product of industrial activity, but as yet the full implications of these changes are still undergoing active research.

Decreasing stratospheric ozone concentrations

As already outlined, ozone (O_3) is a minor constituent of the stratosphere but a very crucial one. The amount present at any one time depends on a balance between the rate at which ozone is being created and the rate at which it is being destroyed. Usually there is a natural equilibrium between the processes involved.

There is evidence, however, that the natural equilibrium could be interfered with by Man, unintentionally increasing the rate of erosion or loss of ozone in two ways. Supersonic aircraft fly in the stratosphere and emit NO and NO_2 in hot exhaust gases into a stable atmospheric environment which does not mix very much with the troposphere; hence any products emitted into this layer may remain airborne for years rather than weeks. Under such conditions the following reactions occur:

$$NO + O_3 \rightarrow NO_2 + O_2 \text{ and } NO_2 + O \rightarrow NO + O_2$$

This could deplete the ozone layer and increase the amount of ultraviolet radiation reaching the earth's surface to levels which would be unsuitable for growing crops and which would cause an increase in the incidence of skin cancer. At the moment, however, such a danger is small owing to the few aircraft operating at this level.

The second potential danger to the ozone layer arises from the use of certain chemicals known as chlorofluorocarbons. Such gases are used as propellants in a wide range of aerosol sprays including hair sprays, deodorants, paint sprays and fly killers, and some 6 billion are produced each year. Although the chlorofluorocarbons are non-toxic and inert in the troposphere, they are carried up to the stratosphere by the atmosphere's natural mixing and there they are decomposed (under conditions of ultraviolet radiation) into a free chlorine atom, which can react with ozone breaking it down into ordinary oxygen:

$$Cl + O_3 \rightarrow ClO + O_2$$

The United States National Research Council's Committee on Impacts of Stratospheric Change recommended that chlorofluorocarbons should not be used in aerosols after January 1978, while the American Food and Drug Administration banned them from interstate trade from April 1979. Sweden was the first country to ban the use of these propellants in 1979. In 1982 the World Meteorological Organisation issued the following statement, summarising current views:

'Without regard for other modifying factors, the long-term steady-state effect of a continued release [of chlorofluorocarbons] at the 1977 world rate of release would be about 5–10% average ozone depletion and the full range of uncertainty could be larger.'

There will be a time-lag for the maximum ozone reduction after emissions have stopped; furthermore, there may well be a persistence of the reduction effect for several decades after this.

The problem was further highlighted when in 1985 a 'hole' the size of the United States was discovered in the ozone layer over the Antarctic. Here there has been a reduction in ozone concentrations of some 50% since 1979. The situation may be unique, but scientists are working fast to identify the exact causes.

3 Energy in the atmosphere

It was Aristotle some 2,000 years ago who first observed that the difference in heating between the equatorial and polar regions of the earth is the ultimate driving force for the general circulation of the atmosphere. This has never been doubted, for the sun provides 99.7% of the heat energy required for the physical processes operating in the earth-atmosphere system (the remainder mainly arising from geothermal energy which manifests itself in volcanic eruptions and hot springs, together with man-made heat unintentionally released into the atmosphere).

The energy in the atmosphere appears in four forms:

(1) *Kinetic energy* – the energy which the moving atmosphere possesses by virtue of its *motion*.

(2) *Potential energy* – the energy which a body of air possesses by virtue of its *position*, owing to the body doing work to overcome the earth's gravity.

(3) *Latent heat energy* – the heat energy absorbed and held in storage in a liquid or solid during the processes of condensation and freezing respectively; energy is required to melt ice (i.e. change its *state*) and evaporate water, and such energy is released when the water vapour subsequently condenses or the water freezes.

(4) *Thermal energy* – the energy stored within a mass of air owing to its thermal condition and consequent molecular motion; such energy only manifests itself where there is a temperature difference between the mass and its surroundings.

The earth can be thought of as a gigantic but imperfect heat engine. It receives a large energy input from the sun, uses some of it to maintain the atmospheric circulation against the effect of friction, uses another fraction to sustain life on earth, and radiates the remainder back to space. The thermal energy is transferred in the atmosphere in five ways:

(1) *Convection* – the heated atmosphere is physically transported from one position to another, particularly in rising thermals.

(2) *Conduction* – heat energy is transferred through the medium by molecular impact, while the medium itself (air) does not move. The more energetic, hotter molecules set their neighbours into more violent agitation by colliding with them. This is a relatively slow process in air, but quite rapid in soil or water.

(3) *Latent heat transfer* – the heat energy absorbed by the melting or evaporation of water in one location may be released elsewhere in the atmosphere when the water vapour subsequently condenses or the water freezes.

(4) *Radiation* – energy is transferred by the process of waves moving through space at the velocity of light (3×10^8 m/sec).

(5) *Advection* – heat energy may be transferred horizontally by the mass movement of the atmosphere (the winds); for example, southerly winds transfer warm air polewards in the northern hemisphere.

Every body with a temperature above absolute zero (0° Kelvin or −273° Celsius) emits radiation in all directions in the form of waves which travel through space at the uniform speed of 3×10^8 metres per second (186,000 miles per second). Different types of radiation have their own characteristic *wavelength*, λ (the distance between successive troughs or crests of the wave motion, as shown in Fig. 3.1). Such wavelengths range in size from several kilometres for long radio waves to billionths of a centimetre for X-rays. Most of the radiation from the sun and the earth has wavelengths in the vicinity of those of visible light, and the standard unit for measuring this is the micron (μm), where one micron is one-millionth of a metre (10^{-6} m) or one-thousandth of a millimetre (10^{-3} mm). Ninety-nine per cent of the sun's radiation falls between the wavelengths 0.15 and 4.0 μm.

The behaviour of radiation is summarised in two laws (see Note, p. 23): the amount of radiation emitted by a body is proportional to the fourth power of its absolute temperature (T^4), and the maximum emission from a body is in a wavelength inversely proportional to its temperature ($1/T$). Thus the sun emits much more radiation than the earth (because of its temperature), with maximum intensity at shorter wavelengths than that emitted from the earth. In meteorology, solar radiation is frequently referred to as short-wave, and terrestrial radiation to space is often referred to as long-wave (or infrared).

Solar radiation

The sun is the source of all radiation on earth. It is radiating continually in all directions to space, and the earth intercepts only a fraction (1/2,210-millionth) of its total output from a distance of some 149,450,000 km. If the earth could be viewed from the sun, it would appear as just a speck in the solar system, with a diameter of a 5p piece observed from a distance of 265 metres!

Fig. 3.2 shows the spectral distribution of solar radiation, in terms of what is received at the outer edge of the atmosphere. The sun emits radiation over a wide range of wavelengths, but 99% of it lies in the region of 0.15–4.0 μm (short-wave radiation); 9% of the radiation occurs in wavelengths of less than 0.36 μm, too short to be observed by eye and known as *ultraviolet*, 45% lies within the visible part of the spectrum 0.36–0.7 μm, and 46% occurs at wavelengths which are too long to be seen, but can be felt, in the *infrared* region. The radiation spectrum peaks in intensity in the middle of the visible part of the spectrum at approximately 0.5 μm; the sun therefore appears white, a mixture of its component colours.

The amount of *insolation* (or *in*coming *sol*ar radi*ation*) received by the earth is governed by four astronomical factors:

(1) *The solar constant* The flux (or amount) of solar radiation at the outer boundary of the earth's atmosphere, received on a surface perpendicular to the direction of the sun (at the mean earth-sun distance) is known as the *solar constant*. This has a value of 1,360 $\pm$ 20 watts per square metre (Wm^{-2}), (or 1.95 cal cm^{-2} min^{-1}), according to long-period records from established observatories. However, recent estimates of the solar constant from the Nimbus-6 earth radiation budget experiment reported in 1977, suggest a value of 1,392 Wm^{-2}, some 1.6% higher. Variations in this value may be caused by gradual long-period changes in the earth's orbit around the sun (due, for example, to the gravitational pull of other planets in the solar system), and have been attributed by some as the possible cause of Ice Ages.

Fig. 3.1 The wavelength λ is the distance between successive wave peaks or troughs.

Fig. 3.2 Spectral distribution of short-wave solar and long-wave terrestrial radiation. Note that both scales are logarithmic; the same graphs plotted on arithmetic scales are shown in the inset.

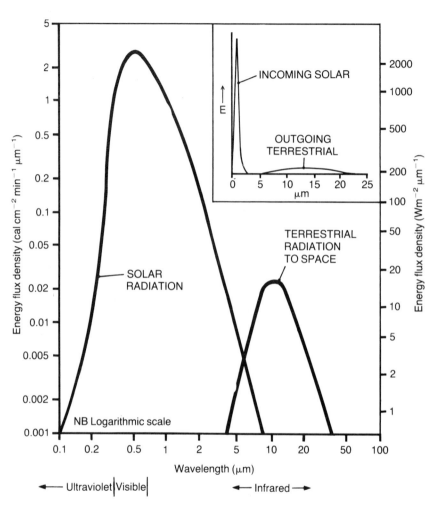

(2) *Distance from the sun* Because of the eccentricity of the earth's orbit around the sun, causing variations in the earth's distance from the sun, differences of up to 6% occur in the value of the solar constant according to the time of year. At present it has a maximum value of about 1,403 Wm^{-2} (2.01 cal cm^{-2} min^{-1}) at the perihelion on 3 January (when the earth is at a distance of 147×10^6 km from the sun), and 1,312 Wm^{-2} (1.88 cal cm^{-2} min^{-1}) at the aphelion on 6 July (when the solar distance is some 152×10^6 km). In theory this should make the northern hemisphere winters slightly milder than the southern hemisphere winters, and southern hemisphere summers warmer than those in the northern

hemisphere, but such seasonal contrasts are usually masked by other factors linked to the atmospheric circulations and land/sea temperature differences in the two hemispheres.

(3) *Altitude of the sun* The angle between the sun's rays and the earth's surface greatly affects insolation levels. The greater the sun's altitude in the sky the more concentrated is the radiation intensity for a given area on the earth's surface, and the smaller will be the depletion of the beam due to absorption and reflection by the atmosphere. Consider the difference in light intensity obtained by shining a torch directly on to a wall at right-angles, and that obtained when the same torch is shone on to the wall at an acute angle. In the earth-atmosphere system the crucial factors are the latitude, the season and the time of day.

(4) *Length of day* Solar radiation is only available to the earth during daylight hours. Clearly the longer the day the greater the amount of insolation a given location will be able to receive. This is governed solely by latitude and time of year.

There are four terrestrial factors which tend to deplete the theoretical amount of insolation at the earth's surface:

(1) *Depletion of insolation due to the atmosphere* Radiation passing through the atmosphere is subject to both scattering and absorption. The scattering of radiation by air molecules disperses the radiation in all directions, so that the radiation received at the earth's surface comes from all parts of the sky, and the daytime sky appears bright.

Like all gases, the different components of the air absorb certain wavelengths of radiation and are transparent to others. Most of the short-wave ultraviolet radiation (which is harmful to life on earth) is absorbed in its path through the upper atmosphere. Solar radiation of wavelengths greater than 0.34 μm, where the intensity of the radiation is greatest, is hardly absorbed by the atmosphere at all, and is transmitted almost undiminished, apart from the effect of scattering. That part not reflected is then absorbed by the ground, which raises its temperature. This in turn tends to heat the air above it by conduction and convection.

(2) *The effect of cloud surfaces* Cloud cover can form a significant barrier to the penetration of direct solar radiation, but this effect depends upon the amount of cloud present, its type and its thickness. The amount of depletion depends on the amount of reflection, absorption (by the ice and water particles present) and scattering (producing diffuse radiation at the surface). The reflectivity (*albedo*) of different cloud types varies greatly. High-level clouds and cloudsheets have an albedo of 21%, middle-level cloudsheets (between 3 and 6 km) an albedo of 48%, low-level cloudsheets an albedo of 69% and deep convective clouds an albedo of 70%, although this depends very much on cloud thickness.

A very small percentage (approximately 1.5%) of the incoming radiation is actually absorbed by the clouds themselves. However, by its properties of reflection and absorption, a sheet of cloud will prevent some of the long-wave radiation from earth being lost to space at night. The presence of clouds, therefore, considerably diminishes the diurnal range of temperature.

(3) *The effect of land and sea surfaces on insolation*   The radiation absorbed by the surface of the earth depends upon the nature of the surface, in particular its albedo and its heat capacity. The albedo of a surface may be defined as the fraction of the intensity of the reflected to the incoming radiation. Typical values for land surfaces are 5–45%, while forests have an albedo of 5–20%, grass 10–20%, desert sand 25–30% and fresh-fallen snow 75–95%. Water surfaces normally have low values of albedo, but these depend on the roughness of the water surface and the angle of the sun. When the sun is high in the sky, the albedo of a calm water surface, such as the sea, may be only 5–10%, but when the sun is low in the sky, much higher percentages (over 50%) may be reflected back to space by the water surface. The radiation that is absorbed by a water body is usually absorbed over a depth of up to ten metres, for water has a high transparency factor. The heat energy may then be carried down to considerable depths by the turbulent mixing in three dimensions of the water by the action of waves and currents.

The response of the land surface to insolation depends upon the *heat capacity* of the material that comprises the surface. The heat capacity is the heat (in calories) required to raise the temperature of the material by 1°C (*specific heat* is the heat required to raise the temperature of one gram of the substance by 1°C). The specific heat of water is much greater than the specific heat of most other commonly-occurring substances in the natural environment (1.0 cal gm^{-1} deg C^{-1} or 4.18 J gm^{-1} K^{-1}, compared with the specific heat of sand, for example, which is 0.2 cal gm^{-1} deg C^{-1} or 0.84 J gm^{-1} K^{-1}). Thus water must absorb five times as much heat energy to raise its temperature by the same amount as a comparable mass of sand. When cooling, the same amount of heat is released; in this way the oceans act as a very effective thermal reservoir for much of the world's heat energy. The range of temperatures over ocean areas is therefore much less than the range over land surfaces, and the difference in thermal response between land and sea areas helps to explain the continentality effect on the large scale and sea-breezes on the local scale.

(4) *The effects of elevation and aspect on insolation*   Both elevation and aspect are very important factors in determining the amount of insolation received at a particular location on the local scale. A hillside location changes the angle of incidence of the sun's rays upon the earth's surface, and the aspect determines the degree of shading or exposure at a particular site. The slope and aspect together will therefore determine the period of direct solar radiation and its total for a given latitude and time of year. This is illustrated in Table 3.1, which compares the daily insolation on north- and south-facing slopes at a latitude of 45°N on three days of the year with those likely to be experienced on a horizontal surface. At such a latitude the total daily insolation will be increased on a slope with a southerly aspect by 2% in midsummer, by 29% at the equinoxes and by 93% in midwinter (assuming a slope angle of 20°), while a northerly exposure decreases the insolation by 14%, 39% and 97% respectively.

The chief effects of altitude are to lengthen the period of direct radiation each day, while because of the smaller depth of atmosphere above a high-altitude site, the depletion of insolation by the atmosphere and its constituents will be reduced.

Table 3.1 A comparison of the daily insolation on north- and south-facing slopes at 45°N on three days of the year (cal cm^{-2} day^{-1}) compared with the insolation received on a horizontal surface.

Date	Horizontal surface	Southerly slope of 20°		Northerly slope of 20°	
	cal	cal	%	cal	%
22 June	577	590	102	495	86
21 March	315	408	129	191	61
22 December	68	131	193	2	3

(1 cal cm^{-2} day^{-1} = 0.484 Wm^{-2})
Source: Crowe (1971) *Concepts in Climatology* (Longman) p. 28.

Terrestrial radiation

Whereas the sun emits short-wave radiation to space, the earth radiates long-wave or infrared radiation to space, principally in the wavelengths 5–80 μm, with a peak emission at 10 μm (see Fig. 3.2). The total emission is some 350–400 Wm^{-2}, which is much less than the solar output.

The atmosphere is only very partially transparent to the long-wave radiation from the earth's surface. It absorbs 94% of the long-wave emission, allowing only some 6% to escape directly to space (see Fig. 3.3). The radiant energy absorbed by the atmosphere is partially re-radiated back to the earth surface, thus increasing the total energy received there, and as a consequence raising the surface temperature by some 38°C above the value it would have if there were no atmosphere.

Water vapour and carbon dioxide are the main constituents of the atmosphere that absorb the outgoing long-wave radiation. Water vapour absorbs principally in the wavelengths 5.5–8.0 μm and beyond 20 μm, while carbon dioxide absorbs at wavelengths 4–5 μm and 14–16 μm. The band between 8 and 13 μm is almost transparent to long-wave radiation, and is called the *atmospheric window*. Radiation from the ground or from the cloud tops passes directly through the troposphere and out to space almost unimpeded. This fact is used by infrared sensors on board meteorological satellites to detect surface and cloud top temperatures from space.

The radiation and energy budget of the earth-atmosphere system

Figure 3.3 shows how the global radiation and energy balances are achieved in the earth-atmosphere system. Assuming an arbitrary figure of 100 units of energy arriving at the top of the atmosphere (the incoming flux of solar radiation), the figures indicate how these 100 units are used and distributed.

It can be seen that the incoming short-wave radiation is not all used by the earth and its atmosphere. Thirty per cent of the incident solar radiation is reflected back to space by the clouds and, to a lesser extent, the earth's surface. This energy is therefore lost from the system. Of the remaining 70 units, 20 are absorbed by the clouds and the atmosphere, and 50 by the oceans and land. This is used partly to heat directly the overlying atmosphere (6 units), and partly to maintain the hydrological cycle through evaporation (24 units), heating the atmosphere when the water is subsequently condensed in clouds. The remaining 20 units are used to heat the underlying surface and will be lost subsequently as long-wave (infrared) radiation to the atmosphere (14 units) and to outer space (6 units).

A small amount of the heat energy absorbed by the atmosphere (about 1 unit) is converted into kinetic energy to maintain the atmospheric and oceanic general circulations against friction. Finally, some 64 units of energy are radiated back to space by the atmosphere. It will be seen that the energy inputs and outputs to and from all parts of the system are in balance (otherwise they would either heat up or cool down over time); 100 units arrive at the outer edge of the atmosphere and 100 units are eventually lost to space; the earth gains 50 units and loses a total of 50.

Fig. 3.3 The radiation and energy budget of the earth-atmosphere system, indicating average values for the entire globe.

The heat balance of the global atmosphere

Not every part of the earth balances its budget in the vertical as described above. There is an equally important energy transfer required in a horizontal sense from equatorial regions towards the poles.

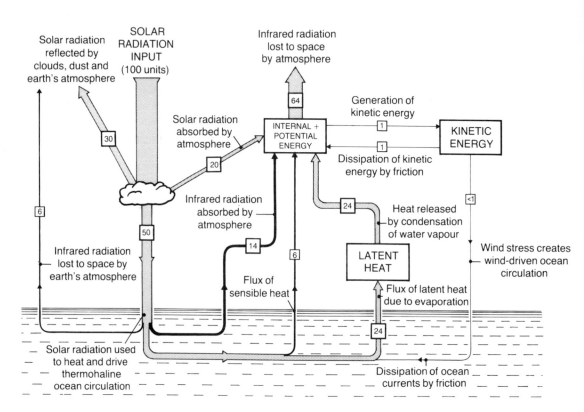

Analysis reveals that for the earth-atmosphere system as a whole the incoming short-wave radiation on average exceeds the outgoing long-wave radiation equatorwards of 35° latitude, while the long-wave radiation exceeds the short-wave radiation polewards of 35° in both hemispheres. Since all latitudes tend to maintain the same mean annual temperature from year to year, there must be a continual poleward transfer of energy from those latitudes equatorwards of 35° – where there is an excess of radiant energy – to those latitudes polewards of 38° – where there is a deficit, as shown in Fig. 3.4. The transfer of this energy, which reaches a maximum at latitude 35°, is the prime function of the general circulation of the atmosphere (see Chapter 15). Between 70% and 90% of this necessary energy transfer is in fact performed by atmospheric circulations; the rest is transferred by ocean currents.

Fig. 3.4 The latitudinal distribution of net radiation at the outer edge of the earth-atmosphere system, and the poleward energy transfer required to offset the latitudinal imbalance.

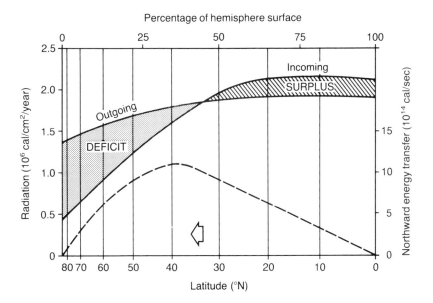

Note

The behaviour of radiation is summarised by two important laws:

(1) *Stefan-Boltzmann Law* The flux of radiation from a black body (i.e. one that emits the maximum amount of radiation for its temperature at all wavelengths) is directly proportional to the fourth power of its absolute temperature:

Flux, $F = \sigma T^4$

$\sigma =$ Stefan-Boltzmann constant $= 8.14 \times 10^{-11}$ ly min^{-1}K^{-4}
$= 5.67 \times 10^{-8}$ Wm^{-2}K^{-4}

(2) *Wien Displacement Law* The wavelength of the maximum intensity of emission λ_{max} from a black body is inversely proportional to the absolute temperature T of the body:

$$\lambda_{max} = \frac{2897}{T} \times 10^{-6} m = \frac{2897}{T} \mu m$$

4 Atmospheric motion

Wind is air in motion over the surface of the earth. It moves in a spectrum of eddies ranging in scale from the turbulence visible within cigarette smoke to swirls of continental dimensions as contained within cyclones and anticyclones. It acts to equalise horizontal differences in pressure, temperature or humidity, although such equalisation is never attained, for new differences are continually being created. The behaviour of each eddy, however ephemeral or however large, obeys known physical laws; this is the fundamental assumption upon which all modern meteorology and weather forecasting is based.

It should be emphasised at the outset, however, that weather systems are not isolated entities. All atmospheric motions are interconnected by the general circulation of the atmosphere; the surface flows and upper flows are linked by patterns of ascending and descending motion, and major disturbances in one area may well have repercussions elsewhere.

Isobars and pressure

The horizontal distribution of mean *sea-level* pressure (values are corrected to sea-level equivalents to eliminate variations arising from differences in altitude of the weather stations) is usually portrayed on synoptic charts by means of *isobars*, which are lines connecting places with equal pressure. The isobars are normally drawn at 4-mb intervals, but there are no rules about this.

It is usually found that when such pressure maps are drawn, the isobars form closed patterns around centres of high pressure (known as *anticyclones*) or low pressure (cyclones or *depressions*); the isobars are usually smooth curves except in the vicinity of fronts, where major atmospheric discontinuities reveal themselves at the surface as discontinuities in the pressure field. An outward extension of high pressure into a region of predominantly low pressure is known as a *ridge*, while an extension of low pressure into a region of higher pressure is known as a *trough*, as shown in Fig. 4.1. An area of almost uniform pressure between two highs and two lows is known as a *col*. Lines joining places with equal barometric tendency (where the pressure is rising or falling by the same amount in a given period of time) are known as *isallobars*. Normally the absolute difference in pressure between the centres of adjacent highs and lows is small, and sea-level pressure values outside the range 950–1050 mb are rare.

If one examines the patterns of pressure distribution and wind on a surface chart, it will become apparent that the wind blows approximately parallel to the isobars with the lowest pressure to the *left* of the direction of the wind in the northern hemisphere, and the wind speed is greatest where the isobars are most closely spaced. The first relationship was originally formulated by the Dutch meteorologist Buys Ballot in 1857, who showed that 'if you stand with your back to the wind in the Northern Hemisphere, the lowest pressure lies to your left, but to your right in the Southern Hemisphere' (Buys Ballot's Law). In other words, winds blow clockwise around an anticyclone in the northern hemisphere and anticlockwise around a depression (but vice versa in the southern hemisphere).

Fig. 4.1 Some common patterns of sea-level isobars. Note that the isobars have been drawn at 10-mb intervals and that no fronts are shown.

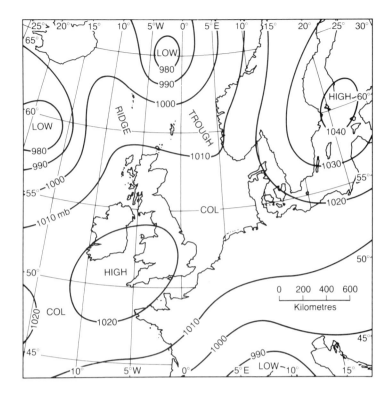

Why should this happen? In areas of undulating topography, water will always flow downhill from high ground to low ground across the contours, under the influence of gravity. In the atmosphere, however, the apparent paradox exists that the air tends to flow *along* the pressure contours *at right-angles* to the pressure gradient force causing the flow.

It is important to note at this point that, in meteorology, wind directions are always quoted in terms of the direction from which a wind is blowing, rather than the direction to which it is moving, so that a westerly wind is one blowing from the west. Wind speeds are normally quoted in units of knots or metres per second (where $1 \text{ m s}^{-1} = 3.6 \text{ km h}^{-1} = 1.94 \text{ knots} = 2.24 \text{ mph}$).

There are two types of forces operating on the atmosphere to produce the patterns of winds:
(1) *Driving forces* These forces exist regardless of whether or not the air is moving:
   (a) in the vertical, gravity (acting downwards) and the vertical pressure gradient force (acting upwards) – these act in opposite directions and normally there is a balance between the two, so that *on average* vertical motions are gradual;
   (b) in the horizontal, the horizontal pressure gradient force arises from spatial differences in atmospheric pressure.
(2) *Steering forces* These arise as the motion of the air begins:
   (a) the rotation of the earth about its axis produces the so-called Coriolis force, which deflects all bodies, including air, to the right of their initial motion in the northern hemisphere, and to the left in the southern hemisphere;
   (b) according to the degree of roughness of the surface over which the air is flowing, frictional forces will act to reduce the wind speed predicted from the prevailing pressure gradient and to produce a component of flow across the isobars; and

(c) if the winds flow around curved isobars, a centripetal acceleration will produce a further force to deflect the motion inwards towards the centre of rotation to maintain the curved flow.

Conservation of angular momentum

Any body of air that moves polewards over the surface of the earth develops an increase in its westerly component of motion. Conversely, any body of air that moves equatorwards must acquire an increased easterly component of motion. This arises from the principle of the conservation of angular momentum on a rotating earth.

All bodies in motion possess a property called *momentum*. The momentum M of a body moving in a straight line is a product of its mass m and its velocity v, or $\quad$ M = mv

If a body is moving in a curved or circular path, its *angular momentum*, M_a, is defined as the product of the body's mass m, its linear velocity v and the radius of curvature of its path, r, or
$$M_a = mvr$$
If the body's angular velocity ω is known, then as $v = \omega r$, an alternative formula for M_a is $\quad M_a = m(\omega r)r = m\omega r^2$

Unless an unbalanced force acts on a body to change its angular momentum, the angular momentum of that body will remain constant over time. This is an important concept known as the *Principle of conservation of angular momentum*. A simple example of this principle can be obtained by whirling a ball on the end of a piece of string in a circle; the ball on the end of the string has a certain mass m, a velocity v, and a radius of curvature r, determined by the length of the string. If the length of the string is reduced (by winding the string around an arm, for example) the mass of the ball will remain constant, but the value of r decreases; to compensate, its velocity v will increase.

Applying this principle to the atmosphere, the surface of the earth is rotating in space at a known velocity about the axis of rotation, shown in Fig. 4.2. This velocity is a product of the earth's angular velocity (360° every 24 hours, or 2π radians every 24 hours) and the distance from the earth's axis of rotation. For any latitude ϕ, this distance is equal to $r\cos\phi$, where r is the radius of the earth ($r\cos\phi$ decreases from r at the equator to zero at the poles). Thus if the atmosphere has no relative motion with respect to the earth (i.e. a state of calm), it nevertheless possesses angular momentum about the earth's axis owing to the earth's rotation in space of $v_\phi r\cos\phi$, where v_ϕ is the linear velocity of the surface of the earth at latitude ϕ about the earth's axis (as shown in Fig. 4.2).

Normally the atmosphere is moving with respect to the surface of the earth as wind. The *absolute angular momentum* of the body of air will then be the sum of the angular momentum which it would have if it were still (i.e. the angular momentum of the earth's surface at that particular latitude) plus the angular momentum due to its own rotation about the earth's axis. If the west-east component of motion of the wind (i.e. the component of motion in the same sense as the spin of the earth) is V, then the absolute angular momentum of a body of air moving over the surface of the earth will be
$$mVr\cos\phi + v_\phi r\cos\phi \text{ or } m(V + v_\phi)\, r\cos\phi$$

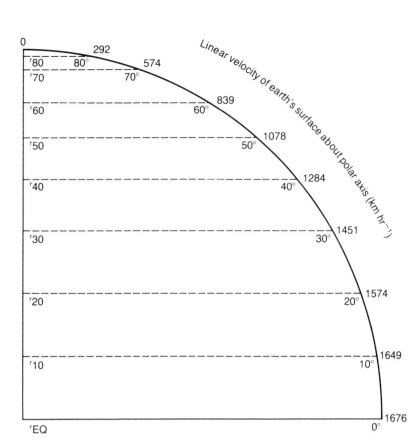

Fig. 4.2   The linear velocity of the earth's surface about the polar axis, at 10° latitude intervals.

r_{30} = radius of latitudinal circle 30° ($r_\theta = r_{EQ} \cos\phi$)

To illustrate the application of this principle of the conservation of angular momentum by the atmosphere, let us put some figures into the formula and investigate the behaviour of the Hadley circulation of the tropics. If it is assumed that air rises at the equator in the Hadley circulation and (for the sake of simplicity) is stationary with respect to the surface there (i.e. V=0), its absolute motion about the earth's axis will be a speed v_ϕ (here v_o) of 1,676 kmh^{-1} = 465 m/sec (the speed of the earth's surface) from west to east in space. As the air moves polewards aloft, its distance from the earth's axis decreases. When it reaches latitude 30° (the vicinity of the westerly subtropical jet stream aloft), this distance will be 0.866 of its original value (as rcos 30=0.866r). To maintain the constancy of its angular momentum, its 'velocity × radius of curvature per unit mass' must remain constant, so its absolute velocity must increase to 1,935 kmh^{-1} (i.e. 1,676 × 1/0.866) to compensate for the reduction in radius. The speed of the earth's surface at latitude 30°, however, is only 1,451 kmh^{-1} (i.e. reduced by the same proportion as the radius, see Fig. 4.2). Thus if the absolute angular momentum is to be conserved, the air would be moving west to east relative to the earth's surface at a speed of 484 kmh^{-1} (or 1,935 − 1,451 kmh^{-1}) or some 268 knots. This overestimates the velocity of the westerly subtropical jet stream, as it does not incorporate the effects of internal turbulence and friction. The conservation of absolute angular momentum argument is the main theoretical explanation of the high-level subtropical jet stream at the poleward limit of the Hadley circulation.

Coriolis force

In 1889, Ferrel summarised the effect of the Coriolis force quite succinctly when he stated: 'if a body moves in any direction upon the earth's surface, there is a deflecting force arising from the earth's rotation which deflects it to the right in the northern hemisphere and to the left in the southern hemisphere'. This 'deflecting force arising from the earth's rotation' may be considered to be a consequence of moving objects, such as masses of air conserving their angular momentum with respect to the surface of the earth, which is itself rotating. Bodies moving over the surface of the earth on straight-line paths are apparently deflected to the right of their line of motion in the northern hemisphere. There must be a force that generates the deflection. This apparent force is known as the *Coriolis force*, after the nineteenth-century Greek mathematician Coriolis who formulated the idea. The Coriolis force (perhaps better called the Coriolis effect) is an apparent force which needs to be introduced into any analysis of motion on a rotating frame of reference such as the earth to explain the apparent deflections of straight-line trajectories.

This apparent deflecting force will act on all bodies moving over the surface of the earth, and unless compensated will cause them to curve continuously to the right in the northern hemisphere and to the left in the southern hemisphere. Normally only the horizontal component of this force is considered; it always acts at right-angles to the direction of motion of the body. It cannot change the speed of movement, only its direction of motion.

The geostrophic wind

Above the layer of the atmosphere affected by surface friction (approximately 1–1.5 km), the horizontal flow of the atmosphere tends to be smooth and reasonably uniform. In the absence of any forces arising from curvature of the flow or from any thermal effects, the uniform motion implies that the wind is blowing under conditions of *balance* between the two forces operating on it, the Coriolis force and the pressure gradient force. The motion of the air under such a balance is known as geostrophic motion and the resulting wind known as the geostrophic wind.

If a pressure field is set up with a pressure gradient force acting from the region of high pressure to the region of low pressure as shown in Fig. 4.3, then a body of air initially at rest will experience a force which will accelerate it from high to low pressure. The body of air will start to move, but as soon as it moves it will appear to an earthbound observer to suffer a deflective force at right-angles to its direction of motion: the Coriolis force. It will therefore be deflected to the right of its initial path by an amount proportional to its velocity. The body of air will continue to be accelerated towards the region of low pressure under the influence of the pressure gradient force, and the Coriolis force will continue to increase in magnitude as a consequence. The Coriolis force will ultimately become of sufficient magnitude to counterbalance the pressure gradient force as shown in Fig. 4.3. The body is then acted upon by equal and opposite balanced forces, and it will continue to move at a uniform speed in a straight line parallel to the isobars as the *geostrophic wind*. (See Note on p. 31 for formula for geostrophic wind.)

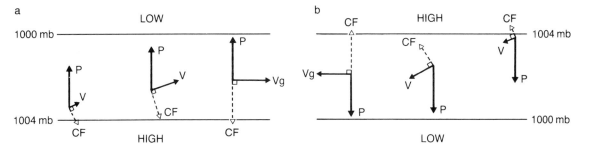

Fig. 4.3 The development of geostrophic balance from near-rest conditions for (a) cyclonic and (b) anticyclonic flow.

Towards the equator where the Coriolis parameter tends towards a value of zero, the geostrophic balance breaks down. In low latitudes the wind direction and strength may be just as much affected by the local temperature distribution as by the local pressure distribution. The geostrophic wind formula is valid only for those situations where the isobars are straight and there is no friction; it also ignores the effects of vertical motion (but these can be ignored in the majority of situations). The effects of curvature and friction are both important steering influences, however.

The effects of friction on wind speed and direction are especially important in the lowest kilometre of the atmosphere. Friction will act in the opposite direction to the motion of the wind, decreasing its speed, and as a consequence of this the Coriolis force acting upon the body of air will be reduced. A new equilibrium of forces is then established as shown in Fig. 4.4. The pressure gradient force is now balanced by the combination (or resultant) of the Coriolis force and the friction force. The result is a drift of air across the isobars towards the lower pressure. The effect of friction in reducing wind speed is greatest over land, where the angle between the isobars and the air is typically some 30°; this may be reduced to 20° at a height of 300 metres and to 10° at 600 metres as the frictional influence decreases. Over sea areas, where the effect of friction is less, the normal angle between the isobars and the wind direction is some 15°.

Fig. 4.4 The effect of friction on the geostrophic balance. The pressure gradient force balances the resultant of the Coriolis force and the friction force.

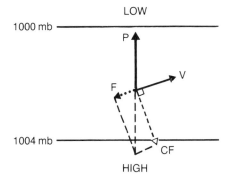

P – Pressure gradient force
V – Wind velocity (Vg – geostrophic wind)
CF – Coriolis force
F – Friction

The lengths of the arrows are drawn proportional to the magnitudes of the forces or velocity involved.

Gradient wind

If the isobars are curved rather than straight then the air motion is subject to another steering force, the centripetal force or acceleration, as well as the pressure gradient force and the Coriolis force. Under conditions of balance between these three forces, the resultant airflow is known as the *gradient wind*.

The centripetal acceleration upon a body moving in a curved trajectory acts inwards along the radius of curvature (in the opposite sense to the centrifugal force acting outwards) and has a magnitude of V^2/r per unit mass, where V is the velocity of the body and r is the radius of curvature of the motion. In a low pressure system in the northern hemisphere the Coriolis force is normally weaker than the pressure gradient force, and the difference between the two provides the necessary centripetal acceleration inwards to maintain the curved flow. In the case of anticyclonic flow, the centripetal acceleration acting inwards is provided by the Coriolis force exceeding the pressure gradient force, as shown in Fig. 4.5. Thus the difference between these two forces provides the force acting inwards. The different contributions of the Coriolis force in each case imply that the wind speed around low pressure centres must be less than the geostrophic value (as the Coriolis force is proportional to the wind speed V, which is less than the pressure gradient force would suggest), a condition known as *subgeostrophic flow*. In the high pressure case, the Coriolis force is greater than the pressure gradient force, producing wind speeds greater than the geostrophic value, known as *supergeostrophic flow*. In reality this effect is masked by the fact that the pressure gradients within high pressure systems are normally less than those within low pressure systems anyway.

Convergence and divergence

Fig. 4.5 The balance of forces producing gradient wind flow around (a) low pressure and (b) high pressure in the northern hemisphere. The lengths of the arrows are drawn proportional to the magnitudes of the forces or velocities involved.

While most meteorological charts are drawn to show the horizontal component of airflow at one particular level of the atmosphere, the air usually has a vertical component of motion also. It has been shown that friction has the effect of causing air to tend to flow across isobars in the direction of the lower pressure. Such a flow towards the centre of a low pressure system produces *convergence*, where there is a net accumulation of air in a limited horizontal area, for example when air flows into the centre of a mid-latitude depression or a tropical cyclone, and even when air flows into a thunderstorm. *Divergence* occurs where there is a net outflow of air from a limited horizontal area, as for

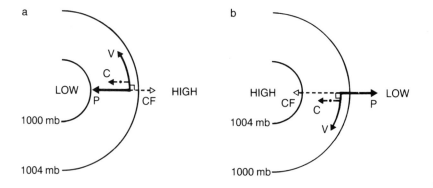

P – Pressure gradient force
V – Gradient wind
CF – Coriolis force
C – Centripetal force

example in the centre of an anticyclone where the air is 'spreading out' from the centre. Divergence and convergence can also occur in the trough-and-ridge patterns of atmospheric flow in the upper atmosphere, and these are very important in giving rise to patterns of mass ascent or descent in the atmosphere.

In general, if the air is converging at the surface it must rise, while if it is diverging at the surface it is usually accompanied by descending air from above (Fig. 4.6). If the air is converging at the top of the troposphere, it cannot rise (because of the tropopause) but tends to subside to preserve its continuity; if it diverges in the upper troposphere, it is normally accompanied by ascending air beneath. Thus convergence at the surface leads to rising motion in the atmosphere and divergence above (as in a depression), while divergence at the surface must be accompanied by air sinking from above, with mass convergence aloft. Because of the vertical motions induced, surface convergence is usually associated with cloud development, and perhaps precipitation; divergence at the surface is normally accompanied by sunny, cloudfree conditions. In the middle troposphere there is a level usually at about 600 mb, at which the horizontal divergence or convergence is effectively nil.

Fig. 4.6 A schematic illustration indicating how patterns of divergence and convergence at the surface and in the upper troposphere are linked by vertical motions.

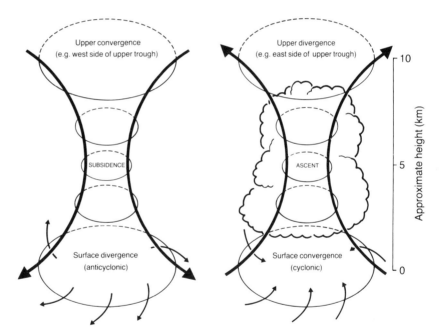

Note
The geostrophic wind V_g occurs when the pressure gradient force is equal in magnitude to the Coriolis force, or

$$\frac{1}{\varrho}\frac{dp}{dn} = 2\Omega\sin\phi V_g$$

where ϱ is the air density, dp/dn is the local pressure gradient (the change in pressure p over a distance n, measured at right-angles to the isobars), Ω is the angular velocity of the earth, and ϕ is the latitude. In other words,

$$\text{the geostrophic wind } V_g = \frac{1}{2\Omega\sin\phi\varrho}\frac{dp}{dn} = \frac{1}{\varrho f}\frac{dp}{dn}$$

where f is the Coriolis parameter.

5 Atmospheric moisture

Water is the most abundant liquid on earth. It is a necessity for life on this planet, it is involved in almost every meteorological process of significance and it is a fundamental factor in determining climates on every scale from the local to the continental. Yet although water is such a ubiquitous liquid it is also the least typical, for four main reasons:

(1) It is less dense as a solid (ice) than as a liquid (water). Ice at 0°C has a density of 0.917 g cm^{-3}, while water at that temperature has a density of 0.999 g cm^{-3} (the difference mainly arising because the crystalline structure of ice contains holes, some of which become filled with water molecules upon melting).

(2) The maximum density of water occurs at 4°C (strictly 3.98°C), rather than at 0°C as would normally be expected (with densities at the two temperatures of 1.000 and 0.999 g cm^{-3} respectively).

(3) Water has higher values of specific heat and latent heat than all other naturally occurring substances. (Specific heat is the amount of heat required to raise the temperature of a unit mass of a substance by 1° Kelvin or 1° Celsius; latent heat is the heat required to melt or evaporate a substance at constant temperature.) This means that temperature changes within water are very slow.

(4) Water exists naturally in the atmosphere in three phases or states: solid (ice), liquid (water) and gas (water vapour). It is continually changing phase, from solid to liquid by the *melting* of snow, hail and ice, or from liquid to solid as the result of *freezing*; it changes from a liquid to a gas as the result of *evaporation*, and from a gas to a liquid by means of *condensation*.

The total amount of water within the earth-atmosphere system is estimated to be some $1,384 \times 10^6$km³; of this amount, 97.2% is contained within the oceans, 0.6% is ground water, 0.02% is contained within rivers and lakes, 2.1% is frozen in ice caps and glaciers, and only 0.001% is contained within the atmosphere. Water vapour is by far the most important variable constituent of the atmosphere, with a distribution which varies both in time and space. The water vapour content of the atmosphere rarely exceeds 3% by mass, with the highest values occurring in the tropics and the lowest values in polar regions, and with a universal decrease with height. This odourless, colourless gas plays a major role in all atmospheric processes.

The average precipitation over the surface of the globe is some 85.7 cm per year, but such a figure disguises enormous spatial variability. Iquique in Chile went fourteen years without any rainfall being recorded during the period 1899–1913, while in March 1952 a total of 187 cm fell on the island of Reunion off the coast of Madagascar in a 24-hour period (compare for example the mean annual rainfall of Manchester of only 81 cm). Such variability is due to the operation of the general circulation of the atmosphere, the variability of its component weather systems, combined with the effects of local circulations and local topographic features.

Fig. 5.1 The principal processes within the hydrological cycle. The small diagram shows the main *stages* (in rectangles, with the percentage of the total water present in each stage as indicated) and *processes* (in circles, with the rates given in units of 10^{15}kg yr^{-1}) of the hydrological cycle.

The hydrological cycle

At any one time the mean water content of the atmosphere is sufficient to produce some 2.5 cm of precipitation over the globe, or an average of some ten days of rainfall. This suggests that there must be continual recycling of water between the land, the oceans and the atmosphere; this is known as the hydrological cycle (Fig. 5.1). Evaporation from water bodies and transpiration from vegetation (usually combined and called *evapotranspiration*) are continually adding water to the atmosphere. Some of this may condense producing clouds of different types, sizes and heights, and some of these may produce precipitation.

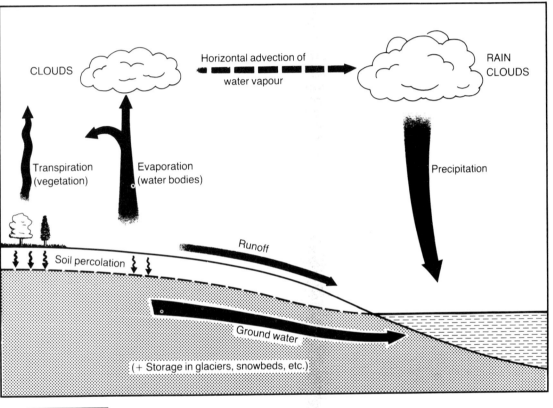

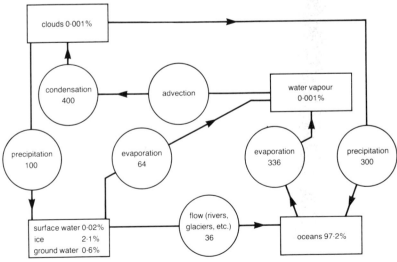

(Not all clouds give rain, and the precipitation will not necessarily occur in the same location at which the evaporation occurred, because of the horizontal transport of water vapour in the winds.) Some of the precipitation evaporates as it falls through the atmosphere; the remainder will fall upon either the ground, a water surface or a vegetation surface. The water which eventually reaches the earth's surface will either evaporate, percolate into the surface to the water table (the level of saturation within the soil), or run off over the surface as sheetflow or in confined channels as river flow. Some of the soil moisture will be taken up by the root system of the vegetation and will eventually be transpired; there will be some storage of water in the soil, and there will be some lateral throughflow of soil water into streams and lakes. Evaporation will then occur and the hydrological cycle will repeat itself.

For a particular location, the moisture gain from precipitation will be balanced over a period of time by the losses from runoff, evapotranspiration and change in soil water storage. For the globe as a whole there is a long-term balance between total precipitation and total evaporation.

The hydrological cycle is simple in concept, but deceptively complex in detail. There are still gaps in the complete understanding of the processes which integrate to form the cycle, particularly where these processes are affected by peculiarities of the local environment (for example the effects of forest cover on local evaporation and runoff rates in different parts of the world, or the effects of an urban area on precipitation). There are also difficulties in measuring or estimating some of the meteorological processes involved; for example, there is no universally accepted method of measuring or estimating evaporation, while the measurement of precipitation at sea, in forested areas, in upland areas and in polar regions still presents formidable difficulties.

Water vapour

Water vapour is a gas which is always present in the atmosphere. The amount of water vapour which the air can hold varies; we speak of dry airmasses and moist airmasses, and in so doing we are describing the concentration of water vapour within the air or its *humidity*.

Water vapour, like any other gas, exerts a pressure according to its concentration; this pressure is called vapour pressure. The total pressure of the atmosphere can therefore be thought of as the sum of (a) the pressure exerted by the dry air; and (b) the pressure exerted by the water vapour, or vapour pressure. Whenever dry air is made to come into contact with a surface of liquid water or ice, evaporation of the water will take place into the air; the resultant water vapour evaporated into the air causes a vapour pressure, and as more evaporation takes place, so the vapour pressure will increase.

For any given temperature there is a limit to the amount of water vapour that can be taken up into the atmosphere in this way. When this limit is reached for the prevailing temperature conditions the air is said to be *saturated*, and the vapour pressure has reached its maximum value for that temperature; this is the *saturation vapour pressure* (SVP). if the vapour pressure is less than the SVP for a given temperature, the air is described as *unsaturated*.

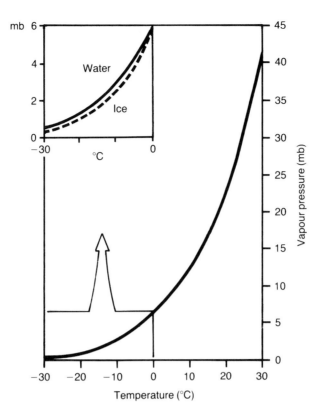

Fig. 5.2 The variation of saturation vapour pressure (SVP) of air over water, with temperature. The inset shows the detail of the variation of SVP over water and ice at temperatures below 0°C.

Figure 5.2 shows how the SVP over a surface of water varies with temperature. It can be seen that the SVP increases rapidly with temperature, so that warm air when saturated holds more water vapour than does cold air.

Measures of atmospheric humidity – some definitions

It has been stated that 'in meteorology air can be regarded very largely as dilute water vapour'. There are five important measures of the humidity content of the atmosphere.

1 Absolute humidity

This is the total mass of water vapour in a given volume of air (usually expressed in grams per cubic metre).

2 Humidity mixing ratio

This is defined as the mass of water vapour (expressed in grams) contained in 1 kg of dry air; 1 kg of dry air usually occupies 1 cubic metre, and the usual values of the humidity mixing ratio in temperate latitudes are between 5 and 50 gm per kg.

3 Relative humidity

This is defined as the ratio of the amount of water vapour actually contained in the air to that which it could contain at saturation,

35

expressed as a percentage; or in terms of vapour pressure, the relative humidity is equal to

$$\frac{\text{vapour pressure of the air}}{\text{SVP of the air with respect to water at that temperature}} \times 100\%$$

Human comfort depends more upon relative humidity than on absolute humidity, with a critical value at about 80%; above this value the air feels damp or 'clammy' even with a low moisture content. Relative humidity values vary from 100% in most cloud and fog to 10% or less over deserts during the day.

4 Dew-point temperature

This is the temperature at which air would become saturated with respect to water if cooled at constant pressure. This is uniquely determined by the vapour pressure of the air, and therefore the dew-point temperature is that temperature at which the vapour pressure of the air is equal to the SVP of that air with respect to water. If the air temperature is above the dew-point temperature the air is unsaturated; the closer the two temperatures are together, the closer the air is to saturation.

Note the condition of 'cooling at constant pressure', for when a parcel of air rises through the atmosphere, not only does its temperature fall but so does its dew-point temperature, even though the parcel may be unsaturated. This is because the decrease in pressure which the parcel suffers affects the partial pressures of its constituents proportionately. Hence the vapour pressure must fall as the parcel rises, and since the dew-point temperature is determined uniquely by the vapour pressure, it too must fall. In practice the dew-point temperature decreases at a rate of 1.7°C/km.

When a dew-point temperature is below 0°C it is sometimes called the *frost-point* temperature with respect to ice.

5 Wet-bulb temperature

The wet-bulb temperature is defined as the lowest temperature to which an air sample can be cooled at constant pressure by evaporating water into it. If the air is saturated, evaporation cannot occur and there will be no cooling. In this case the wet-bulb temperature of the saturated air will be the same as the air temperature and the dew point. If the air is unsaturated, evaporation will cause cooling and the wet-bulb temperature will be less than the air temperature.

The measurement of atmospheric humidity

There are two main types of instrument used in meteorology for measuring atmospheric humidity.

1 Hygrometer

Some substances, such as human hair, react to changes in humidity by expanding or contracting in size or length. The length of human hair changes by $2\frac{1}{2}\%$ between 0% and 100% relative humidity; thus the change in length of a piece of hair of sufficient length can be used to measure changes in the relative humidity.

2 Psychrometer

The whirling psychrometer consists simply of two ordinary thermometers mounted side by side in a sling, shaped like a football rattle, with one of the thermometers having a bulb kept permanently moist using a wick drawing water from a container of distilled water. When air is forced to blow across the instrument, the evaporation of water from the wick causes the temperature of the wet-bulb thermometer to be lower than that of the dry bulb measuring the air temperature, and the difference in the two temperatures gives a measure of the humidity, which can be obtained accurately from hygrometric tables or a humidity slide rule.

Latent heat

The latent heat of a substance is the amount of heat energy required to melt or evaporate it, without changing its temperature. This energy is basically used in breaking intermolecular bonds and rearranging the structure of the substance.

Latent heat exchanges are vitally important in the atmosphere, for heat is absorbed in changes from ice to water to vapour, and heat is released in changes from vapour to water to ice. Evaporation in the atmosphere causes a cooling, and condensation causes a heating of the atmosphere.

The atmosphere therefore contains a vast storehouse of heat in latent form. There is a net input into the storehouse in low latitudes where evaporation within the trade winds region exceeds precipitation (see Chapter 13), and a net output in middle and higher latitudes in the form of excess precipitation. The change of phase of water into and out of its vapour phase is a fundamental link in all energy transformations and on all scales of atmospheric motion from the hemispheric downwards.

Evaporation

Evaporation is the process whereby liquid water or ice changes to water vapour; it is a process that proceeds continuously from the earth's free water surfaces, soil, snow and ice fields, in contrast to precipitation which tends to occur sporadically over relatively short periods of time. Evaporation occurs whenever the vapour pressure in the air is less than its saturation value; it also needs a vapour pressure gradient between the evaporating surface and the atmosphere. Within 1 mm or so of the surface, the upward movement of water vapour takes place by the diffusion of individual molecules, and above this it occurs by turbulent air motion (eddy diffusion).

The rate of evaporation depends primarily upon four factors:
(1) the difference in saturation vapour pressure between the evaporating water surface and the vapour pressure of the air – the greater the difference the greater will be the rate of evaporation;
(2) the temperature of the evaporating surface;

(3) the wind velocity – the water vapour is usually diffused by turbulent airflow (in conditions of very light winds, a shallow layer above the evaporating surface gradually becomes saturated and decreases the overall evaporation rate, but in conditions of strong winds the moisture is readily diffused through a much deeper layer of the atmosphere); and

(4) the availability of a continuous supply of water at the evaporating surface.

The optimum conditions for high evaporation rates are therefore low humidity, high temperatures and strong winds.

Evapotranspiration

There is considerable moisture loss from areas of the earth covered by soil and vegetation. Evapotranspiration is the combined process of evaporation of water from the soil surface together with transpiration by growing plants. It is a slow, continuous and complex process governed by (a) the atmospheric factors that control evaporation, and (b) plant factors, such as the stage of the plant growth, leaf area, leaf temperature, root development and soil moisture.

There is a fundamental difference between the *actual* evapotranspiration and the *potential* evapotranspiration. Potential evapotranspiration represents the maximum amount of water that could be evaporated from vegetation and land surfaces when it is not limited by the available water supply. The actual evapotranspiration rate depends on the availability of water; it is the amount of water that is actually evapotranspired from an environment, and this may well be limited by the availability of soil moisture. There is little difference between them when the soil is moist, but a great difference between them in dry areas and at times of soil moisture deficit.

Evaporation climatology

On a global scale evaporation amounts decrease with increasing latitude because of the reduction in available energy for the process. In middle and low latitudes differences arise between land and sea areas. The maximum oceanic losses occur in the trade-wind belts at 10°–20° north and south where wind speeds and temperatures are both high; values are at a maximum in the western Pacific Ocean and central Indian Ocean where some 200 cm of water may evaporate per year where sea temperatures are high and winds strong. Over land areas maximum values of evaporation occur in equatorial regions because of high radiation values there combined with high transpiration losses from the vegetation. A secondary maximum occurs in middle latitudes in the zone of the prevailing westerlies.

Annual evaporation amounts over the British Isles vary from 38 cm per year in Scotland to 50 cm in south and south-east England. Potential evapotranspiration reaches a maximum of 64 cm over most of south-east England, and as most of this occurs between May and September, seasonal water deficits of 12–15 cm may result, necessitating irrigation, which may be required in nine years out of ten during the summer months.

6 Atmospheric stability and instability; clouds

Clouds are the fundamental building blocks of weather systems and can be looked upon as nature's own three-dimensional representation of the weather map. Their character depends upon the type of motion occurring within them; their form depends upon whether they consist of frozen or liquid droplets. Clouds are the physical manifestation of the atmosphere in action. Climatologists must therefore understand them in order to interpret their existence when observed from the ground, from weather satellite imagery and from weather charts.

The character and development of different cloud types are dependent on the relative buoyancy of the air that forms them compared with the surrounding environmental air. When air rises to produce the clouds, it does so for one of three reasons:
(1) It has become relatively lighter than the surrounding environmental air as a result of its warmth and humidity, producing *thermally-induced* convective clouds.
(2) It has been forced to rise over some obstacle to its movement, for example a line of hills, producing *mechanically-induced* orographic clouds.
(3) It has been forced to rise because of air converging at the surface, as within a depression for example, producing a variety of *dynamically-induced* clouds.

In any of these cases the air cools as it rises, since its ascent through levels of progressively lower pressure makes it expand. Expansion requires the use of energy; this energy can only be obtained from its own internal energy, and this process must therefore lead to a drop in temperature. Ascending air will therefore expand and cool, while sinking air will contract and warm.

When a 'parcel' of air is buoyant with respect to the surrounding atmosphere, this air is said to be statically *unstable* (or just unstable); when it shows negative buoyancy or a tendency to sink through the surrounding atmosphere, the atmosphere is said to be statically *stable* (or simply stable).

It is a fallacy simply to assume that warm air rises and cold air sinks, for it is possible that air at sub-freezing temperatures can rise spontaneously under the right circumstances and warm tropical air can sink. It is *relative* temperature (i.e. the temperature of a volume of air relative to its surroundings), or more correctly, *relative density* that determines vertical motions. Consider the motion of a hot-air balloon; it rises because the relative temperature of the air within the balloon is higher than the environmental air outside – the air in the balloon is less dense than the surrounding air and is thus buoyant. Stability and instability are normally ascertained by considering the distribution of temperature in the atmosphere with height. Temperature is a relatively easy parameter to measure, and since air temperature is directly proportional to air density, a vertical profile of temperature can readily be compared with a vertical profile of density.

Lapse rates

The distribution of the temperature of the environment with respect to height (as measured by a radiosonde) is normally referred to as the *environmental lapse rate* (ELR). It is the detail of this which will determine the stability or otherwise of the atmosphere.

As a 'parcel' of air rises through the atmosphere, it will cool. The amount of temperature change depends very strongly on the moisture content of the air parcel at the earth's surface (i.e. the relative humidity at the surface is important). Any parcel of air in which the relative humidity is not 100% (i.e. which is not saturated) will cool as it rises at a specific and constant rate, called the *dry adiabatic lapse rate* (DALR). Any parcel which is unsaturated and sinks, will warm at the DALR. This lapse rate is 1°C per 100 metres for unsaturated air, regardless of the temperature.

If the temperature within the parcel of air cools sufficiently, the air will become saturated and normally condensation of liquid water will begin to occur. The condensation of water within the parcel will release latent heat of condensation which will offset the normal decrease of temperature with height. When saturated air is forced to rise it will therefore cool at a new rate, known as the *saturated adiabatic lapse rate* (SALR). This is not a constant rate of temperature change like the DALR, for it varies with the moisture-holding capacity of the air (which increases with temperature). At temperatures of, say, 20°C, at a pressure level of 1000 mb, the SALR is approximately 0.43°C per 100 metres (i.e. less than half the DALR), while higher up in the atmosphere, at for example 300 mb with temperatures of −40°C, the SALR is 0.90°C per 100 metres – close to the DALR. Here little latent heat release occurs on condensation to offset the normal cooling within rising air because of the low water vapour content of the air at these temperatures.

On temperature-height diagrams or tephigrams, the DALR is always represented by straight lines (i.e. a constant decrease of temperature with height), while the SALR is represented by convex curves (indicating how the rate of cooling is dependent on the temperature).

These lapse rates are referred to as being *adiabatic*, which means a temperature exchange process where there is no loss or addition of heat to or from the surroundings. An adiabatic lapse rate therefore refers to a lapse rate of temperature for a parcel of air for which there is *no mixing* with the surrounding environmental air, and no exchange of heat, momentum or water; the parcel of air will heat or cool at a rate which is predictable and independent of environmental temperature.

These assumptions are valid if (a) the parcel is large enough that mixing processes at its outer limits are small in terms of the temperature of the overall parcel; (b) the adjustment for decreased temperature is relatively rapid; (c) there are no compensating motions around the parcel; and (d) precipitation does not fall from the parcel during the process, thus altering its water content.

Near the earth's surface, in the layer of air adjacent to the ground, most processes are non-adiabatic; this is because of the tendency of the air to become readily mixed with the surrounding air by turbulence. When a parcel of air moves vertically in the atmosphere, the temperature changes that take place are approximately adiabatic, as air is a poor conductor of heat, and mixing of a parcel with its surroundings is usually slow. The air parcel will therefore tend to retain its own thermal identity, which distinguishes it from the surrounding air. This is especially true within the centres of large clouds away from the lateral mixing (or entrainment) which may be present on the edges of the cloud.

In reality, if a parcel of air is forced to rise through the atmosphere or undergoes natural convection, it is normal for it to be unsaturated at the bottom of its ascent and to reach saturation after rising to a specific height. At this height, known as the *condensation level* or cloud base, a cloud will form; above this level it will cool at the SALR. A sinking parcel will warm at the SALR and then at the DALR if originally saturated. It is very rare that an air parcel is either saturated from ground level upwards, or dry throughout its ascent, so the normal ascent path curve will be a combination of the DALR and SALR, as shown in Fig. 6.1.

However, the ELR varies in time and space and is affected by many different interactions at different levels: there may be two different airmasses above a station in a frontal situation, ground heating may warm the lowest layers, or there may be a temperature inversion at the surface or aloft. On average the ELR is of the order of 6.5°C per km in the troposphere.

Fig. 6.1 A schematic forced ascent curve for a convective situation. A parcel of air with a surface dry-bulb temperature of 20°C and a dew-point temperature of 15°C will cool at the DALR until it reaches saturation. At the condensation level (cloud base) it will continue to cool at the SALR. Note that saturation occurs at a temperature of less than the dew-point temperature of 15°C.

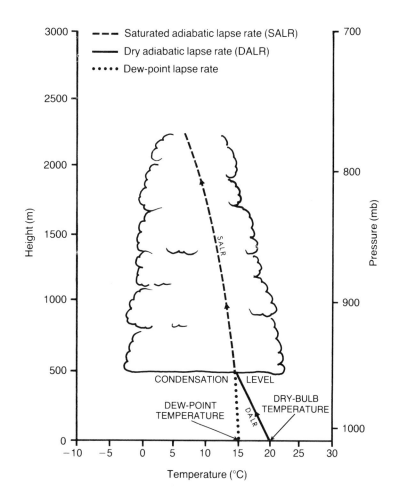

The tephigram

In order to assess whether the atmosphere is stable or unstable and to ascertain the likely heights and depths of clouds, meteorologists normally use a tephigram, a graph of temperature t, against entropy ϕ (hence t-ϕgram). This looks complicated at first sight, but it is in fact simply a variety of temperature-pressure (or temperature-height) diagram (see Fig. 6.2).

Like any other graph it has two axes, although these are oriented at 45° to each other rather than the normal 90° of most graphs:
(1) The nearly horizontal lines correspond to different atmospheric *pressure* values (in mb); the approximate altitude of the various pressure levels is indicated by the scale on the right of Fig. 6.2.
(2) The straight lines sloping from bottom left to top right correspond to temperatures (in °C); the 0°C isotherm is shown with a bold line.
Superimposed on these are three sets of construction lines:
(1) The straight, dotted lines sloping from bottom right to top left are DALR lines.
(2) The convex curves represented by dashed lines sloping away from bottom right to top left are SALR lines.

Fig. 6.2   A tephigram.

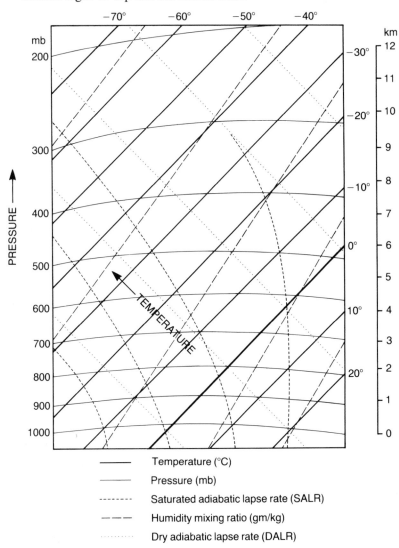

———	Temperature (°C)
———	Pressure (mb)
- - - - - - - -	Saturated adiabatic lapse rate (SALR)
– – –	Humidity mixing ratio (gm/kg)
· · · · · · · ·	Dry adiabatic lapse rate (DALR)

(3) The straight, thin, dashed lines which slope from bottom left to top right are *humidity mixing ratio* lines (gm of water vapour per kg of dry air), or lines of constant humidity.

To use the tephigram, the following procedure is adopted:

(1) Plot each air temperature (from a radiosonde ascent or similar) at its corresponding pressure level and join up the points with straight lines (line E–E′ in Fig. 6.3); this represents the ELR;

(2) Plot each of the dew-point temperatures (if available) at its corresponding level and join up the values with dashed lines (line d–d′ in Fig. 6.3); the differences between the air temperature and the dew-point temperature at each level indicate the humidity of the air at that level.

(3) Using the DALR lines, draw a line parallel to these from the surface air temperature (line D–D′ in Fig. 6.3); this shows the temperature which a parcel of surface air would undergo if forced to rise and if it remained unsaturated.

Fig. 6.3 The use of a tephigram for constructing the forced ascent curve, and assessing the height of cloud base and cloud top.

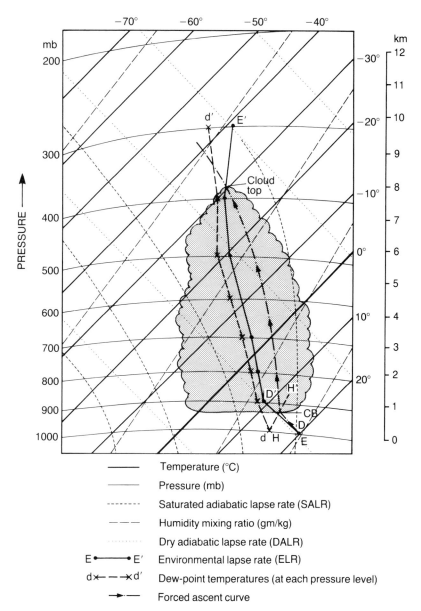

——————	Temperature (°C)
——————	Pressure (mb)
- - - - - - - -	Saturated adiabatic lapse rate (SALR)
— — —	Humidity mixing ratio (gm/kg)
··············	Dry adiabatic lapse rate (DALR)
E•———•E′	Environmental lapse rate (ELR)
d✕— —✕d′	Dew-point temperatures (at each pressure level)
—•—	Forced ascent curve

43

(4) Using the mixing ratio lines, draw a line parallel to these through the surface dew-point temperature (line H–H').

(5) The intersection of these two lines indicates the level at which the rising parcel of air becomes saturated, giving the condensation level and thus the cloud base (CB).

(6) Using the SALR lines, interpolate an SALR line from the point of intersection CB, upwards; this shows the temperature change which the rising parcel of air will undergo. If the atmosphere is unstable (as here), the intersection of this SALR line with the ELR will indicate the height of the cloud top.

Absolute stability

The atmosphere is said to be absolutely stable when the ELR is less than both the DALR and SALR, so that the temperature within any parcel of air which is forced to rise from the surface is lower than that of the surrounding atmosphere (and is thus denser). An example of a vertical temperature profile through a stable atmosphere is shown in Fig. 6.4. Stable air is usually associated with anticyclonic conditions,

Fig. 6.4 Absolute stability. Any parcel of air that is forced to rise from the surface would always be colder – and therefore denser – than the environment and would tend to sink back to its original position. Convection is suppressed, and the only cloud likely to develop is stratiform.

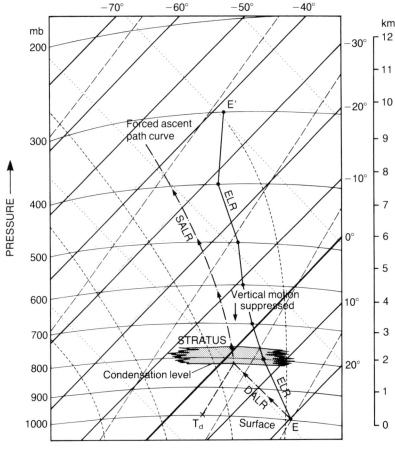

——— Temperature (°C)

——— Pressure (mb)

- - - - - Saturated adiabatic lapse rate (SALR)

– – – Humidity mixing ratio (gm/kg)

·········· Dry adiabatic lapse rate (DALR)

•—•— Forced ascent path curve

E•——•E' Environmental lapse rate (ELR)

T_d Dew-point temperature

and convection tends to be suppressed by the sinking air within the anticyclone. The stability may be helped by a temperature inversion (a condition where temperature increases with height, 'inverting' the normal profile). Such *inversions* may arise from the following causes:

(1) a warm airmass being undercut by a cold airmass, as in a warm or cold frontal situation;
(2) when the surface loses heat by long-wave radiation to space on clear nights – this chills the overlying air in contact with the ground, cooling it below the temperature of the air above, unaffected by the chilling, so that the air temperature increases from the surface upwards;
(3) warm air passing over a cold land or sea surface is chilled from below, giving rise to a low-level temperature inversion;
(4) dynamic causes, such as the subsidence in the return flow of the Hadley circulation of the tropics, forming the trade wind inversion; and
(5) warm, dry stratospheric air overlies the cooler troposphere at the tropopause.

In general, stable atmospheric conditions are either cloudfree or produce layered, stratiform clouds, because of the tendency of the air to sink.

Absolute instability

The atmosphere is said to be absolutely unstable if the ELR is greater than both the DALR and the SALR. The measured air temperature falls rapidly with height, so that any air parcel cooling at the DALR will always be warmer and less dense than the surrounding air. Its buoyancy will give it an upward impulse, so that convection is encouraged, and some form of cumuliform (convective) cloud is the usual end-result. Unstable air characteristically continues to move away from its original level once it is set in motion.

The upward motion within the unstable air normally occurs within limited depths of the atmosphere to a level of equilibrium where the SALR and ELR lines intersect, as shown in Fig. 6.5. The main exceptions to this occur in thunderstorms where deep convection may occur right to the level of the tropopause; this is particularly true in equatorial regions.

Neutral equilibrium

The condition of neutral equilibrium occurs when the DALR is the same as the ELR in unsaturated air, and the same as the SALR within saturated air. Any forced vertical displacement of an air parcel will take it into a region of the atmosphere where its temperature is the same as that of the environment, so there will be no upward or downward impulse due to density differences. This condition is not common.

Conditional instability

Usually the atmosphere in temperate latitudes is neither absolutely stable nor absolutely unstable, but is conditionally unstable. This occurs

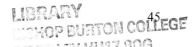

45

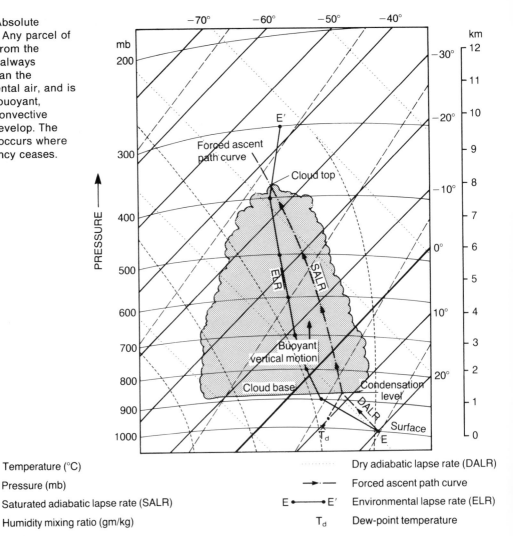

Fig. 6.5 Absolute instability. Any parcel of air rising from the surface is always warmer than the environmental air, and is therefore buoyant, allowing convective cloud to develop. The cloud top occurs where the buoyancy ceases.

——	Temperature (°C)	
——	Pressure (mb)	
- - - - - -	Saturated adiabatic lapse rate (SALR)	
– – –	Humidity mixing ratio (gm/kg)	

··········	Dry adiabatic lapse rate (DALR)	
➤ — · —	Forced ascent path curve	
E ●——● E′	Environmental lapse rate (ELR)	
T_d	Dew-point temperature	

when there is a lower stable layer of atmosphere with an unstable layer higher up. If some mechanism can overcome the lower stability of the atmosphere, the stability can be triggered off and natural convection can occur aloft. The instability is conditional on the stability of the lower layer being overcome to initiate vertical motion. Such a situation is illustrated in Fig. 6.6. Airflow over a range of hills may provide such a trigger, by forcing the air upwards above the stable level; moistening of the low-level air (by evaporation from the earth's surface) until it is saturated provides another mechanism.

Clouds

Clouds are the visible aggregates of minute particles of water or ice, or both, held in suspension in the free air. They were given no universally acceptable scientific names until the beginning of the nineteenth century. In 1803 an English pharmacist and naturalist, Luke Howard, proposed a system of classifying cloud types, based essentially on their shape and height. His descriptive classification, which took no account of the origin of the clouds, is still the one used in twentieth-century meteorological reporting, and is used in the *International Cloud Atlas* (WMO).

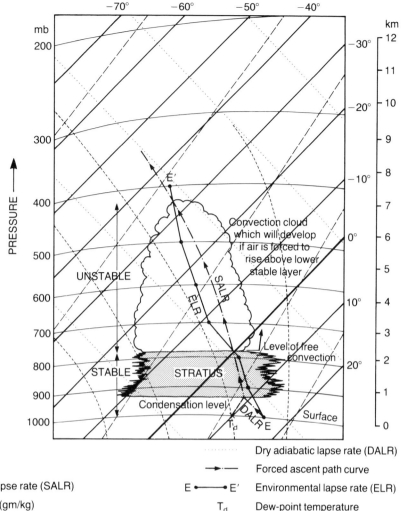

Fig. 6.6 Conditional instability. The atmosphere is stable up to about 785 mb and unstable above this (to 425 mb). Convective cloud will only develop if the air is forced to rise above the lower stable layer (if it is forced to rise over a range of mountains 3 km high, for example).

———— Temperature (°C)	············ Dry adiabatic lapse rate (DALR)
———— Pressure (mb)	→·— Forced ascent path curve
-------- Saturated adiabatic lapse rate (SALR)	E •——• E′ Environmental lapse rate (ELR)
– – – Humidity mixing ratio (gm/kg)	T_d Dew-point temperature

Howard proposed four basic Latin names: *cumulus* (meaning a heap or pile) for convective clouds, *stratus* (a layer) for layered clouds, *cirrus* (a filament or hair) for fibrous clouds, and *nimbus* (rain-yielding) for rain-clouds. He used the prefix *alto-* for middle-level clouds (occurring from 2 to 7 km in altitude). Using composite names (for example *cirrostratus, cumulonimbus*), he proposed a total of ten types, or genera, of clouds:

High cloud
(cloud base at 5–13 km
in temperate latitudes)
Medium cloud
(cloud base at 2–7 km
in temperate latitudes)
Low cloud
(cloud base 0–2 km in
temperate latitudes)

1. cirrus (Ci)
2. cirrocumulus (Cc)
3. cirrostratus (Cs)
4. altocumulus (Ac)
5. nimbostratus (Ns)
6. altostratus (As)
7. stratocumulus (Sc)
8. stratus (St)
9. cumulus (Cu)
10. cumulonimbus (Cb)

Each one of these can take a range of forms, and the interested reader is referred to works such as *Cloud Types for Observers* published by the Meteorological Office (1982) for detailed descriptions and photographs of some of the hundreds of cloud types that nature produces.

It should be realised that clouds are not static components of the sky, but are continually changing. A cloud is not one isolated entity drifting across the sky with the wind; it is rather a visible manifestation of physical processes at work within the atmosphere, some tending to form the cloud, others tending to dissipate it; when the formative processes dominate, the cloud grows.

Two important factors determine the appearance of a cloud:
(1) The *stability* of the atmosphere within which the cloud forms. Stability determines the nature of the vertical motion in the atmosphere; if it is stable the air must be forced upwards which will lead to smooth, slow and usually widespread ascent giving rise to layered, stratiform cloud. If the atmosphere is unstable, portions of the air will rise spontaneously in rapid and localised motions, producing scattered cumuliform clouds.
(2) Whether the *water content* of the cloud occurs in a liquid or solid state, and whether there is precipitation from the cloud. Ice clouds have blurred edges and in general are wispy, tenuous clouds, whereas those formed of liquid water tend to have sharper, better developed outlines. When precipitation begins, droplets begin to appear which are much larger than the original cloud droplets present owing to the action of gravity. Soon after the formation of precipitation, the largest particles appear below and the smallest above. Streamers of precipitation beneath a cloud appear as fallstreaks (fibrous and small, rather like cirrus), and the cloud base will appear to be diffuse with little structure if the rain is widespread.

There are two main processes of dispersal of clouds: evaporation of the cloud droplets, usually arising from mixing with the dry surrounding air, and the fallout of precipitation.

Unstable cloud forms

Cumuliform clouds develop in conditions of atmospheric instability through the formation of rising *thermals*. These are envelopes of rising air from a locally warm surface. The air in contact with the heated surface forms a bubble of warm air which breaks away and rises through the surrounding cooler air. The thermals tend to be roughly hemispherical or mushroom-shaped, as shown in Fig. 6.7, varying in width from tens to hundreds of metres across.

As the thermal rises and expands, friction between the rising air within the thermal and the relatively still air outside it causes a tumbling movement that appears to be constantly turning the atmosphere inside out. Thermals are normally invisible below the condensation level, where they are known as dry thermals, and are a source of uplift used by glider pilots. Above the condensation level the water vapour condenses into a visible cloud of tiny water droplets. The condensation causes a release of latent heat which further heats the thermal and helps to offset the reduction in buoyancy arising from the mixing with cooler air on the leading edge of the thermal together with the evaporation of droplets (causing cooling) on the margins of the cloud. At the cloud-base the thermals are normally rising at speeds of 1 m/sec, but this may reach 5 m/sec or more within the cumulus clouds, while within thunderstorms the upcurrents may attain speeds of at least 30 m/sec.

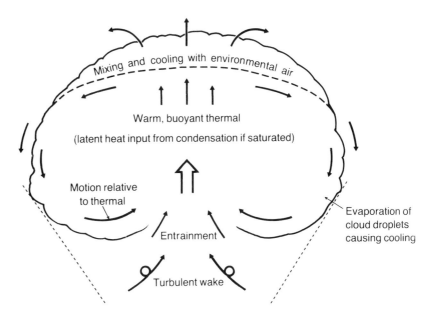

Large cumulus clouds usually contain a number of thermals, which rise one after the other through the main body of the cloud, partly composed of the remnants of former thermals. The newer, more vigorous thermals will break through the top or flanks of the cloud as growing turrets, giving rise to the typical cauliflower-like appearance of cumulus clouds, until arrested by the cooling from the mixing and evaporation, they either evaporate or lose their buoyancy and sink back into the main cloud tower. The upward penetration of thermals may also be arrested by a high-level stable layer, such as an inversion, which will cause the cloud to spread out laterally beneath it (e.g. the anvil at the top of a thunderstorm cloud).

If the air is only unstable for a small depth above the condensation level, small 'fair weather' cumuli result, with no precipitation. When the air is unstable to great heights, the cumulus will grow both vertically and laterally, and may well develop into a cumulonimbus cloud producing precipitation. The structure of thunderstorm systems is treated in detail in Chapter 8.

Stable cloud forms

Stable atmospheres tend to produce stratiform clouds of one type or another. These characteristically have wide horizontal extents compared with their depths, diffuse outlines and weak vertical air motions which are forced either dynamically by turbulence or by topography. Stratiform clouds associated with frontal depressions are discussed in Chapter 10.

Stratus cloud is usually formed by advection (movement) of a moist airmass over a cool surface under stable atmospheric conditions. For example, when a moist airstream flows from a warm sea over a cool land surface, the increased friction over the land will induce greater vertical turbulence within the stable layer. Given a wind speed of some 2.5–5 m/sec, the turbulent air is cooled at the surface, the cooling may spread through the moist layer, producing condensation aloft (where the air is cooled resulting in saturation) and stratus cloud (extending to an inversion which normally caps the mixed layer). Stratus cloud formed in this way will normally have a cloud-base close to the surface (rarely above 500 metres) and will disperse through heating or increased wind speed. Stratus may also form from fog which has lifted.

Fog is defined as a state of atmospheric obscurity in which the visibility is less than 1 km, and may be considered as a form of stratus with its cloud base at ground level. There are four main types of fog. The general characteristics of these are summarised in Table 6.1.

The influence of topography on airflow and cloud development is a complex one, although under stable conditions the resultant cloud forms are relatively simple. With strong winds and stable conditions, lens-shaped wave clouds may develop downwind if the hills are of sufficient magnitude.

Table 6.1 Summary of fog types affecting the British Isles.

Type of fog	Season of occurrence	Areas affected	Mode of formation	Mode of dispersal
Radiation fog	Autumn and winter	Inland areas, especially river valleys and low-lying damp ground	Cooling due to radiation from the ground on clear anticyclonic nights in conditions of light winds	Heating of the ground by the sun or increased wind
Advection fog (a) over land	Winter and spring	Often widespread inland	Warm air cooled by movement over cold land	Change in airflow or heating of the land
(b) over sea	Spring and early summer	Sea and coastal areas	Warm air cooled by movement over cool sea surface	Change in airflow or heating of the coast
Frontal fog	All seasons	Inland, especially high ground	Warm airmass in contact with cold airmass in a weak circulation	Increase in intensity of the circulation or passage of front
Upslope or hill fog	All seasons	High ground	Low cloud forming below the summit of the hills	Change in circulation

7 Precipitation

Precipitation (see Table 7.1) is the main source of all fresh water on earth. Its distribution, however, varies widely in time, space, intensity and amount, and it is an important component of the climate of any environment. A knowledge of how precipitation develops in the atmosphere is a fascinating subject in itself, and with the increasing interest which is developing in acid rain and its environmental consequences, such knowledge is becoming even more important.

Water vapour is always present in the atmosphere and often in large amounts. In order that this gaseous reservoir can be tapped to produce precipitation, cooling and condensation must first take place to form clouds, and the droplets must then grow by some mechanism until they are large enough to fall as precipitation. Not all clouds give rain, however. Whereas evaporation is a slow, continuous, ubiquitous process, precipitation is a process that is intermittent and sporadic. Over the world as a whole the greatest precipitation is in areas where air is converging at the surface – the intertropical convergence zone of near-equatorial latitudes and regions of frontal depressions in middle latitudes.

Table 7.1 Precipitation types and their characteristics.

Precipitation type	Droplet characteristics	Cloud type from which derived
Rain	Water droplets with diameter 0.5–4.0 mm	Ns, As, Sc, Ac
Drizzle	Fine water droplets with diameter 0.1–0.4 mm	St, Sc
Snow	Loose aggregates of ice crystals; at low temperatures these are small, at temperatures near 0°C they may be large	Ns, As, Sc, Cb
Sleet	Partly melted snowflakes, or rain and snow falling	Ns, As, Sc, Cb
Hail	Concentric shells of ice forming particles with diameter 5mm +	Cb

Condensation

Until the 1930s it was thought that cloud droplets grew and grew by continuous condensation to produce raindrops and thus precipitation; this is now known to be untrue. As air cools, its relative humidity increases until at saturation its relative humidity is 100%. This hardly ever occurs in nature without the condensation of water taking place. However, under laboratory conditions, perfectly pure and clean moist air can be overloaded with water vapour, or *supersaturated* (where the vapour pressure of the air exceeds the saturation vapour pressure). This implies that condensation has not taken place directly at the dew-point temperature. A sample of very clean air, under such conditions, can have a relative humidity of up to 700% without condensation occurring. Humidities of this order are never encountered in the atmosphere, so it is clear that simple cooling of the air to its dew-point temperature cannot account for the condensation that produces the clouds, still less for precipitation.

In reality the air is never pure and clean; there are always impurities present to provide a surface upon which water can condense. At ground level such surfaces are provided by the land, vegetation and such objects as spiders' webs, upon which dew and frost are deposited. In the atmosphere there are *condensation nuclei* which allow condensation to occur naturally, and because of these there is very little supersaturation in the atmosphere, where relative humidities rarely exceed 100%. Indeed, most condensation nuclei have an affinity for water (i.e. they are hygroscopic); for example, condensation can occur on salt nuclei at relative humidities as low as 78% (a reason why salt-cellars clog-up on humid days).

The need for condensation nuclei in the free air was not fully explained until 1941, when Simpson showed that even if some 5,000 water molecules could somehow be brought together by chance, the resulting droplet would have a diameter of only one-millionth of a centimetre (0.01 μm), and that such a droplet would evaporate immediately unless the relative humidity of the air around it reached the highly improbable value of 125%.

Condensation nuclei are present in the atmosphere in large numbers and their sizes cover a wide spectrum. They consist of solid particles, droplets of solutions, and of mixed particles that are partly soluble, partly insoluble. They are generally classified according to size and there are three types as listed in Table 7.2:

Table 7.2 Characteristics of condensation nuclei.

Type	Diameter (μm)	Mean concentrations	
		Number per m^3	Number per cc
Aitken nuclei	0.01–0.4	4×10^{10}	4×10^4
Large nuclei	0.4–2	10^8	10^2
Giant nuclei	2–60	10^6–10^3	0.5–1

(1) *Aitken nuclei*   These have diameters of less than 0.4 μm, and originate primarily from combustion processes, both natural and manmade (hence the high concentrations of Aitken nuclei in polluted urban air). Concentrations vary from 1 million per cubic metre (10^6m^{-3}) over oceans to figures of 10^{12}m^{-3} near industrial areas. Because the saturation vapour pressure (SVP) over a water droplet is inversely proportional to its radius (small droplets have high SVP values), only a small proportion of these minute nuclei play an active role in cloud formation.

(2) *Large nuclei*   These have diameters of between 0.4 and 2 μm, and consist of ammonium sulphate, ammonium chloride or sulphuric acid; they are largely hygroscopic and have typical concentrations in the range 10^6 to 10^{9-3}.

(3) *Giant nuclei*   These have diameters greater than 2 μm, and consist either of mixed nuclei containing a good deal of sulphuric acid or of sea-salt particles derived from breaking waves and bursting foam

bubbles. They occur with typical concentrations of 10^6 nuclei per cubic metre. There has been considerable argument over the last two decades concerning the importance of sea salt as a source of condensation nuclei, but it is now apparent that salt particles contribute only a small percentage of the total number of nuclei involved in cloud formation; the remainder result from combustion, photochemical reactions in the atmosphere and the weathering of rocks.

Concentrations of these nuclei vary enormously; air over the oceans and at higher levels contain fewer nuclei than air at low levels over towns and industrial areas. Weather conditions also play a crucial part in nuclei concentrations: atmospheric turbulence with a strong wind will mix up the nuclei, whereas stable, stagnant conditions tend to concentrate them (as with pollution). Many nuclei can also be washed out of the atmosphere by rainfall itself.

Having established the viability of condensation within the atmosphere, there are three processes which operate either alone or in combination in the atmosphere to produce the necessary cooling of the air to produce saturation and condensation:
(1) *Adiabatic expansion* (see Chapter 6).
(2) *Contact with a cold surface*   When warm, moist air blows over a cold land surface it may be chilled to its dew-point temperature, producing condensation (and perhaps fog or low cloud).
(3) *Mixing of airmasses*   If two airmasses, both close to saturation but with different temperatures, are forced to mix (as in a frontal depression), condensation will occur.

The formation of precipitation

The formation of precipitation is a complex but very interesting process. Rain is produced by the condensation of excess water vapour in the air under conditions of saturation; the condensed moisture forms clouds of little droplets which in time grow sufficiently large to fall to the ground under the influence of gravity. However, not all droplets within a cloud are the same size and droplet size is a critical factor in the development of precipitation. The fall speed of drops depends upon two factors: the *weight* of the droplet and the counteracting effect of *air resistance*. For a large and heavy body, air resistance is a secondary factor and it will fall like a stone, but for a small body like a cloud droplet the air resistance is all-important and it will fall like a feather at its *terminal velocity* (the steady velocity that prevails when the effect of gravity on the droplet is balanced by the effect of air resistance).

Some typical fall speeds of cloud droplets, drizzle drops and rain drops (classified according to size) are listed in Table 7.3. It can be seen from this that cloud droplets averaging some 10 μm (0.01 mm) in diameter would have insufficient time to reach the ground from middle-level clouds in the atmosphere even in the whole lifetime of a depression. In reality the actual fall speeds of the droplets will be less than those quoted, for the terminal velocities relate to conditions in still air and are negligible compared with the magnitudes of the updraughts and other motions affecting the clouds.

A comparison of the relative sizes of cloud droplets and raindrops is shown in Fig. 7.1. Even if chance processes caused an increase in the

Fig. 7.1 The comparative sizes, concentrations and terminal velocities of droplets and nuclei involved in condensation and precipitation processes. (r: radius in microns; n: average number per litre; V: terminal velocity in cm/sec.)

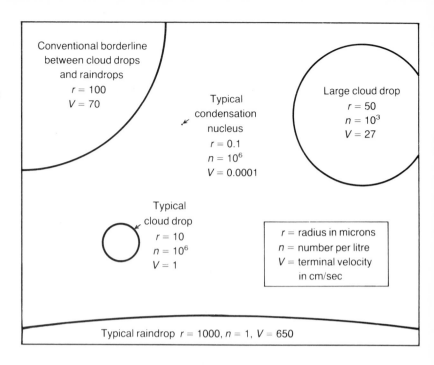

Conventional borderline between cloud drops and raindrops
$r = 100$
$V = 70$

Typical condensation nucleus
$r = 0.1$
$n = 10^6$
$V = 0.0001$

Large cloud drop
$r = 50$
$n = 10^3$
$V = 27$

Typical cloud drop
$r = 10$
$n = 10^6$
$V = 1$

r = radius in microns
n = number per litre
V = terminal velocity in cm/sec

Typical raindrop $r = 1000$, $n = 1$, $V = 650$

Table 7.3 The sizes and fall speeds of different water droplets.

Type of droplet	Diameter (mm)	Terminal velocity (cm sec^{-1})	Time to fall 100 metres
Cloud	0.01	0.3	5 days
	0.04	5.4	6 hours
Drizzle	0.10	27	1 hour
	0.40	170	10 minutes
Rain	1.00	390	4 minutes
	2.00	690	2.3 minutes
	4.00	930	1.8 minutes

total water content of a cloud droplet by a factor of 8, the diameter would only be doubled and the fall speed increased by a factor of 4; the resultant droplet would still be extremely small and not at all like a raindrop. The mass of a raindrop only 1 mm in diameter (1,000 μm) is 1 million times that of a cloud droplet of diameter 10 μm; the problem of the theory of precipitation formation is to explain how this concentration of mass of water can occur as a continuous process within a strictly limited time period. Condensation alone is not enough. The diameter of an active salt nucleus is about 1 μm; when condensation occurs it will take one second to grow to the size of a small cloud droplet of diameter 10 μm; it will take some 500 seconds to grow to a large cloud droplet of diameter 100 μm and three hours or more to grow to the size of a small raindrop with a diameter of 1 mm. This argument assumes no loss from evaporation during the process. Condensation will produce the cloud droplets, but acting alone it is far too slow to produce raindrops. If no process existed for collecting condensed water into a few big drops, each the equivalent of some 1 million small droplets, clouds would remain in suspension in the atmosphere almost indefinitely!

There are currently two main theories which can explain the rapid and continuous transformation of cloud droplets to raindrops.

The Bergeron-Findeisen process

This theory was first suggested by a Norwegian meteorologist, Bergeron, in 1933 and was subsequently confirmed by the German, Findeisen, in 1938. It is based on the assumption that ice plays a critical role in the development of precipitation. There are four stages in the argument:

(1) At levels within potential rainclouds where the temperatures are below freezing, at say $-5°C$ to $-10°C$, it is usual to find a mixture of water droplets (supercooled below their freezing point) and a few ice crystals. It is important to note here that while ice will melt into water at 0°C with the addition of heat, water does not necessarily freeze into ice at 0°C. For this to happen it needs the presence of freezing nuclei, which are much less common than condensation nuclei. Water can in fact be cooled to temperatures as low as $-40°C$ before freezing occurs spontaneously. At temperatures between 0°C and $-10°C$ the number of ice particles is usually very small compared with the number of water droplets; the concentration of ice particles increases as temperatures decrease.

(2) At temperatures below 0°C the saturation vapour pressure of air over ice is lower than the saturation vapour pressure of air over a surface of supercooled water, as shown in Fig. 5.2 and detailed in Table 7.4. The difference between the two (some 10%) is small (the greatest difference between the two being of the order of 0.27 mb at a temperature of $-12°C$), but this difference is critically important in a cloud with a mixture of both water droplets and ice crystals, for air that is saturated with respect to a water surface will be supersaturated with respect to ice.

Table 7.4 Variation of saturation vapour pressure with temperature over water and ice surfaces.

	Temperature (°C)					
	0	-4	-8	-12	-16	-20
SVP over water (mb)	6.11	4.55	3.35	2.44	1.76	1.25
SVP over ice (mb)	6.11	4.37	3.10	2.17	1.51	1.03
Difference (mb)	0.00	0.18	0.25	0.27	0.25	0.22

(3) In such a cloud, water will preferentially condense on the ice particles, which will grow, while the droplets will dwindle and evaporate. The ice particles will normally grow into hexagonal star-shaped crystals.

(4) The ice crystals will grow as snowflakes, gathering additional water by accretion until their mass is sufficient for them to fall rapidly to earth, melting into raindrops in transit (if the air temperatures are above freezing).

Time is of the essence in such a process; a snowflake large enough to fall at an appreciable rate can form from 1 million cloud droplets in ten minutes, and a supercooled cloud can be transformed in a similar time-period. The process is further enhanced by the fact that the enlarged ice particles or snowflakes throw off new particles of ice by splintering, and if a supercooled droplet touches a fragment of ice the whole mass will freeze immediately; the process is thus self-multiplying.

The Bergeron-Findeisen process is most favoured in those clouds with temperatures in the range $-10°$ to $-30°C$. The presence of freezing nuclei in the cloud is vital for the process to operate. Two kinds of nuclei have been identified in the atmosphere: (1) those that induce freezing of the liquid water drops; and (2) those that induce the direct formation of ice crystals from water vapour. The origins of these nuclei are still controversial, but it is generally considered that the major sources are fine soil particles, such as eroded particles of kaolinite.

The theory suggests that all rain has its origin in melting snowflakes or ice crystals. There are two pieces of evidence that reinforce this point of view: (1) rainclouds are nearly always thick enough to reach above the freezing level; and (2) reports from aircraft and high altitude stations have shown that quite often when it is raining at low levels it is snowing at higher levels.

The theory has thus been vindicated by observational evidence, but it may not be the only process at work in producing raindrops. The Bergeron-Findeisen process was advocated for the temperate latitudes, but a number of reports from tropical regions since World War II have shown that rain is occasionally observed from clouds which may only be some 2 km deep, with tops with temperatures above $0°C$, where it is impossible for ice crystals to develop and for the Bergeron-Findeisen process to operate.

Collision and coalescence process

This process has been proposed to explain the problem of rainfall from 'warm' clouds, but it is not an insignificant factor in clouds with ice crystals present. It is suggested that if a cloud consists of a large number of droplets being transported through it by turbulence and convection, collision between the droplets is bound to occur. Observations of the spectrum of sizes of cloud droplets within large tropical cumulus clouds indicate that although most of the droplets are small, there are always present some large droplets derived from large hygroscopic nuclei, such as salt particles. When such droplets swirl through the cloud within convection currents they will grow as a result of collision and subsequent coalescence with smaller droplets. The larger the droplets, the greater is the chance of a collision and therefore the faster the growth rate.

If the cloud is deep with a high water content, when the big drops approach the top of the cloud they will be too heavy to be sustained by the updraughts and will fall through and out of the cloud, growing larger by more collisions in transit. Some drops reach a critical size with a radius of 3 mm at which they become unstable and break up owing to the stresses imposed by their motion, thus providing a fresh supply of large drops. In this way a chain reaction is set up and a heavy shower may well result. The collision and coalescence process is believed to be responsible for the typical tropical shower in conditions where convection is strong and all of the cloud is at a temperature above $0°C$.

In general, droplet growth by condensation alone is regular but gradual; no coalescence will occur with droplets of less than 19 μm radius as they are too small, but the process is most effective for droplets greater than 30 μm. Beyond a radius of 40 μm the droplets will grow much more rapidly by collision and coalescence than by condensation. The rate of growth by collision and coalescence depends upon the following factors: (1) the efficiency with which the droplets sweep up their smaller neighbours; (2) the amount of liquid water in the air; and (3) the fall speed of the drops. The process works in conjunction with, and is complementary to, the Bergeron-Findeisen process in clouds with tops above the freezing level. Within such clouds the ice crystals with their complex dendritic shapes may well interlock on collision, forming snowflakes which may then grow in size in a similar manner. Like the Bergeron-Findeisen process, this too is a sufficiently quick process to produce raindrops at the observed rates.

Acid rain

The subject of acid rain (or more correctly 'acid deposition') has received increasing interest in recent years. Some of the major components of atmospheres polluted by industrial emissions include sulphur dioxide (SO_2) and nitrogen oxides (NO and NO_2). When particles of these substances form condensation nuclei, the result of water condensing upon them is a dilute solution of sulphuric or nitric acid. 'Pure' rain water has a pH of 5.6 (less than the neutral pH value of 7, due to the natural absorption of carbon dioxide by rain water). Recently-published information has shown that much of the rain which now falls over the British Isles has a mean pH below 5.0, it is sometimes as low as 4, and may be even lower for short periods (the lowest value on record in the UK is a pH of 2.4 – more acid than vinegar! – recorded at Pitlochry in Scotland).

The consequences of acid rain are beyond the scope of this book, but acid deposition affects water quality (a number of Scandinavian lakes and rivers have lost their fish stocks), vegetation (especially forests), and – in the long term – soils.

Rainfall types and intensities

Rainfall may arise from a number of synoptic situations, but it can generally be classified into one of three types:
(1) *Cyclonic* – due to the passage of a frontal depression.
(2) *Convective* – due to instability in the atmosphere (it is often of a showery nature).
(3) *Orographic* – due to the motion of air across an area of locally high ground.
Rainfall intensities are officially classified as *light* if the rain falls at a rate less than 0.5 mm/hr, *moderate* if the rate is between 0.5 and 4 mm/hr, and *heavy* if greater than 4 mm per hour.

PART TWO   WEATHER SYSTEMS

8   Thunderstorm systems

Thunder is the sound resulting from the violent and rapid expansion of the air as it is intensely heated to temperatures of 10,000°C or more along a channel only a few centimetres across, along the path of the lightning flash. The lightning flash is an enormous spark caused by the discharge of static electricity either between a cloud and the ground, between two clouds, or more rarely from one part of a cloud to another. There is a delay of some 3 seconds for every kilometre of distance separating the observer and the original flash, as the velocity of light is 3×10^5 km/sec while the speed of sound is only 3.3×10^{-1} km/sec. The flash is therefore seen almost immediately, while the sound travels approximately one-third of a kilometre every second. The normal rumbling effect of thunder is caused by the difference in time taken for sound to reach the observer's ear from various parts of the flash, combined with echo effects.

It is estimated that there are some 16 million thunderstorms over the earth each year, and in any one hour it is likely that some 2,000 are occurring over different parts of the earth. Their distribution is not even, however; few are recorded polewards of about 60° latitude, while in general numbers tend to increase equatorwards. Numbers are locally reduced over cool sea areas and where dynamic factors influence the stability of the atmosphere – very few occur within the subsident air of the subtropical anticyclones, for example. Kampala in Uganda averages some 242 days with thunderstorms per year, one of the highest averages anywhere.

The conditions which favour the development of thunderstorms are basically the same as those which favour the growth of vigorous cumulonimbus clouds:

(1) a deep, unstable – or potentially unstable – layer in the atmosphere, preferably from the ground to the tropopause;
(2) a plentiful supply of water vapour, especially near the ground where much of the cloud air originates; and
(3) strong winds in the high troposphere (at the level of outflow from the storm).

In addition, two extra factors are required for the generation of electrical charge within the thunderstorm: part of the cloud must lie in the temperature range $-20°$ to $-40°$C so that large quantities of ice pellets can develop; and there must be little vertical wind-shear within the cloud, in order that a deep, convective column with a vertical axis can develop.

The trigger action required to set off the deep convection may be of several kinds, either operating alone or in conjunction with others:

(1) Heating from below over land or sea produces rising cells of warm, moist, unstable air. This has a marked diurnal and seasonal variability, with maximum frequency and intensity in the afternoon in summer.
(2) Uplift over hills and mountain ranges may trigger off conditional instability.

(3) Convergence of air due to thermal or dynamic causes may result in intense convection (where sea breezes converge from the west and east coasts of Florida, for example, or within the cloud clusters which form the intertropical convergence zone in the tropics).

(4) Frontal ascent, where the air ahead of an active cold front is particularly unstable, may cause thunderstorms to develop along the line of the front (especially important in the development of squall-lines).

Thunderstorms are local (meso-scale) weather systems, where local environmental conditions influence patterns of temperature and airflow at scales of up to tens of kilometres in size; they are normally too small and localised to be shown on synoptic-scale weather maps.

Knowledge of the structure of thunderstorms and their associated weather is important as they are important components of many other weather systems, including tropical cyclones, the intertropical convergence zone and active cold fronts. Thunderstorms are usually classified according to their organisation, size and intensity.

The airmass thunderstorm

Airmass thunderstorms develop as a result of surface heating within warm, humid, unstable airmasses where individual cumulonimbus clouds grow to thunderstorm proportions. Much of the knowledge of the structure and dynamics of these comes from detailed aircraft and ground-based observations from the 'Thunderstorm Project', an extensive and comprehensive study undertaken in Florida in 1946 and south-west Ohio in 1947. Using data from a large number of case studies, the classic model of the evolution of a typical airmass thunderstorm was developed. It was shown that a thunderstorm undergoes a characteristic pattern of evolution, and that it consists of an agglomeration of *cells*. These thunderstorm cells are between one and a few kilometres across and contain vigorous chimneys of rising and descending air, i.e. updraughts and downdraughts. The typical lifetime of an individual cell is some 30 minutes to one hour, though a large thunderstorm, which is a cluster of continually evolving cells, may persist for up to twelve hours.

The life cycle of a thunderstorm cell can be summarised in terms of three stages. These are illustrated in the time-lapse photographs on p. 62; the circulations within the cell are shown in Fig. 8.1.

Cumulus stage

In this initial stage, the cumulus cloud is built up by the successive ascent of bubbles of warm air rising from a heated surface in a cell some 1–5 km in diameter and a top at about 6 km. As can be seen from Fig. 8.1a, updraughts prevail throughout the cell; these have a typical vertical velocity of some 10 m/sec, rising to a maximum of 60 m/sec at the top of the cloud where accelerations are greatest. Outside the cloud slow subsidence prevails. The temperatures inside the cloud are higher than those outside it (because of the instability), and this effect is increased by the release of latent heat of condensation within the updraughts. No precipitation and no lightning occur, for although rain or snow may develop, the updraughts are so vigorous that they are held in suspension.

Mature stage

The mature stage of the thunderstorm cell is reached as soon as rain starts to fall. As can be seen from Fig. 8.1b, both updraughts and downdraughts occur together in the bottom half of the cell. The downdraught is induced by the chilling effect and frictional drag of the precipitation particles (often frozen) falling through the cell, but once it has started it can continue without this frictional drive. The updraughts reach their maximum speed in the middle and upper parts of the cell, sometimes reaching up to 320 km/hr; they can prove a major cause of turbulence within the cloud and are very hazardous for aircraft. Temperatures within the unstable updraught are normally higher than those outside the cloud (helped by the release of latent heat of condensation), while temperatures within the downdraught are lower than those outside (dry air entrained from outside the cloud into the downdraught causes some of the precipitation to evaporate, and the resultant cooling enhances its negative buoyancy). Horizontal temperature contrasts of some 4°–5°C within the cloud help to accelerate the updraught.

The cold downdraught reaches the surface as a cold gust just before the onset of heavy precipitation; there is a marked drop in temperature accompanied by squally winds (often seen before a storm when dust is picked up and tree branches start to stir in the strong, turbulent wind) and a darkening of the sky (due to the great depth of cloud overhead obscuring the sun). The gusts are due to the cold air from the downdraught sinking to ground level and then spreading out laterally in the form of a slipper or wedge of cold dense air, undercutting the surrounding warmer surface air.

Fig. 8.1 Stages in the development of an airmass thunderstorm cell.

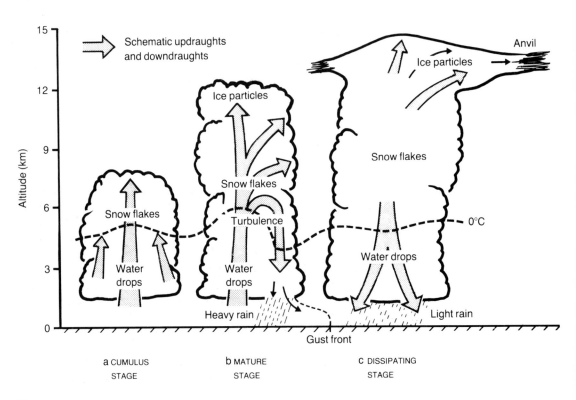

a CUMULUS STAGE

b MATURE STAGE

c DISSIPATING STAGE

Frequently the tops of such developing thunderstorm clouds reach the level of the tropopause (at 12 km or more) and sometimes because of the great buoyancy of the updraughts they may briefly overshoot into the stratosphere. The cloud at this level is composed of ice crystals and snowflakes and takes on the form of the characteristic 'anvil' of high-level cirrus cloud projecting downwind; this is due to the strong winds at these latitudes distorting the top of the cloud. The anvil – the main outflow region of the cloud – assumes a fibrous, wispy appearance because of its ice-crystal composition and it may extend downwind for tens of kilometres.

During this mature stage of development everything develops to its maximum intensity: the lightning activity reaches its climax, the turbulence within the cloud due to the downdraughts and updraughts reaches its maximum, and the heaviest rain, and perhaps hail, falls from the cloud.

Dissipating stage

During the dissipating stage, the anvil cloud top assumes its greatest development, but at lower levels the supply of warm, moist air feeding the cloud becomes exhausted (this may be influenced by cooling from the downdraught and its associated precipitation). The updraught finally ceases, and the entire lower part of the cell consists of gentle downdraughts with negligible vertical motions at higher levels. The downdraughts in turn weaken as the mass of water available to feed them is removed. The cloud air slowly reverts to the temperature of the surrounding atmosphere and the cloud gradually dissipates.

It has been estimated that only 20% of the water vapour condensed in the updraught reaches the ground as precipitation; the rest either evaporates in the downdraught or is left behind in the dissipating cloud which subsequently evaporates. However, if a typical thunderstorm of this type produces some 6 mm of precipitation in the form of rain and hail over an area of 64 km^2, then this represents a total mass of some 400,000 tonnes of water which has circulated within the cloud system. The latent heat of condensation released in such processes is enormous, representing an equivalent amount of energy to that released in the explosion of twelve atomic bombs of the size that dropped on Hiroshima.

Hail

When the thunderstorm circulation is particularly vigorous, hailstones are often produced from the cloud. These are transparent or partially opaque quasi-spherical lumps of ice that range in size from 5 mm in diameter (smaller particles are termed 'ice pellets') to 10 cm or more. The largest hailstone ever recorded fell at Coffeyville, Kansas, USA on 3 September 1970. It weighed 758 gm and measured some 190 mm in diameter and 444 mm in circumference. The heaviest recorded hailstone to fall in Britain fell at Horsham in Sussex on 5 September 1958, weighing 142 gm; 50 acres of apple trees were destroyed by the hailstorm and small pits were left in lawns marking where the hailstones had fallen and melted.

If such a hailstone is dissected and examined in polarised light to display its internal structure, it will be seen to consist of a series of

A time-lapse view of a
thunderstorm cell
evolution. (a) to (c) show
a mature cell developing
in the background and
producing an anvil cloud,
with a new cell
developing from the
cumulus stage to the
mature stage in the
foreground. It is rare for
such thunderstorms to
develop in this way in an
otherwise cloudless
environment. *Kindly
supplied by Carol
Unkenholz and Prof R. S.
Scorer*

a

b

c

more or less concentric onion-like shells of clear and opaque ice around a central nucleus, which is often an ice pellet (see photograph on p. 64). Hail forms in regions of violent updraughts and high concentrations of supercooled water droplets (i.e. droplets at subfreezing temperatures) within cumulonimbus clouds. The internal layered structure of a hailstone is largely controlled by the time it has spent in different regions of the cloud, each with different proportions of ice crystals and supercooled water droplets. A hailstone will frequently be picked up by a strong updraught and suspended in space against the force of gravity, whereas lighter droplets will ascend rapidly in the upcurrents. There will therefore be many collisions with the moving drops in a few seconds. When the hailstone is in an environment with a high liquid water content, the water accumulates on the nucleus faster than it can freeze, and a wet layer is formed which produces a clear layer of ice when it eventually freezes. When the hailstone falls through air with smaller and fewer drops, they may freeze immediately on impact, trapping bubbles of air, producing the opaque ice. Within a severe thunderstorm the hailstones may be swept through successive updraughts and downdraughts and recycled through large temperature changes several times, which accounts both for the layered nature of the hailstones and for their size. The probability of hail from a storm increases both with the intensity and the vertical extent of the storm.

Lightning

One of the most spectacular features of a thunderstorm is the associated lightning; this is responsible for some 150 deaths per year across the world and a considerable amount of damage to property and forests. Lightning is essentially a brief but massive discharge of electricity of about 20 coulombs, involving a potential difference of some 10^8–10^9 volts. Although Benjamin Franklin demonstrated the electrical character of thunderstorms over 200 years ago and the distribution of charge within the storm has long been known (the upper parts are mostly positively charged, while the central and lower regions are negatively charged, sometimes with a secondary centre of positive charge near the cloud base in the vicinity of the rain), scientists are still not certain of the processes by which the electrical charges are separated within the cloud and how they are concentrated in certain regions. There are various theories, but many fail because they are incapable of producing the necessary potential difference in the limited time available. Most workers agree, however, that the presence of ice particles in the upper region of the developing thunderstorm cloud together with active precipitation are important prerequisites.

Four main mechanisms appear to be responsible for the separation of the charge:
(1) Charges are separated when supercooled droplets collide with ice particles; both carry negative charges on their lower surfaces and positive charges on their upper surfaces, and when the cloud particles collide with the downward-moving precipitation particles, negative charges will be transferred to the latter by induction.
(2) Supercooled waterdrops freeze from the outside; thus when the water inside eventually freezes, expansion occurs and the outer ice shell splinters. Ice splinters carrying a positive charge will be carried

A thin section cut through a giant hailstone. The photograph, taken in reflected light, shows the onion-like shells of clear and opaque ice, caused by its passage through different regions of the hailstorm. *Kindly supplied by Dr K.A. Browning*

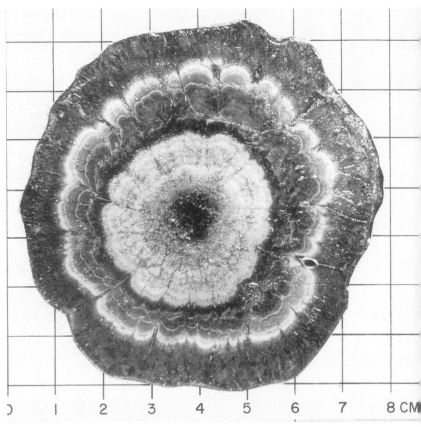

A satellite view of a well-marked squall line in the midwest United States on 31 May 1985. Note the large storms along the squall line (from which a number of severe tornadoes developed) interspersed with a larger number of small cells. *Kindly supplied by NOAA*

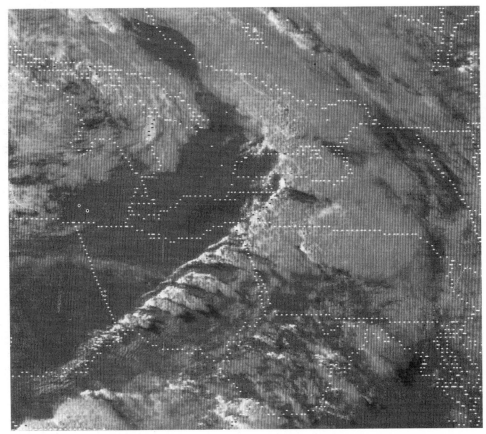

to the top of the cloud in the updraughts, while the ice crystals with their negative charges will fall to the base of the cloud.

(3) Falling cloud droplets or ice crystals may selectively capture negative atmospheric ions.

(4) Charges separate when large raindrops break on reaching their maximum size by coalescence (at 3 mm radius).

Cell development and movement

Many thunderstorms consist of several cells in different stages of development; radar observations have shown that the lifetime of an individual cell is of the order of half an hour. Radar and satellite imagery have also demonstrated that new cells tend to form most readily in the neighbourhood of the downdraughts from pre-existing cells, ahead of the cold air of the gust front. The cold downdraught spreads out laterally at the ground and the leading edge takes the form of a miniature cold front. This converges with the warm, potentially unstable environmental air, causing it to rise, and a new cumulus cell may well develop. This process is particularly effective where the downdraughts from two adjacent cells converge. The new cell is thus triggered on the forward side of the downdraught and this cell may then go through the same life cycle, while the old cell dissipates in the rear. Such a storm may persist for several hours, even though the lifetime of each cell is limited. In conditions with little wind, the storm may move irregularly, according to the growth and decay of its cells. When the wind field is well defined the storm will tend to travel more or less with the wind.

Multi-cell thunderstorms

A multi-cell thunderstorm is a large thunderstorm system comprising a number of cells at different stages of development. Although most of the updraughts and downdraughts within the individual thunderstorm cells similar to those described for airmass thunderstorms can still be identified (using radar) in multi-cell thunderstorms, some degree of *organisation* is present. Thunderstorms in this category tend to be more severe than the airmass thunderstorm. Many severe thunderstorms of this type develop over central USA in conditions when a warm, moist, southerly airflow from the Gulf of Mexico at low levels is overlain by a drier westerly flow aloft from the Rockies; the wind is here veering with height, i.e. it is changing direction in a clockwise sense.

In such a situation, it is found that while individual cells move in the direction of the mid-tropospheric winds (the winds at the level of the main cloudmass), the storm as a whole drifts systematically to the right of the environmental winds in the mid-troposphere, as shown schematically in Fig. 8.2. Low-level inflow into the storm occurs preferentially along the right side of the storm (normally from the south) and new cells develop here, while old cells tend to dissipate on the left flank of the storm, where the availability of warm, updraught air is limited. It is this pattern of development and decay of the component cells which gives the storm an effective propagation to the *right* of the mid-tropospheric winds. On average, in situations with winds veering with height, large multi-celled storms move at an angle of

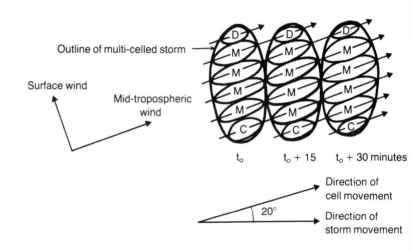

Fig. 8.2 A schematic illustration of the patterns of growth and decay of cells within a multi-celled storm moving to the right of the mid-tropospheric winds. The outline of the storm is shown at fifteen-minute intervals as it moves from left to right across the diagram; note that the new cells form on the right of the storm and old cells dissipate to the left. (C: cumulus stage; M: mature stage; D: dissipating stage)

some 20° to the right of the mean wind in the 850–500 mb layer. In the southern hemisphere, there is evidence from South Africa that similar storms move to the left of the mid-tropospheric winds.

Squall lines

A squall line (or instability line) is a line of well-developed thunderstorms, usually triggered in middle latitudes by a cold front. The thunderstorms are normally of varying structures and are often at different stages of development along the squall line. Such a system is normally associated with severe weather – heavy precipitation, strong winds, lightning, hail and occasionally tornadoes. They are frequently observed in summer over mid-latitude continental areas, especially central and eastern USA. Here they develop when an elongated tongue of warm, moist, conditionally unstable air in the warm sector of a depression lies ahead of an active cold front and beneath the eastern side of a trough in the upper westerlies (producing divergence aloft to get rid of the air flowing through the system). In the tropics they have been well documented in West Africa south of the Sahara.

The trigger mechanism to release the instability in the atmosphere is usually provided by the cold front sweeping into the moist warm-sector air at low levels and causing simultaneous development of thunderstorms along its leading edge. This usually appears on the radar or satellite image as an unbroken line of storms with a distinct leading edge; the convective activity is dominated by a small number of large storms interspersed with a larger number of small cells (see photograph on page 64).

The basic structure of a squall line is shown in cross-section in Fig. 8.3. Despite the varying configurations along the length of the squall line, it is nevertheless highly organised in cross-section with warm, moist, unstable air being forced to rise ahead of the cold gust front, which is itself produced by the sinking of cold, dense air from the downdraught behind it. The unstable air is lifted beyond its condensation level (usually marked by a dark and well-defined cloud-base) and the air then rises spontaneously forming deep cumulonimbus clouds. Massive amounts of water are rained out, and some of the precipitation falls into the downdraught air, whereupon evaporation occurs, with the resultant cooling invigorating the downdraught. The air within the system converges at the surface and diverges aloft. The system is thus organised and self-propagating; the processes responsible for the updraughts and downdraughts are complementary, allowing the squall line to travel across country as an open system with a marked two-dimensional organisation. Such systems have been observed for hours on radar screens.

The gust front shown in Fig. 8.3 is usually a marked feature of the circulation; at its passage there is usually a rapid temperature fall (of some 5°–10°C), an abrupt pressure rise (or surge), strong gusty winds (sometimes exceeding 25 m/sec) and a marked wind shift.

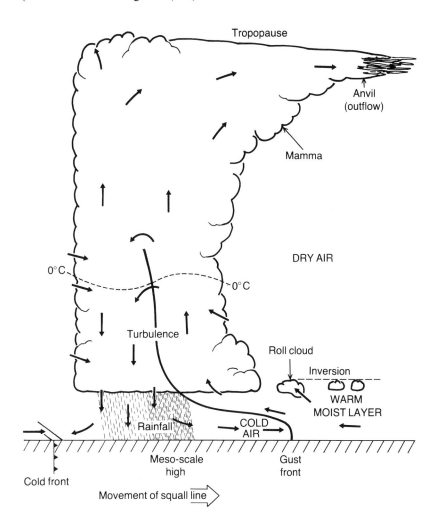

Fig. 8.3 A schematic cross-section through a squall line.

Supercell thunderstorms

Much research has been undertaken in the last 25 years or so, concerned with understanding and modelling the circulations within the really severe steady-state local storms which produce violent weather, hail and occasionally tornadoes. The use of radar, scanning the storms in both the horizontal and the vertical planes, has allowed a greater understanding of their anatomy both in terms of two-dimensional cross-sections and – more recently – of three-dimensional models.

The supercell thunderstorm is a large, violent storm dominated by one huge cell or supercell in a mature stage of development, which may persist in a steady state for hours. The supercell storm is more highly organised, larger, more persistent and more severe than all other types of thunderstorm. Air is continually being fed into the storm from below and emitted aloft (effectively turning the troposphere upside-down) while it propagates continuously to the right of the mean tropospheric winds (in the northern hemisphere) – unlike the discrete 'jumps' in one direction of the multi-celled storm. The term 'supercell' was first used for such storms by Browning in 1962, describing the Wokingham storm of 1959, from which large hailstones fell continuously for four hours along a 200-km-wide path over south-eastern England.

For their development, supercell storms require the following conditions:

(1) an atmosphere which is potentially unstable (often convection is limited by an inversion, but when this is overcome by either surface heating or circulation changes, explosive convection can result);
(2) convergence at low levels and a divergent circulation aloft; and
(3) strong vertical wind-shear, with the wind changing in strength and veering in direction with height.

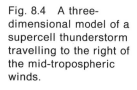

Fig. 8.4 A three-dimensional model of a supercell thunderstorm travelling to the right of the mid-tropospheric winds.

The main features of supercell thunderstorms are shown schematically in Fig. 8.4. This emphasises the fact that such thunderstorms are frequently asymmetric both in shape and in the distribution of their weather elements, with a 'left' and a 'right' side; it also stresses the necessity for strong vertical wind-shear in the

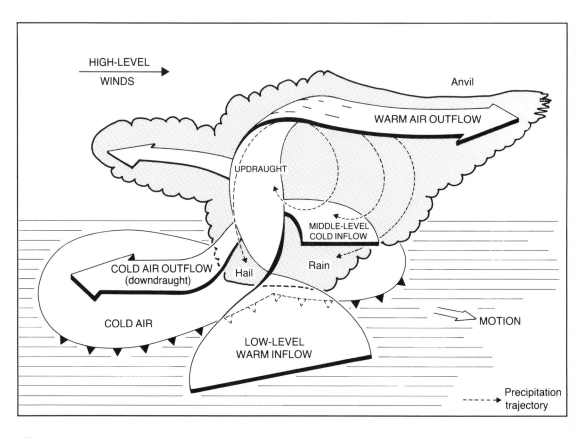

environment for such storms to develop. Both the updraught and downdraught air are derived from air approaching the storm with strong components of motion from its right side, while the outflows have a component of motion to the left of the storm's motion. The warm, moist, updraught air enters the storm from the right flank at low levels, twists cyclonically through some 270° while tilting slightly towards the rear before leaving the storm in the anvil, at right-angles to the direction at which it entered the storm. This is primarily due to the veering of the wind with height. The cold downdraught air is fed into the storm from the right at mid-tropospheric levels, ahead of the updraught; this undergoes a cyclonic turning through some 90° around the updraught before leaving the storm from the left rear side. The air entering the storm at these levels is dry and suitable for maintaining the downdraught by evaporative chilling, which is further augmented by the cooling from the evaporation of raindrops falling into it from the updraught above.

Rain droplets forming in the updraught region of the cloud are swept up into the storm by the violent circulation and held in suspension above, from where they may be recirculated up and down through the cloud several times (shown by the pecked lines in Fig. 8.4), often producing large hailstones. When they have achieved sufficient size their fall speeds become sufficiently great to fall through the updraught. Most of the hail tends to occur beneath the region of the updraught, while most of the rain falls towards the left forward flank of the storm and into the downdraught.

Tornadoes

Tornadoes are perhaps the most violent and frightening by-products of intense convective systems such as supercell thunderstorms and squall lines. They contain some of the highest windspeeds ever recorded, they strike with little warning and in a very short time a path of total destruction is left in their wake. A tornado normally appears as a narrow, black funnel cloud extending almost vertically from the base of a deep cumulonimbus cloud to, or nearly to, the ground (see photograph, page 70). Tornadoes are small in extent and ephemeral; Table 8.1 indicates typical dimensions and velocities. The fierce cyclonic winds within these narrow vortices are due to the sudden and enormous

Table 8.1 Features of tornadoes.

Feature	Characteristic magnitude	Typical range
Diameter	100 metres or less	2 m to 3 km
Path length (distance travelled across terrain)	3 km	A few metres to hundreds of km
Duration	4 minutes	A few seconds to several hours
Windspeed	90 ms^{-1}	80 ms^{-1} to 225 ms^{-1}
Speed of motion	10–20 ms^{-1}	0 to 20 ms^{-1}
Direction of travel	Southwest to northeast	Variable
Pressure fall	25 mb	20 to 200 mb

A tornado funnel cloud extending from the base of a cumulonimbus.
Kindly supplied by NOAA

drop in pressure within them; typically the pressure drop exceeds 25 mb, but pressure drops of 200 mb are not uncommon! The condensation within them resulting from this sudden pressure drop (and the consequent cooling) makes them visible. The pressure at the surface within a tornado is approximately the same as that at the base of the parent cloud.

Tornadoes leave an enormous amount of damage in their wake. This is due both to the extremely violent winds involved and the sharp drop in pressure during their passage which can cause buildings to explode. The resultant debris is then spun around and ejected at high speeds causing further damage. The intense upcurrents within them have the power to uproot trees and lift objects through the air, performing feats which may appear incredible to the unacquainted. There are numerous well-substantiated reports of animals having been carried through the air, of railway engines having been lifted bodily off the lines on which they were travelling, of buildings being lifted and moved on their foundations (giving rise to such newspaper headlines as 'Garage collides with car'!) and even of chickens losing their feathers during the passage of a tornado (owing to the explosion of the pocket of air contained within each quill). The debris contained within the funnel cloud adds to its dark appearance.

On average 100 people are killed each year by tornadoes in the USA, and they cause over $150 million of damage to property each year – but these figures disguise enormous variability. In 1973, one of the worst years on record, 1,107 tornadoes were reported in the USA causing 87 deaths and $600 million worth of damage. In the so-called 'super-outbreak' of tornadoes of 3–4 April 1974, which extended over thirteen states from Georgia to Michigan in the American mid-West, some 148 tornadoes occurred in 16 hours, 10 minutes. This was described by the US National Weather Service as 'the most devastating outbreak of tornadoes ever recorded anywhere in the world'; the total path was 4,157 km, 323 people were killed and 5,484 injured.

The USA tends to experience more tornadoes than anywhere else in the world. Every state has at some time experienced them, but there is a preferred region of tornado development in the Great Plains area of the mid-western and eastern Gulf States (known as 'Tornado Alley'), where conditions in summer often favour the development of severe storms (with warm, moist air from the Gulf of Mexico at low levels, overlain by cooler, drier air from the Rockies to the west). Tornadoes have a maximum incidence in early summer (most occur in May and June), and 80% occur between 14.00 and 22.00, with a peak incidence in the late afternoon at 17.00.

Tornadoes also occur elsewhere in the world and are not uncommon in the UK. Since 1971 Britain has averaged some 18 tornadic days each year, with an annual average of 45 separate tornadoes; in 1981 there were 152 reported tornadoes on only 12 days, including 105 on 23 November 1981 from a very vigorous cold front – Europe's biggest tornado outbreak on record. In general, however, they tend to be much less severe than those in the USA; most develop from violent convection in well-defined cold fronts associated with rapidly deepening depressions in the winter half of the year.

The reasons for tornado development are still largely uncertain and these vortices remain a great meteorological enigma. To quote the Meteorological Office's *Meteorological Glossary* of 1972: 'While the conditions required for the formation of a tornado are similar to those required for a severe thunderstorm . . . the precise conditions which cause tornadoes (rather than merely thunderstorms) are not yet known'. Despite an extensive literature which associates their development with the presence of such features as hail, lightning and rapid cumulus development, there is still no acceptable theory to explain both their formation and their maintenance.

It is reasonably certain that their development is associated with (a) great instability, (b) strong convergence, and (c) very vigorous and persistent updraughts within the cloud. Recent radar evidence has shown that the most violent tornadoes form beneath the twisting updraughts of supercell thunderstorms. As already outlined, the inflow converges and feeds the updraught which twists cyclonically through 270°. It appears that in the right conditions, the updraught and the convergence may reach sufficient magnitudes that in order for the air to conserve its angular momentum a tight vortex of small radius results, leading to a sudden drop in pressure and the development of the funnel cloud. If the inflow layer is restricted to a shallow surface layer beyond the storm by an inversion, for example, on entering the storm circulation the air will suddenly converge and be accelerated within the updraught to high levels (analogous to pulling the plug out of a sink of water) and a vortex will develop. On occasions the tornado circulation may extend into the cloud, forming a rotating tornado cyclone.

9 Local wind systems

Two further examples of meso-scale circulations induced by local temperature differences are the land and sea breeze and the mountain-valley wind system.

The land and sea breeze

Land and water surfaces have different thermal responses to the same amount of insolation, and most land surfaces have a much greater diurnal range of temperature (i.e. high maximum and lower minimum temperatures) than water bodies, which tend to exhibit much more uniform temperatures throughout the day (see Fig. 9.1). The four main reasons for this are as follows:

(1) Whereas the insolation is used to heat up the surface of the land, the same energy is absorbed by a large volume of water; short-wave incoming radiation penetrates to a depth of some 10 metres in most water, but up to several hundreds of metres in clear tropical waters.

(2) The volume of water being heated by the insolation is further increased by the natural motion of the water and the convection within it.

(3) Much of the energy is used as latent heat (through the evaporation of the water) rather than direct (or sensible) heating of the water. Evaporation has the effect of cooling the water surface, which further encourages surface mixing.

(4) The thermal capacity (or heat capacity) of water is exceptionally large (see Chapter 5). It requires up to four times as much heat to raise a unit volume of water through the same temperature interval as a unit volume of soil.

For these reasons, temperature gradients are set up between the land and the sea, and these have a diurnal reversal (the land is warmer than the sea during the day and the sea warmer than the land at night). In the right synoptic situations, temperature differences induce local air

Fig. 9.1 The diurnal variation in temperature of a land and water surface under cloudfree conditions. Note the much greater temperature range of the land surface.

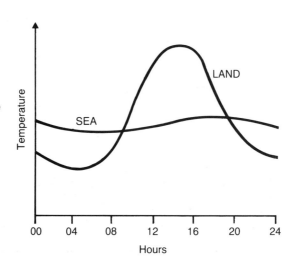

density and pressure gradients, which provide the driving force for breezes to become established across the shoreline with a diurnal rhythm. The *sea breeze* blows from the sea to the land during the day, with a compensating offshore flow aloft; the weaker *land breeze* blows from the land to the sea at night (again with a weak return flow aloft). Similar circulations can develop in the vicinity of large inland water bodies, such as the Great Lakes, producing *lake breezes*.

In the early morning, under calm, cloudfree conditions, there is no pressure gradient between the land and the sea, and in the vertical section (Fig. 9.2a) the isobaric (pressure) surfaces are horizontal. As the day proceeds, the air over the land surface heats up and expands relative to that over the cooler sea. Because the decrease in air density with height (or vertical pressure gradient) is greater in cool air than in

Fig. 9.2 Pressure distributions and resultant patterns of ascent and descent associated with the development of land and sea breezes. (H: high pressure; L: low pressure)

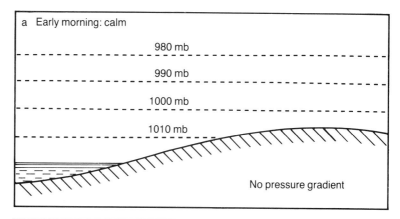

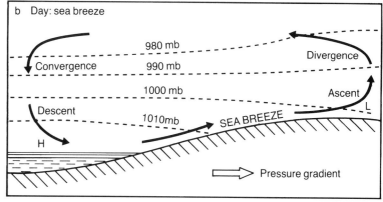

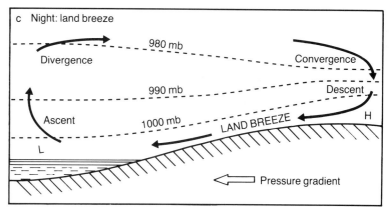

warm air (discussed in Chapter 12), the initially horizontal pressure surfaces become tilted as shown in Fig. 9.2b. At a height of 1 km or so, the pressure is higher over the land and air begins to flow seawards. The divergence aloft over the land causes the pressure to fall at the surface as air rises to take its place. Over the sea the air converges aloft, increasing the pressure at the surface; air sinks over the sea and the development of the surface pressure gradient of approximately 1 mb per 50 km is sufficient to give rise to the landward flow of the sea breeze.

At night, cooler land temperatures cause the air to subside and diverge at the surface (helped by cold air drainage off the sloping coast) while over the sea there is convergence and weak ascent (as shown in Fig. 9.2c). The flow of air at night is thus reversed, from land to sea at the surface, with a landward flow aloft. This circulation tends to be weaker than the sea breeze (partially owing to the smaller temperature difference between the land and sea at night compared with the daytime difference, as shown in Fig. 9.1).

The structure of the sea-breeze circulation is shown schematically in Fig. 9.3a (note the exaggeration of the vertical scale in the diagram). The leading edge of the sea breeze is marked by a *sea-breeze front*, a convergence line separating the land air from the cool sea air; this gradually advances inland as the day progresses. The structure of the sea-breeze front is very narrow, usually only some 100–200 metres wide, and with an overall slope of some 1 in 10.

Fig. 9.3 Land- and sea- (lake-) breeze circulations (a) during the day, and (b) during the night. Note that the vertical scale is exaggerated compared with the horizontal scale.

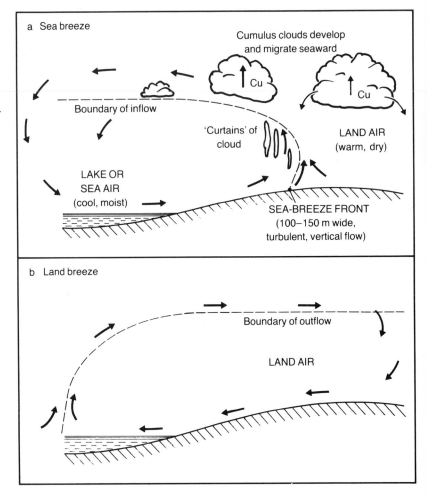

At the passage of a sea-breeze front over a weather station, the following changes are normally observed: (1) the wind direction changes (it may be northerly or northwesterly ahead of the front along the south coast of England, but southerly within the sea air); (2) windspeed increases; (3) there is a decrease in temperature; (4) the relative humidity increases, as the land air is replaced by sea air; and (5) there is a change in visibility (the sea air is often hazy in summer).

The warm, inland air rises ahead of the wedge-like advance of the cool sea air, with turbulent upcurrents of some 1–2 m/sec. These upcurrents are a favoured source of lift for glider pilots. If the land air is sufficiently moist, the rising air is normally marked by a line of cumulus cloud. The narrow region of ascent within the cooler, moist sea air is often marked by a wispy curtain of vertical cloud, rising to the inversion separating the warm, dry land air aloft and the cool, moist sea-breeze air below.

The sea-breeze system gradually moves inland at speeds of 2–5 m/sec, and can be traced across country from surface weather observations. By 21.00, under favourable conditions, the circulation may stretch for hundreds of kilometres in length, parallel to the coast, and may have extended 40–50 km inland. Where two sea breezes converge from different coastlines, the convection may be much more accentuated, and showers may develop in these areas although surrounding areas remain dry. The front itself may not be regular, especially in undulating terrain. Indentations exceeding 1 km or more may exist, there may be gaps in some areas and there may be diffuse sections in its structure. In some parts the front may move gradually; elsewhere it may move in a series of pulsations as it moves through gaps in the terrain.

Given the right synoptic conditions, sea breezes can occur on most coasts equatorwards of about 50° latitude, and on average occur on some 2–3 days out of 10 in West European summers. Sea breezes are more common and better developed in the tropics and subtropics, however, where local heating of the land is especially effective. In Jakarta they occur on 7–8 days out of 10. In the tropics such circulations may extend 200 km or more inland, and may generate showers from the convection along the sea-breeze front. On peninsulas (such as Florida), sea breezes may converge from both sides and produce deep convection, showers, and even thunderstorms, where the two systems meet.

The mountain-valley wind system

Airflow within mountainous terrain is rarely simple and often complex in form. The mountains act as obstacles to large-scale regional airflow, providing local shelter in some areas, while elsewhere it gusts and eddies around summits and escarpments. At low levels, when the wind is in the right direction, it may be channelled (or funnelled) through valleys at high speeds, while at higher levels the mountains may generate lee waves (and lenticular lee-wave clouds) in the air above and behind them.

However, when the large-scale regional winds are light, when the skies are cloudfree and the scale of the relief is great, the differential heating of the mountains and valleys may generate its own local mountain-valley wind circulations with the diurnal rhythm.

At night the valley surfaces radiate long-wave energy to space, and cool down, chilling the air in contact with them. This cool, stable air drains downhill into the valley bottoms because of its density, producing a downslope *katabatic* flow, known as the *mountain wind*. The accumulation of cold, dense air in hollows, depressions and valley bottoms can sometimes lead to frost in the low-lying land, or valley fog when the air is sufficiently moist. During the day, mountain slopes facing the sun are heated; the air in contact with the slopes expands and rises up the valley and the mountain slopes because of its buoyancy as an *anabatic flow* or *valley wind*. This may lead to the formation of convective clouds over the mountains during the afternoon, with clear conditions over the valley (see Fig. 9.4). The winds associated with this anabatic flow are greatest at around 14.00, the time of the greatest influence from surface heating. The flow is a thermally direct, reversible circulation similar to the land/sea breeze. The return flows aloft are usually less marked apart from their influences on cloud formation.

Given a favourable synoptic situation (anticyclonic, cloudfree conditions in the summer months), the intensity of the circulation in a particular valley depends on the following: (1) its orientation (south-facing slopes are heated more effectively than slopes with other aspects); (2) the magnitude of the relief (i.e. difference in height of the valley bottom and adjacent ridge tops); (3) the type and amount of vegetation cover (bare rock heats up more rapidly than green vegetation, while the latter retards surface flows more because of the effect of friction, particularly on forested slopes); (4) the surface conditions (the circulations are best developed when the ground is dry rather than wet, but a snow-cover will accentuate the nocturnal down-valley flows); and (5) the geometry of the valley (whether straight or meandering in form, whether the valley sides are steep or gently sloping, and whether there are constrictions or obstacles to surface flows in the valley). The circulations are best developed in deep, straight, unvegetated valleys with a north-south axis; in other configurations the flows become irregular or incomplete.

In the calm conditions prevailing just after sunrise, the isobaric surfaces across the mountain-valley cross-section are horizontal. As the day progresses and the sun heats the mountain slopes, the air next to the sloping ground becomes warmer than the air at the same height over the valley, locally producing a greater vertical pressure gradient in the cooler free air above the valley than in the warmer air above the slope (similar to the pressure gradients responsible for the land-/sea-breeze circulations described earlier). An upslope pressure gradient develops at the surface from the valley bottom to the slopes, giving rise to an upslope (anabatic) wind during the day, with rising air over the slopes (the thermals often producing clouds), compensated by sinking cloudfree air over the valley. At night the mechanism and the resultant circulation is reversed with cold, stable air sinking from the valley slopes to the valley bottom, compensated by weak ascent over the valley bottom (see Fig. 9.4).

Nocturnal katabatic flows tend to occur on slopes where the angles are 2° or greater, and where there are few large-scale obstacles to air movement. The flows resulting from a single night's cooling in Britain usually have depths from a few metres to up to 150 metres, the shallow flows occurring if there is no wind to cause any mixing of air in the vertical. The rate of flow is typically of the order of just 3 km/hr, but

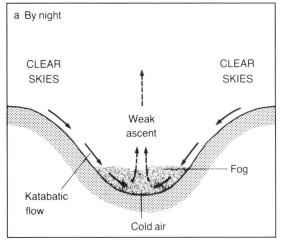 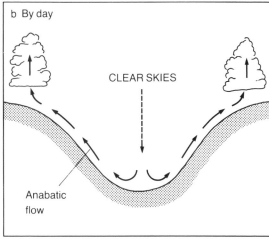

Fig. 9.4 A schematic diagram of the mountain-valley wind circulation: (a) at night, cold air drains as a katabatic flow from the slopes into the valley bottom (where, on saturation, fog may form) with weak ascent above and further cold air drainage down the valley (out of the plane of the cross-section); (b) during the day, warm air rises up the valley sides, producing cloud above the mountain ridges, with compensating sinking motion over the cloudfree valley – the anabatic flow continues up the valley (into the plane of the cross-section).

the rates of flow vary with the geometry of the terrain and the prevailing synoptic situation. The flows commence after sunset and attain their maximum velocities at about 06.00.

It must be borne in mind that although the 'flow of cold air' presents an analogy with the flow of water down slopes, the processes involved are very different. Water has a density 800 times that of air, and with a temperature difference of as much as 10°C, the density of cold air is only some 4% greater than warm air. Cold air thus moves very slowly – it can sometimes be seen by the motion of drifting bonfire or chimney smoke on calm autumn evenings. The katabatic flow may be gradual or it may occur in intermittent surges, where the cold air is blocked by obstacles until a threshold is reached and it plunges forward.

Such flows are responsible for producing local radiation or valley fogs on cloudless nights in the autumn and winter months when the air is sufficiently moist (especially where the local humidity is increased by the presence of a river, lake or other surface water in the valley) and the air is cooled below its dew-point temperature.

Frost may also form in the cold air draining off higher ground into local hollows, valleys or 'frost pockets'. The Chess valley between Rickmansworth and Chorleywood in the Chilterns is one of the best examples of a frost hollow in England, and is due to an unfavourable combination of topography (a large catchment area for cold air drainage) and very dry, porous soils overlying the chalk. In a study of this locality over the years 1930–42, only 2 months out of the 156 were without ground frost on the valley floor, such frosts even occurring during the summer months. A further consequence is that valley bottoms in the British uplands normally have higher diurnal ranges of temperature than the mountain summits; they receive the coldest air at night, while by day the sheltered valleys have the warmest temperatures.

Usually such katabatic flows are weak in this country, but a very cold, strong, outblowing wind is a regular feature of both the Antarctic and Greenland ice-caps, where the intense chilling of the air in contact with the frozen surfaces augments the normal down-valley wind, producing violent and persistent winds in a circulation up to 300 metres deep. At Adelieland, the wind may attain speeds of up to 45 m/sec (exceeding hurricane force), one of the strongest thermally driven circulations on earth.

10 Frontal depressions

Much of the characteristic weather of mid-latitudes is determined by the variable incidence of the weather systems within the prevailing westerly circulation of these latitudes, such as the mobile frontal depressions and the less mobile anticyclones.

In 1863 Admiral Fitzroy, the first director of the Meteorological Office, suggested that depressions formed on the boundary between two great 'airstreams' with markedly different properties: warm and humid airstreams from the subtropics, and colder, drier air from the polar regions. Meteorologists and climatologists would today refer to these airstreams as *airmasses*.

Airmasses

Air that remains fairly stationary over an environment of uniform geographical character (such as a large area of ocean) will tend to develop thermal equilibrium with this environment, and by prolonged contact will take on the temperature and humidity characteristics of the underlying surface. It may thus acquire approximately homogeneous values of temperature and humidity over hundreds of thousands of square kilometres, with small horizontal gradients of these at any particular level. Areas dominated by large anticyclones are particularly suitable for the development of such homogeneous bodies of air, known as airmasses.

For example, in the snow-covered wastes of Siberia and northern Canada during the long winter period, the ground becomes extremely cold. By virtue of contact cooling with the surface and gentle mixing, anticyclonic air stagnating over this 'source region' becomes very cool and dry, forming a Polar continental airmass. In contrast, air over the tropical oceans (in the region of the Azores anticyclone, for example) will gradually acquire the characteristic temperature of the tropical ocean at low levels; after a period of time in the same source region the warmth and moisture will have penetrated into the cloud and subcloud region as a result of convection and turbulent mixing, forming a Tropical maritime airmass.

The airmass concept was originally developed by Bergeron, Bjerknes and their co-workers in the 1920s in Norway, as part of their development of the Polar Front Theory. Today airmasses are usually termed either Arctic (A), Polar (P), or Tropical (T) according to the latitude of their source region and are either maritime (m) or continental (c) according to the underlying environment. Combining these labels gives six possible airmass categories (Am, Ac, Pm, Pc, Tm, Tc), although only five are normally used, as the Arctic category is rarely subdivided.

Figure 10.1 illustrates the principal source regions and trajectories of the airmasses affecting the British Isles, and Table 10.1 lists the main features of each airmass category, and their characteristics over the British Isles.

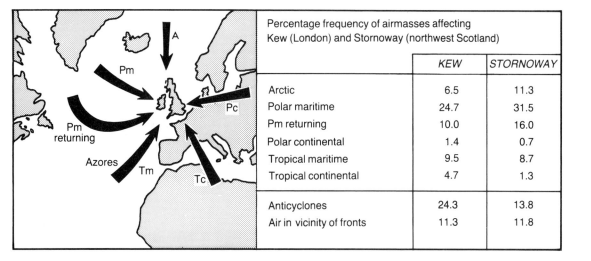

Percentage frequency of airmasses affecting Kew (London) and Stornoway (northwest Scotland)		
	KEW	*STORNOWAY*
Arctic	6.5	11.3
Polar maritime	24.7	31.5
Pm returning	10.0	16.0
Polar continental	1.4	0.7
Tropical maritime	9.5	8.7
Tropical continental	4.7	1.3
Anticyclones	24.3	13.8
Air in vicinity of fronts	11.3	11.8

Fig. 10.1 Source regions and trajectories of airmasses affecting the British Isles, together with their annual frequency of occurrence. (Note that some days cannot be classified; hence the figures do not add up to 100%.)

The *Arctic* airmass has a source region in the high Arctic and produces very cold weather in winter and cold conditions in spring and early summer (it is very rare in summer). It tends to be unstable in its lowest layers by the time it reaches Britain, owing to surface heating as it moves away from its cold source region. This produces showers (often sleet, snow or hail in winter and spring) especially on windward coasts; leeward districts may well enjoy relatively clear skies.

Polar maritime air originates over the northern part of the North Atlantic Ocean, and is the commonest airmass affecting the British Isles. It produces cold or rather cold conditions in all seasons, especially on windward coasts. It is unstable (owing to the surface heating as the air moves to lower latitudes), often producing showers from cumulus or cumulonimbus clouds, with bright intervals in between – the clouds tend to die out inland at night and in winter. If a depression becomes slow-moving west of the British Isles, Pm air may well flow south from its source region well beyond 50°N so that when it approaches the British Isles from the southwest it has been greatly modified; this is normally referred to as a *returning polar maritime* airmass. Because of the modification during its passage, the instability is greatly decreased by the time it reaches Britain and the resultant temperatures tend to be close to the seasonal normal.

Polar continental air originates from northern Eurasia, and produces cold or very cold conditions in winter, and warm conditions in summer (following the temperature of the continent). The air is normally unstable and cloudy in winter, producing snow showers in the easterly winds along the east coast; further west conditions tend to be drier with clearer skies. In the summer months the air is less unstable when it reaches the British Isles, because of the cooling influence of the North Sea; the cloud cover depends on the air's trajectory – whether it has a lengthy passage over the North Sea or not. Inland districts tend to experience warm conditions and clear skies, while temperatures are cooler on the east coast with either an overcast sky of low stratus, or sea fog (in light winds).

Tropical maritime air originates in the vicinity of the Azores anticyclone to the southwest of the British Isles, and brings mild conditions in winter and warm weather in the summer, especially in the east. The air is stable (owing to cooling as it moves northwards), with

Table 10.1 Properties of the major airmasses affecting the British Isles.

Airmass	Source region	Temperature	Typical temperatures in London (°C) Jan.	Typical temperatures in London (°C) July	Humidity	Typical humidity mixing ratios in London (g/kg) Jan.	Typical humidity mixing ratios in London (g/kg) July	Stability in source region	Stability over the British Isles	Synoptic situation producing the airmass over the British Isles	Associated weather types
Arctic (A)	Within the Arctic Circle	Very cold or severe in winter; cold in summer	1	14	Dry	3.1	6.3	Very stable	Unstable	Low over Scandinavia with blocking high over mid-Atlantic	Northerly or northwesterly
Polar maritime (Pm)	Ocean in vicinity of Iceland and Greenland polewards of 50°N	Cold in winter, cool or rather cold in summer	6	18	Rather moist	5.8	8.4	Unstable	Unstable	Deep depression northwest of Scotland, bringing air from vicinity of Iceland over the British Isles	Northwesterly, northerly or cyclonic
Polar continental (Pc)	Northern Eurasia	Cold or very cold in winter; warm or very warm in summer	−2	—	Dry	2.6	—	Stable	Unstable especially in lower layers	Anticyclone over Scandinavia	Easterly
Tropical maritime (Tm)	Azores anticyclone	Mild in winter; warm in summer	11	19	Moist at surface; dry aloft	6.8	10.8	Unstable near surface; stable aloft	Stable	Ridge of high pressure from Azores anticyclone towards the British Isles	Westerly, southerly or cyclonic
Tropical continental (Tc)	North Africa and Mediterranean	Mild in winter; hot in summer	13	22	Dry	4.5	12.1	Unstable	Stable	Anticyclone over central Europe	Southerly

Sources: Barry, R. G. and Chorley, R. J. (1982) *Atmosphere, Weather and Climate* (Methuen) pp. 151, 155 who use data from Belasco, J. E. (1952) 'Characteristics of air masses over the British Isles' in *Met. Office Geophysical Memoirs* 11(87); Lamb, H. H. (1964) *The English Climate* (English Universities Press) pp. 48–50.

dull skies, drizzle and occasional hill and coastal fog in windward areas; conditions further east are normally brighter and sunnier.

Tropical continental air originates from north Africa and the Mediterranean. It is the least common airmass to affect our shores (see Fig. 10.1), but when it does arrive it brings very mild conditions in winter and very warm conditions in summer. The weather is typically cloudy in winter with a cloud cover of stratus, while in summer thunderstorms may occasionally develop if surface temperatures rise sufficiently in the southerly airflow.

Because of the location of the British Isles on the western edge of Europe, airmasses arriving from the west tend to be maritime whereas those with an easterly component are continental in character. As westerly winds tend to be the most frequent in our latitudes, it will be seen from Fig. 10.1 that maritime airmasses are the most frequent over the British Isles. It will be seen that Pm and Pm returning occur on nearly 50% of days at Stornoway in the northwest of Scotland.

As airmasses move away from their source regions they are modified by interaction with the surface over which they are flowing, and this can affect their temperature, humidity and stability. When Arctic and Polar continental airmasses move southwards they are heated at the surface and become more unstable. If Pc air moves out over the Atlantic, the rate of heating may be so great that the instability and moisture are quickly transferred to great heights within the air, so that it is rapidly transformed to Polar maritime. The evaporation from the warmer water surface increases its moisture content.

Tropical maritime or Tropical continental air moving northwards to regions of cooler surface temperatures is normally cooled and becomes more stable, leading to the development of stratus clouds and fog.

The structure of an airmass is also changed by the processes of convergence and divergence associated with the large-scale patterns of air flow. Divergence is associated with anticyclonic motion and tends to stabilise the air and reduce cloud, while convergent cyclonic flow tends to increase the instability and the amount and depth of cloud.

There are a number of difficulties in applying airmass labels in real situations: (1) there is no universal agreement on either an internationally acceptable system of airmass classification or the precise specifications of a particular airmass, mainly because the characteristics of the airmass types differ considerably from continent to continent; (2) the airmass concept was originally developed using only surface data – heavy emphasis is often placed on surface temperatures and humidities, frequently at the expense of more important dynamic features; (3) conditions are rarely uniform in the source areas; (4) many airmasses are transitional in character, owing to modifications arising as they move away from the source regions; and (5) precipitation is more closely related to the dynamics of the atmosphere (instability, stability, presence of inversions, convergence and divergence) than airmass type.

An airmass in its source region is an example of a *barotropic* atmosphere (a homogeneous atmosphere where the isobars and isotherms are parallel in any vertical cross-section); in contrast, at their boundaries where different airmasses converge, strong horizontal gradients of temperature and humidity occur and the atmosphere is *baroclinic* (a condition where isotherms and isobars intersect each other in any vertical cross-section). Here *fronts* are nearly always found.

The Polar Front Theory

The Polar Front Theory is the name given to a series of papers concerning the processes in operation within a mid-latitude depression, produced by a remarkable group of Norwegian meteorologists (V. and J. Bjerknes, Bergeron and Solberg) working in Bergen just after World War I. Together the papers constitute the first major theory of such depressions. The fundamental notion within the Polar Front Theory is that many of the day-to-day weather variations in middle latitudes are connected with the movement and evolution of the boundaries between airmasses which they called *fronts* (analogous to the boundaries between opposing forces in the War).

In his first paper in 1919 entitled 'On the structure of moving cyclones' – one of the most influential meteorological papers ever written – V. Bjerknes introduced the idea of an asymmetrical cyclone with discontinuities in the isobar pattern. He wrote: 'Every moving cyclone has two lines of convergence, which are greater and more conspicuous than the others, and distinguished by characteristic thermal properties'. He called these two lines the *steering line* and the *squall line* (later to be termed the *warm front* and *cold front* respectively) and suggested that the warm and cold airmasses converged along these lines or surfaces. He called the warm region between the two lines the *warm sector*. Regarding the distribution of clouds and rain he noted that in front of the steering line the zones of rain and cloud were due to the ascent of warm air up the slowly inclined steering surface, with the clouds changing continuously from cirrostratus to nimbus (to paraphrase his own words). He stated that the zone of rain along the squall line is caused by ascent of warm air ahead of the cold air, with the rapid ascent giving the rainfall its greater intensity.

In 1922, Bjerknes and Solberg wrote a further paper entitled 'Life cycles of cyclones and the polar front theory of the atmospheric circulation' which presented an elaborate account of the Polar Front Theory as we now know it. Here the two convergence lines were called 'warm front' and 'cold front' for the first time (the warm front can be regarded as the leading edge or front of the warm airmass, while the cold front is similarly the front of the cold airmass). The cold front and warm front are linked in the form of a wave which increases in amplitude with time. The nature of occlusions was explained and families of wave cyclones were identified.

The initial stage of a wave cyclone (or frontal depression) is a slight deformation of the polar front, producing a wave. If the wave is dynamically unstable it grows in amplitude, with the warm air creating a poleward bulge into the cold air which begins to flow around the rear of the wave as shown in Fig. 10.2a. At this stage the wind has a component blowing from cold to warm air behind the wave and from warm to cold ahead of it (such poleward transfer of warm air is an important energy transfer process in the general circulation of the atmosphere). The whole system will tend to move in a direction parallel to the isobars within the warm sector (a useful forecasting rule of thumb).

As the development of the system continues, more and more cold air is replaced by warm air, whose lower density contributes to a decrease in pressure and the development of cyclonic flow around the region of low pressure at the tip of the warm sector (with divergence aloft).

Within 24 hours of the initial disturbance of the front, a well-defined warm-sector depression will have developed with warm front, cold front, and a cloud and weather distribution corresponding to the classic model of Fig. 10.2b, enlarged in Fig. 10.3. The cold air forms a wedge in cross-section, undercutting the warm-sector air owing to its greater density, with the warm air gliding up the frontal surface at the warm front. Cloud belts and precipitation result from the convergence and ascent at the two fronts as shown in Fig. 10.3.

Within the system the air behind the cold front moves faster than the air receding ahead of the warm front. With time the cold front 'catches up' the warm front and the warm air is gradually lifted from the surface and the frontal system begins to occlude. The front that is formed by the merger of the cold front and warm front is called an *occluded front*, as shown in Fig. 10.2c; it is bounded on both sides by cold air of slightly different thermal properties. The process of lifting of the warm air is called *occlusion*.

The different temperatures of the cold air behind the cold front and ahead of the warm front are generally due to their different trajectories. There are two types of occluded front: the cold occlusion (Fig. 10.4a), when the air behind the occluded front is colder than the air ahead of it, and the warm occlusion when the reverse is the case (Fig. 10.4b). The former is the more common over the North Atlantic in summer (in a situation where the air behind the cold front has had a cool oceanic trajectory, while the air ahead of the warm front has had a largely continental, warmer trajectory). The warm occlusion tends to occur over land areas in winter, where cold Polar continental air lies ahead of the system.

The final stage of development is shown in Fig. 10.2d, where as the cold front overtakes the warm front at increasing distances from the centre of the depression, the occlusion grows in extent and the warm-sector air becomes almost totally eliminated at the surface. The depression is transformed into a large, weak vortex, and will gradually fill and dissipate.

Fig. 10.2   Stages in the evolution of a frontal depression according to the Polar Front Theory. The middle diagrams represent surface weather charts at different times; the areas of cloud are shown in grey, the areas of precipitation are shown as pecked lines. Upper and lower diagrams represent cross-sections drawn at the positions of the pecked lines in the middle diagrams.
(a) growing wave;
(b) mature wave;
(c) partially occluded wave; (d) occluded wave. (W: warm; C: cold)

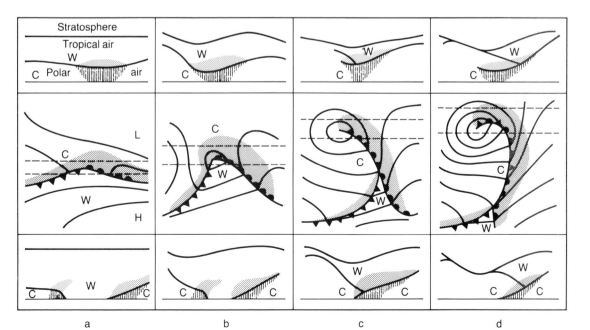

a   b   c   d

Fig. 10.3 An idealised model of a warm-sector depression. Upper diagram: vertical cross-section north of wave depression. Middle diagram: representation of frontal wave and streamlines on surface chart. Lower diagram: vertical cross-section through warm sector. Shading indicates areas of precipitation.

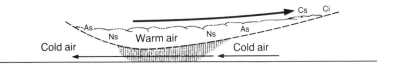

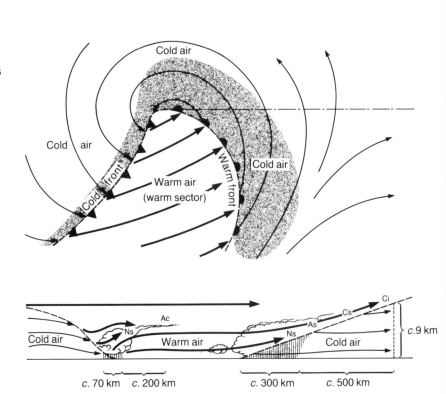

Fig. 10.4 Schematic cross-sections through a cold occlusion (left) and a warm occlusion (right).

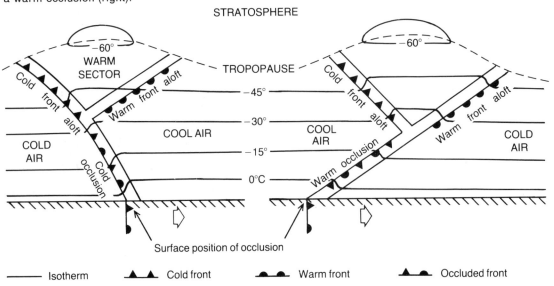

In the classical Norwegian model, the cloud forms at the warm and cold fronts are very different. The effect of the steeper cold front is to set off cumuliform, convective clouds which tend to produce heavy, showery rain of relatively short duration. The slow upgliding of air at the warm front produces sheets of more stratiform, layered cloud and more persistent, generally less intense rain. The sequences of weather which are normally experienced with the passage of a warm and cold front are listed in Table 10.2.

Frequently a succession of waves forms along the polar front, producing a succession of cyclones or lows in various stages of development. These secondary depressions form along the cold front of the main or parent depression. Such families frequently develop over the North Atlantic and Pacific Oceans, with systems usually separated by some 1,500 km or more, but they rarely develop in the southern

Table 10.2 The normal sequence of weather associated with the passage of a warm and cold front.

Element	In advance	At passage	In the rear
Warm front			
Pressure	Steady fall	Fall ceases	Little change or slow fall
Wind	Increases and sometimes backs	Veers and sometimes decreases	Steady direction
Temperature	Steady/slow rise	Rise	Little change
Dew-point temperature	Rises in the area of precipitation	Rise	Steady
Relative humidity	Rises in the area of precipitation	May rise further	Little change
Cloud	Ci, Cs, As, Ns in succession; scud below As and Ns	Low Ns and scud	St or Sc
Weather	Continuous rain (or snow)	Precipitation almost stops	Cloudy, drizzle or light rain
Visibility	Good, except in rain	Poor, often misty	Usually poor; mist may persist
Cold front			
Pressure	Fall	Sudden rise	Rise continues more slowly
Wind	Increasing and backing, becoming squally	Sudden veer, perhaps squally	Backing a little after squall, then steady or veering
Temperature	Steady, but falls in rain	Sudden fall	Little change, variable in showers
Dew-point temperature	Little change	Sudden fall	Little change
Relative humidity	May rise in precipitation	Remains high in precipitation	Rapid fall as rain ceases
Cloud	Ac or As, then Cb	Cb with low scud	Lifting rapidly, followed by As or Ac; later further Cu or Cb
Weather	Rain	Rain, often heavy, with perhaps thunder and hail	Heavy rain for short period, sometimes more persistent, then fair with occasional showers

Source: Meteorological Office (1960) *Handbook of Aviation Meteorology* (HMSO).

hemisphere. When a new secondary wave depression forms on the trailing part of a cold front, it tends to cause a local intensification of precipitation and to retard the movement of the main system.

The Polar Front Theory is fundamentally correct, and it provided a very clear and elegant synthesis of the available observations at the time, but it was essentially a three-dimensional model developed from ground-based observations. Because of this there are several faults in the theory: (1) the upper circulations are very vague because of the lack of upper air observations at the time – upper flow patterns were hardly known in the 1920s and the role of the jet stream was completely neglected; (2) although the sequences of weather are correct, the associated cloudforms and types are rather vague; (3) it lacks a full explanation of why the frontal surface should distort in the way that it does, of the occlusion process (particularly what happens to the warm-sector air lifted off the ground during the occlusion process), and of the large pressure falls which occur in deep depressions (the argument of the replacement of cold air by less dense warm air produces an insufficient pressure fall); and (4) no scheme was suggested for identifying fronts on weather maps according to strict criteria, which has perhaps led to their usefulness being overworked by meteorologists on occasions – there are often differences in the numbers and positions of fronts on synoptic charts of the same weather situation produced by different European meteorological services, even today!

However, the Norwegian airmass model of the development of frontal depressions has lasted a remarkably long time considering the limited amount of information upon which it was first based. It has now been substantially improved by recent observational evidence, and these modifications to the general theory will now be considered in turn.

The vertical structure of frontal zones

According to the models of the Polar Front Theory, a front was envisaged as being a single surface separating the warm and cold airmasses (like an atmospheric 'fault-line'), with the underside of the warm front cloud defining the warm frontal surface. Since World War II knowledge of the vertical structure of fronts has increased owing to new information provided by radiosonde balloon ascents, radar and, particularly, aircraft reconnaissance flights through frontal systems. During the period 1950–5, flights by instrumented aircraft through frontal systems over the British Isles revealed important new facts about fronts which can be summarised as follows (see Fig. 10.5):

(1) All fronts are dual in character, with two approximately parallel surfaces of discontinuity separating the airmasses and forming a frontal *zone*, rather than the single surface suggested by Bjerknes.
(2) The slope of the frontal zone is shallow, with gradients ranging from 1 in 30 to 1 in 140 for cold fronts, and from 1 in 110 to 1 in 200 for warm fronts – the original diagrams illustrating the polar front theory contained much vertical exaggeration.
(3) At the level of the tropopause, the warm frontal zone is some 500 to 1,000 km ahead of, and on the cold side of, the surface warm front; the warm front cloudiness will therefore precede the surface warm front by several hours.

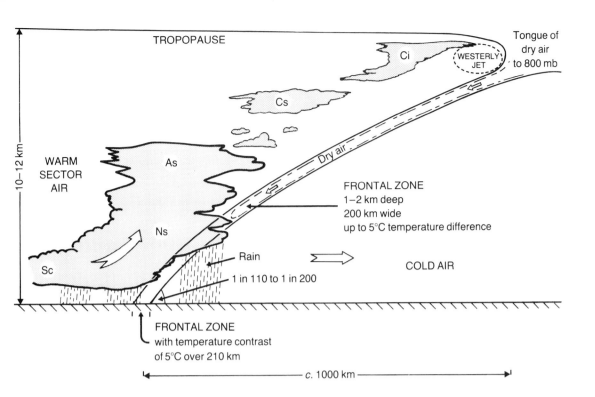

TROPOPAUSE

Ci

WESTERLY JET

Tongue of
dry air
to 800 mb

Cs

10–12 km

WARM
SECTOR
AIR

As

Dry air

FRONTAL ZONE
1–2 km deep
200 km wide
up to 5°C temperature difference

Ns

Rain

Sc

1 in 110 to 1 in 200

COLD AIR

FRONTAL ZONE
with temperature contrast
of 5°C over 210 km

c. 1000 km

Fig. 10.5 A schematic cross-section through a warm front illustrating the main features associated with the frontal zone.

(4) The frontal zone is usually about 1–2 km deep (about 100 mb), with a horizontal width of 80–320 km (averaging some 210 km); frontal zones less than 80 km wide were unusual.

(5) The frontal zone can be considered as a local steepening of the temperature gradient between airmasses, which continues into the airmasses on either side of the front, but at a reduced rate; a frontal *region* was identified within which temperature gradients of some 8°–9°C occurred over distances of 800–1,000 km, with a marked steepening of the gradient within the frontal *zone*, with a temperature change averaging some 5°C over 210 km.

(6) Within the frontal zone there is usually a tongue of dry air extending downwards between the two surfaces of discontinuity; within this dry tongue relative humidities as low as 5% have been recorded down to 800 mb within warm frontal zones and to 700 mb in cold frontal zones (see Fig. 10.6); such dry air probably originates in the lower stratosphere and subsides through the gap in the tropopause at the front.

(7) It is the surface encountered on moving from warm to cold air that is most important in the production of weather at both warm and cold fronts; over the warm front the inclination of the sloping cloud base is often twice as steep as the front itself, and the upper levels of the cloudiness are often observed to lie completely within the warm airmass. The clouds usually intersect the warm boundary of the frontal zone at about 600 mb and do *not* glide up the frontal surface as envisaged by the Polar Front Theory; this helps to explain the problem that the ascent of air at known speeds up gradients of only 1 in 200 is quite insufficient to produce even moderately heavy precipitation. The cloudiness and precipitation appears to be a function of the conditional instability within the

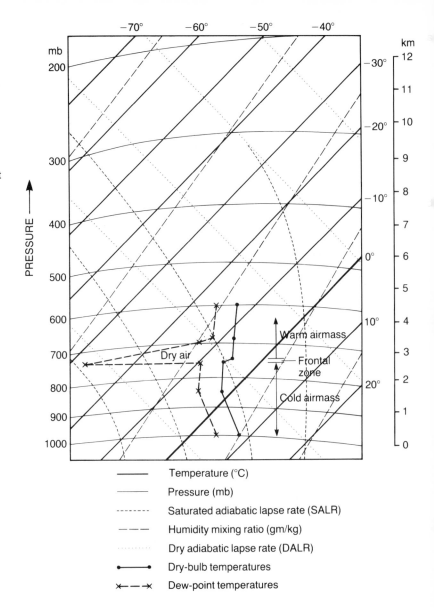

Fig. 10.6 A typical radiosonde ascent through a frontal zone (data for Aughton, 0000 GMT, 1 December 1961). Note the temperature increase across the frontal zone (transition from cold to warm airmass) and the very low humidity in the frontal zone (a dew-point depression of 21°C).

——	Temperature (°C)
——	Pressure (mb)
--------	Saturated adiabatic lapse rate (SALR)
– – –	Humidity mixing ratio (gm/kg)
·········	Dry adiabatic lapse rate (DALR)
•——•	Dry-bulb temperatures
×—–×	Dew-point temperatures

warm airmass which is triggered by the front; the forward edge of the precipitation ahead of the surface warm front is usually very close to the location where the frontal cloud intersects the warm boundary of the frontal zone as shown in Fig. 10.5.

Ana-fronts and kata-fronts

Fronts can be classified according to the vertical motion of the air associated with them. If the air within the warm sector is *rising* relative to the cold and warm front (the classical textbook situation), the fronts are usually active, producing heavy precipitation, and are known as *ana-fronts*. Such fronts are shown schematically in Fig 10.7a. The ana-warm front, with rising air in the warm sector, typically has multi-layered cloud which increases in thickness towards the surface position of the front; embedded within it may be areas of instability and convective cloud.

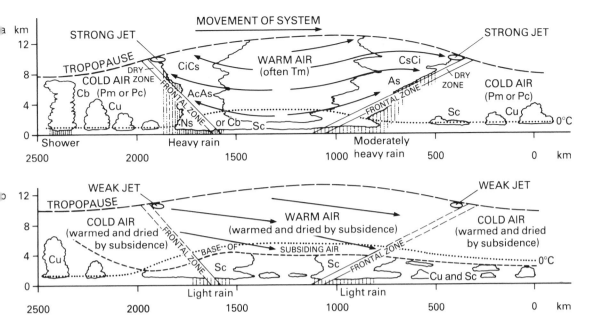

Fig. 10.7 Vertical cross-sections through warm sectors of frontal depressions, showing (a) ana-fronts, with warm-sector air rising relative to the frontal surfaces, and (b) kata-fronts, with warm-sector air subsiding relative to the cold airmasses. Note the great vertical exaggeration in the sections.

If the warm-sector air is *sinking* relative to the cold airmasses, the fronts are less intense and termed *kata-fronts*. These occur when the component of the wind at right-angles to the front is greater than the velocity of movement of the cold front, and occur either when the associated depression is tending to fill, or when the trailing end of a frontal system is moving around the periphery of an anticyclone. A vertical section through a frontal depression with kata-fronts is shown in Fig. 10.7b. The descending air within the warm sector (especially at mid-troposphere levels) both increases the stability of the atmosphere (by decreasing the environmental lapse rate) and restricts the vertical development of middle- and high-level clouds. The kata-warm front cloud is mainly stratocumulus whose depth is often restricted below the freezing level by the subsidence inversion, and precipitation is often in the form of drizzle. The restricted depth of the kata-cold front cloud normally produces only light rain of short duration.

Satellite evidence of frontal cloud patterns and structures

Since the early 1960s weather satellite imagery has enabled meteorologists to view the cloud patterns and structures of frontal depressions in their entirety. In particular, new detail of the *spatial* patterns of the cloud systems has considerably improved the enforced generalisation on these of the Polar Front Theory. The cloud patterns associated with each stage of the evolution of the frontal depression have been well documented for both hemispheres, and valuable new information has been obtained on areas of cyclogenesis (i.e. cyclone formation) and preferred depression tracks, especially over sea areas.

When the frontal depression reaches maturity and begins to occlude (stage (c) of Fig. 10.2), the cloudiness develops a characteristic and diagnostic comma shape, with the bulge of the comma over the centre of the depression. The photograph on page 90, showing an occluding frontal depression approaching the British Isles, well illustrates this.

A Nimbus-3 image of an occluding frontal depression approaching the British Isles, 25 July 1969, with coastal outlines and frontal symbols superimposed. Note the well-developed vortex, the slot of cold air, the well-defined edge to the cold front cloud and the unstable convective cloudiness producing showers in the cold air. *Kindly supplied by Ambassador College*

In general the rear edge of the cold front is well defined as a band of cloudiness trailing from the centre of the comma, with a marked concave curvature and a well-defined edge. This separates the frontal cloud within the warm sector (normally showing almost complete cloud cover) from the more 'speckled' cellular cloudiness associated with convection and showers in the cold air behind the cold front. The edge of the cloud marks the upper edge of the frontal cloud rather than the surface position of the cold front, which is just within the frontal cloud as shown. The instability within the cold airmass behind the cold front is due to the cold air moving southwards and being heated at the surface as it moves over warmer water.

The characteristic pattern of cloud associated with the warm front is much less clearly defined, and in general the surface position of the warm front can seldom be located exactly from satellite imagery alone; it is usually obscured by the warm-sector cloudiness. If a secondary depression (wave depression) develops on the trailing cold front, this is usually clearly evident as a bulge on the cold front cloudiness, with the concave curvature changing to a convex curvature where it forms – this is a very helpful tool for forecasters.

The typical patterns of cloudiness associated with the stages of evolution of a frontal depression in the northern hemisphere are shown diagrammatically in Fig. 10.8. A frontal wave begins to develop on day 1, becomes well-developed by day 2 with pronounced warm sector cloudiness; by days 3 and 4 it has begun to occlude (the convective instability cloudiness and the clear slot of cloudfree air spiralling in towards the centre of the cyclonic vortex are both well marked), and by day 5 the depression has begun to fill, being marked by an occluded front and a region of slowly rotating air behind it.

Recent work, particularly by Streten and Troup in the 1970s using satellite imagery, has shown that there are considerable differences between the structure, the evolution and the climatology of frontal depressions in the southern hemisphere compared with their counterparts in the northern hemisphere, which was not envisaged before. They have shown that there appear to be three preferred areas of cyclogenesis downwind of the three major landmasses: to the east of Brazil over the South Atlantic, to the east of Australia over the South Pacific, and to the east of South Africa over the southern Indian Ocean. These regions all have high frequencies of frontal depressions, and it is suggested that the locations are governed by the mean positions of the waves in the upper atmospheric westerly flow (especially the troughs), which are anchored in quasi-permanent locations by the orographic influence of the Andes.

It has also been shown that far more of these depressions in the southern hemisphere develop in isolation, rather than from waves on frontal cloud bands (the more common situation in the northern hemisphere). There is little evidence of wave cyclone families (i.e. secondary depressions) over the southern oceans. Furthermore, most frontal depressions in the southern hemisphere appear to reach the occluded stage more rapidly than in the northern hemisphere.

Fig. 10.8 The typical patterns of cloudiness associated with the stage of evolution of a frontal depression in the northern hemisphere. (L: low; W: warm; C: cold)

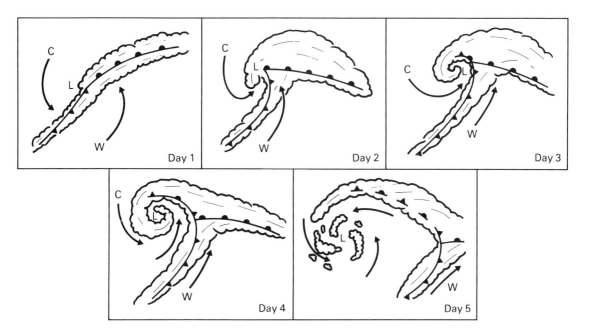

Meso-scale airflows within frontal depressions – the warm conveyor belt

In order to comprehend the spatial variability of precipitation within frontal systems, it is necessary to understand the meso-scale flows within them and the mechanisms producing them. Until the 1960s it was assumed that fronts became more active as the associated depression deepened, and that local variations along a front were simply the results of local variations in topography. In 1963, Wallington investigated the distribution of rainfall along warm fronts and suggested that local variations are due to local (meso-scale) waves on the front itself. These waves produce local convergence in some areas, together with increased vertical motion, augmented by local instability within the slowly rising air in the frontal system. These sweep across country as the depression moves, tracing out the regions of locally increased rainfall in the form of bands.

In the early 1970s Atkinson and Smithson processed records from large numbers of recording rain-gauges, together with surface and upper air data, and identified large meso-scale (200 × 50 km in size) and small meso-scale (50 × 50 km) rain areas at the warm front and within the warm sector of an occluding depression. The small rain areas form where local potential instability is released within the large-scale vertical motion, and form what are known as generator cells. It was thought that upward motion within the clusters of generator cells results from localised cyclonic development and meso-scale fluctuations within the polar front jet above. As the small rain areas move across country within the moving depression, large rain areas are traced out, often occurring downwind of local hills.

Work by Browning and Harrold (before his untimely death), also in the 1970s, using data from radiosonde ascents and radar, has provided new and interesting information on the organisation of airflow within frontal depressions both at the synoptic and meso-scales, which has allowed the flows to be modelled in three dimensions (as opposed to the earlier two-dimensional cross-sections through the systems).

Analysis of airflow within partially occluded depressions has revealed that the production of frontal precipitation occurs mainly within a tongue of warm air originating within the warm sector. This flows parallel to, and in advance of the cold front at low levels (900 mb) before turning and gradually ascending above the warm front to flow parallel to it as shown in Fig. 10.9. This narrow sweep of low-level air is usually referred to as the *warm conveyor belt*. The cross-section shows the conveyor belt ascending from low levels to 500 mb (5–6 km), the low-level flow ahead of the warm front descending from 700 to 900 mb (3 to 1 km) and the westerly middle tropospheric flow at about 500 mb.

The warm conveyor belt is typically some 200 km wide and 1–2 km deep. It begins to ascend within the warm sector, so the rear edge of the warm front precipitation is not often closely associated with the surface position of the warm front. Within the flow the large-scale ascent of the order of 10 cm/sec is locally modified by small-scale convection from the release of potential instability, as the mid-tropospheric air continually over-runs the warm conveyor belt. The amount of instability released is proportional to the humidity of the air from the west, and if the middle-level air is dry little precipitation will occur in the warm sector.

Fig. 10.9 The structure of the warm conveyor belt. (a) A plan view of the large-scale flows which determine the distribution of frontal precipitation; the pressure values indicate the levels at which the flows occur; arrows depict flow relative to the system, the stippling indicates the extent of the warm conveyor belt, with the denser shading depicting the extent of surface precipitation. (b) Vertical section along the line A-B in (a); the fronts are here shown as surfaces rather than as zones, and the extent of convection is indicated.

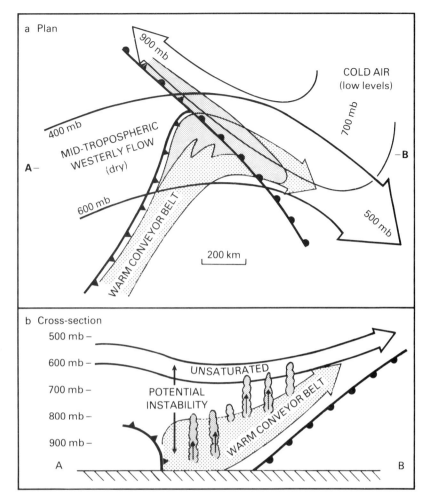

As the warm conveyor belt ascends above the warm front, the depth of the layer of potential instability with convective activity is gradually eroded, until at some 100 km ahead of the surface warm front the ascent becomes uniform. This gives rise to a transition from a convective precipitation regime within the warm conveyor belt to more uniform ascent and more uniform precipitation ahead of the warm front. Radar studies have revealed that the convective regions within the warm conveyor belt display a marked meso-scale organisation with convection occurring in clusters of cells, each some 20–30 km in diameter, which are aligned in bands, typically some 100 km wide. Within the warm sector the bands are aligned parallel to the relative flow within the conveyor belt, as shown in Fig. 10.10; on occasions these bands may be triggered and anchored downwind of certain topographic features producing persistent swathes of heavy rain in fixed geographical locations with respect to the major hills. Ahead of the warm front the convective bands are aligned parallel to the flow within the conveyor belt and hence broadly parallel to the warm front.

Upper atmospheric circulations

In order for the air to converge into the centre of a depression without it filling, there must be divergence of a similar magnitude in the

Fig. 10.10 Organisation of precipitation areas within the warm conveyor belt. Note the transition from uniform rain to convective rain ahead of the warm front. The extent of moderate and heavy precipitation is shown by the changing intensity of shading.

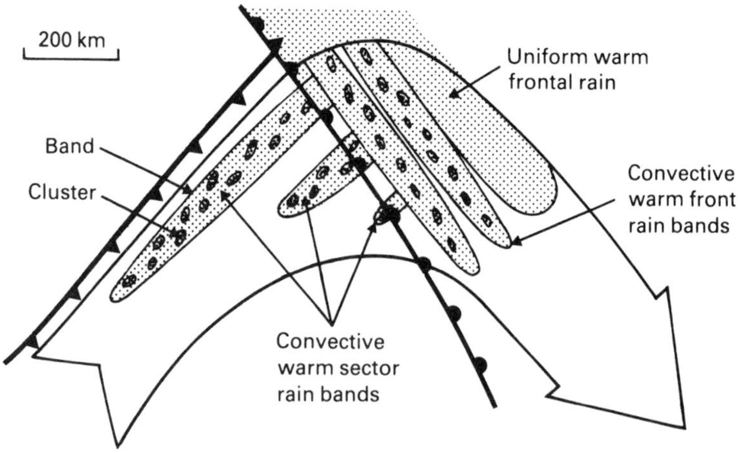

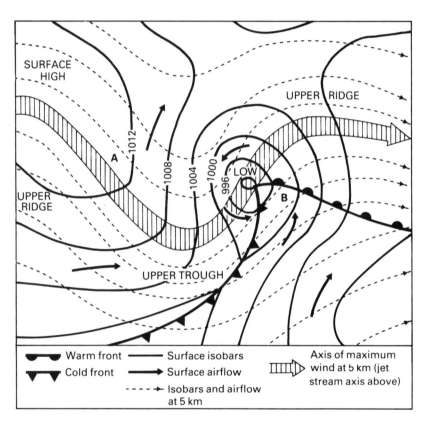

Fig. 10.11 The relationship between the circulation at the surface and at 5 km (500 mb) associated with a frontal depression. The depression lies on the eastern side of an upper trough; at A there is upper convergence, subsidence and surface divergence, while at B there is surface convergence, ascent and upper divergence.

atmosphere aloft. If the depression is deepening the upper divergence must exceed the surface convergence. Mature frontal depressions nearly always occur beneath the eastern (forward) side of a trough in the upper westerlies where divergence is favoured, as shown in Fig. 10.11. On the western (rear) side of an upper trough, convergence normally occurs at high levels, with air subsiding into a surface anticyclone or a ridge of high pressure. If the upper air flow above the depression does not diverge, the surface depression will fill.

11 Anticyclones

It has been said that 'in Britain there is no climate, only weather'. The variability of the climate of the British Isles and of the circulation patterns producing the climate is one of its fundamental characteristics. The mean atmospheric circulation in winter and summer in the vicinity of the British Isles is shown in Fig. 11.1. From these maps it can be seen that, on average, the British climate is determined by the presence of a fairly persistent area of low pressure in the vicinity of Iceland (the so-called 'Icelandic low', although this feature is more the result of the averaging process, representing the fact that mobile depressions crossing the North Atlantic tend to reach their maximum intensity near Iceland), and a more permanent and persistent area of high pressure centred near the Azores (the Azores anticyclone). Between these centres of action lie the prevailing westerlies (both at the surface and in the upper troposphere), with a succession of mobile lows and highs (or ridges of

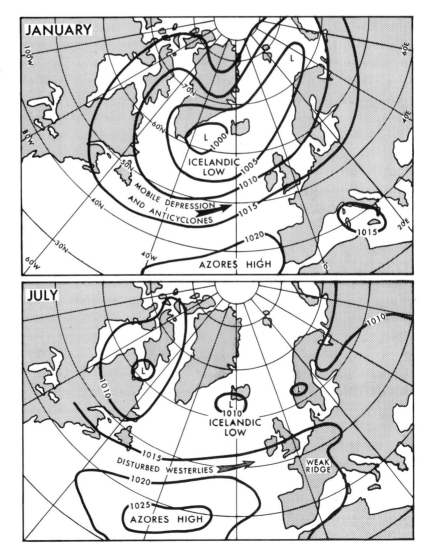

Fig. 11.1 Mean sea-level pressure distribution (in mb) and the main circulation features in the vicinity of the British Isles in January and July.

95

high pressure) embedded within them. Typically, the westerlies are mild and humid, a result of their passage over the warm North Atlantic Drift, which maintains temperatures in Ireland at some 6°C above their latitude mean.

However, this mean circulation pattern is an expression of a wide variety of different synoptic situations. Because Britain lies on the edge of the European landmass, when this circulation breaks down the changing circulation produces conditions that are very different from the average: a northerly flow and an easterly flow from the continent in winter produces anomalous cold, while a southerly flow or an easterly flow from the European mainland in summer tends to produce anomalous warmth.

Most anomalous weather is due to the influence of an *anticyclone* (a region of high pressure) in the vicinity of the British Isles disrupting the prevailing westerlies and diverting frontal depressions. On average the circulation over the British Isles is 'anticyclonic' on some 25% of the days of the year (see Table 11.4).

The term 'anticyclone' was first introduced by Galton in 1861 to describe cells of high pressure with roughly concentric isobars, possessing characteristics opposite to (or 'anti') those found in a cyclone or depression. These contrasts are summarised in Table 11.1. Anticyclones are generally larger (up to some 3,000 km across), slower moving and more persistent than depressions, with weaker pressure gradients and light, variable winds which diverge from the centre of the 'high'. Normally, with relatively clear skies, the weather is quiet, dry and settled. They appear on synoptic charts as either extensive, semi-permanent high-pressure regions or as minor, migratory systems between frontal depressions, which tend to be steered around their flanks.

Anticyclones are dominated by *subsidence* throughout most of the troposphere, but especially between 1.5 and 6 km. The air does not normally sink right to the ground, but down to approximately 0.5–1.5 km above the surface, where it meets air rising by convection and turbulence from the ground. The sinking air originates through

Table 11.1 The contrasting features of anticyclones and depressions.

Feature	Anticyclone	Depression
Surface pressure	High	Low
Wind direction	Anticyclonic (clockwise*)	Cyclonic (anticlockwise*)
Airflow	Diverges at surface (converges aloft)	Converges at surface (diverges aloft)
Vertical air motion	Subsides	Rises
Wind speed	Weak	Moderate to strong
Precipitation	Generally dry	Wet
Cloudiness	Stratus or no cloud	Cloudy
Stability	Stable air, with a subsidence inversion aloft	May be unstable
Temperature gradient	Little temperature contrast across the high	Strong temperature contrasts, especially at the fronts
Speed of movement	Slow-moving or stagnant	Generally mobile, moving west-east

* in the northern hemisphere

horizontal convergence in the upper atmosphere (often beneath the forward side of a ridge in the upper westerlies, see Fig. 4.6 and Chapter 12), inducing compensating divergence at low levels, with subsidence in between. The dry air originates at high levels where there is little water vapour present. It sinks at rates of the order of 1 km per day (but this may be 30 m per day or less, depending on the intensity of the system). This results in the following characteristics:

(1) dynamic warming of the air by compression as it sinks (at the DALR if the air is not saturated, under cloudless conditions);
(2) a decrease in the relative humidity of the air (the air temperature warms by 10°C for every kilometre of descent, but the dew-point temperature of descending air increases by only 1.7°C/km of descent);
(3) an increase of stability of the atmosphere, often with a subsidence inversion at low levels; and
(4) fine, often cloudless conditions.

The general subsidence suppresses upward motion and prevents much precipitation at the surface. The structure of a typical anticyclone is shown schematically in Fig. 11.2 (note that the vertical scale is greatly exaggerated compared with the horizontal scale). Figure 11.3 shows a typical vertical temperature profile through an anticyclone (it is for that shown in the photograph on p. 4). Note the strong radiation inversion formed above the surface under clear night skies and the very dry atmosphere above the subsidence inversion: the difference between the dry-bulb and dew-point temperatures at 613 mb on the midnight radiosonde ascent was 29°C, indicative of very dry air.

In summer, the weather under anticyclonic conditions is normally fine with light winds; the skies are usually cloudfree, apart from small 'fair-weather' cumulus which may develop briefly over the heated land in the middle of the day, and daytime temperatures will rise to high levels because of the insolation. Nights tend to be cool owing to the loss of long-wave radiation to space through the cloudless skies. Any mists that form overnight will dissipate soon after sunrise, although in coastal areas sea fog may develop where the air passes over cool sea waters and is cooled to its dew-point temperature.

In winter, clear, stagnant and stable anticyclonic conditions (with long nights) are favourable for the formation of fog and frost. Pollution may build up beneath the inversion, which acts as a lid on vertical motion, preventing the normal turbulent mixing of air throughout the troposphere. The famous London smog of December 1952, which caused dense fog and severe air pollution (smog being derived from the words 'smoke' and 'fog'), and ultimately led to the passing of the Clean Air Act by Parliament in 1956, developed under such conditions, arising from an anticyclone producing a shallow inversion which persisted over the Thames Valley for several days.

If the surface air is moist in winter, a layer of stratus or stratocumulus cloud may form beneath the inversion. This does not disperse easily, partly because of the weak circulation, and partly because the cloud top loses heat by radiation to space, cools, and forms an increasingly pronounced temperature inversion with the warm, dry, subsident air immediately above. Such a layer of cloud may persist for a day or more, and creates a situation known as 'anticyclonic gloom'.

An anticyclone tends to be one of two general types, depending on whether its origin is thermal or dynamic; see Table 11.2.

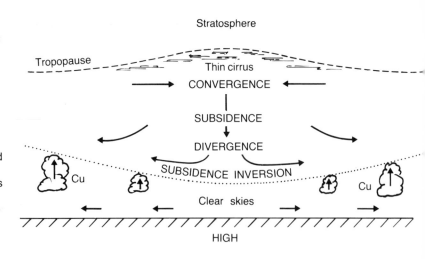

Fig. 11.2 A schematic cross-section through an anticyclone; subsidence occurs down to the level of the subsidence inversion. The shallow layer of air beneath the inversion may be unstable (owing to surface heating) but the air is usually too dry and the layer too shallow to produce cloud. The skies are usually clear, apart from patchy cirrus in the high troposphere.

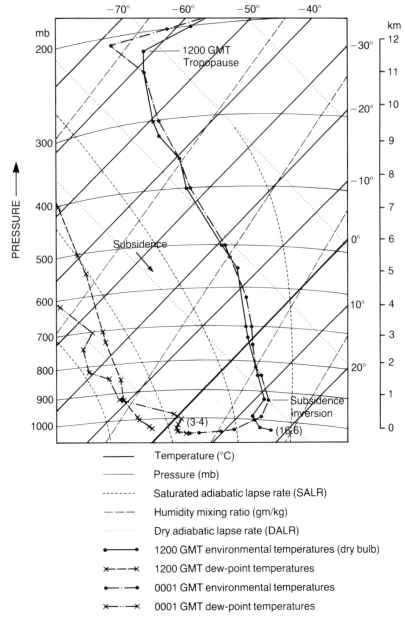

Fig. 11.3 A typical vertical temperature sounding through an anticyclone; radiosonde data for 0001 and 1200 GMT, 17 May 1980, Shanwell (east Scotland). Note the very dry air, especially above the subsidence inversion at approximately 1000 mb; below this level the air is unstable (but too dry for cloud formation) at 1200 GMT, while at 0001 GMT there is a strong surface radiation inversion with temperature increasing from 3.4°C at the surface to 12.4°C at 1,000 mb. Figures in parenthesis indicate surface temperatures at the times of the two ascents. (The synoptic chart for 1200 GMT on this day is shown in Fig. 11.6 and the corresponding satellite image on p. 4.)

———— Temperature (°C)

———— Pressure (mb)

- - - - Saturated adiabatic lapse rate (SALR)

— — — Humidity mixing ratio (gm/kg)

· · · · · Dry adiabatic lapse rate (DALR)

●——● 1200 GMT environmental temperatures (dry bulb)

✕- -✕ 1200 GMT dew-point temperatures

●—·—● 0001 GMT environmental temperatures

✕—··—✕ 0001 GMT dew-point temperatures

Table 11.2 The major characteristics of cold and warm anticyclones.

Feature	Cold anticyclone	Warm anticyclone
Characteristics	Shallow anticyclone with circulation extending up to 2–3 km	Deep anticyclone, slow-moving and associated with blocking in higher latitudes
Origin	Persistent radiational cooling of land surface and chilling of the overlying atmosphere	Convergence in the upper troposphere with subsidence beneath throughout the depth of the troposphere
Intensity	Decreases with height	Increases with height
Regions of formation	High-latitude continental interiors, e.g. Siberia, Greenland and northern Canada	Subtropical belt 30°–40° latitude, e.g. Bermuda-Azores, Sahara, North Pacific and southern hemispheric subtropical oceanic anticyclones, often with ridges extending polewards
Troposphere	Cold	Warm
Tropopause	Low	High
Stratosphere	Warm	Cold
Persistence	More mobile in location and less persistent than warm anticyclones	Days, weeks or months

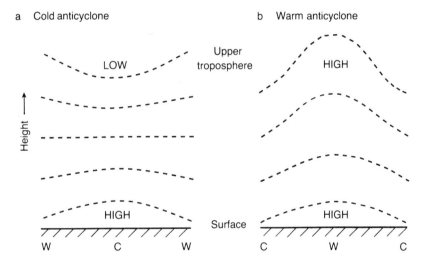

Fig. 11.4 A schematic diagram of the vertical pressure distribution in (a) a cold anticyclone, in which high pressure weakens aloft, with low pressure at high levels, and (b) a warm anticyclone, in which the high pressure intensifies aloft. Isobars are shown as pecked lines. (W: warm; C: cold)

Cold anticyclones

Cold anticyclones are thermal in origin, developing over continental interiors (such as Siberia, Greenland and northern Canada) in winter, and for most of the year over the poles.

They result from persistent radiational cooling of the land surface and chilling of the overlying atmosphere, producing a shallow anticyclonic circulation extending up to about 2–3 km. The anticyclone decreases in intensity with height, as shown in Fig. 11.4 (for explanation, see Chapter 12). The lower troposphere is cold, with normal temperatures at higher levels; inversions are common, and the air is very stable. The depth of the anticyclone is a function of the depth of the atmosphere affected by the surface chilling – this may be absent from the middle troposphere upwards.

The formation of these cold anticyclones is a result of convergence at high levels as a result of the 'contraction' of the lower troposphere while it is being cooled by contact with the cool ground. They may be considered to be the opposite of thermal lows which develop at the surface owing to surface heating.

Within these highs, the winter sky is often cloudless and temperatures very low ($-20°$ to $-50°C$). 'Surface' pressures in the Siberian anticyclone may be as high as 1,060 mb when corrected to sea-level values. The cold anticyclones tend to be more mobile than warm anticyclones. The Siberian high is likely to be displaced more frequently, and to experience more incursions from low pressure systems than the Azores anticyclone, for example.

Warm anticyclones

Warm anticyclones result from convergence in the upper troposphere and subsidence beneath. This produces warmer than normal temperatures in the middle and lower troposphere, although in the upper troposphere temperatures may be colder than normal owing to the upward bulge of the tropopause. These deep highs intensify with height as shown in Fig. 11.4.

Warm anticyclones develop chiefly in the subtropics and mid-latitude regions. The subtropical high pressure cells centred at approximately 30° latitude (including the Azores, Sahara and North Pacific highs in the northern hemisphere, and the South Atlantic, South Pacific and South Indian Ocean highs in the southern hemisphere) are of this type. These result from convergence and subsidence beneath the westerly subtropical jet stream at the poleward limit of the Hadley circulation of the tropics. In middle latitudes these form beneath the forward side of a ridge in the upper westerlies and may be associated with blocking action.

Blocking anticyclones

Blocking occurs when a complete anticyclone cell (rather than simply a ridge of high pressure) breaks away from the Azores anticyclone and establishes itself in higher latitudes (around 50°–70°N) for a period of several days. The blocking anticyclone blocks or diverts the normal westerly flow at all levels, and depressions are prevented from following their normal paths, being steered around the edge of the high. Once established, the system may persist for a week or more, and this usually results in marked local departures from the average temperature, precipitation and sunshine.

Blocking highs are warm anticyclones, and thus their influence extends high into the upper troposphere, disrupting flows aloft, where the circulation changes from the normal *zonal* (west-east) pattern to a more *meridional* (north-south) looping flow. The waves in the upper westerlies become distorted with the westerly jet stream splitting or bifurcating around the cut-off circulation (or block), one limb diverted northwards and one southwards around the blocking anticyclone (see Fig. 11.5). For a blocking anticyclone over central Europe, for example, the main depression track would lie over Scandinavia, with a second

Fig. 11.5 A schematic diagram of a blocking anticyclone over Scandinavia. The upper westerlies split upwind of the block and flow around it steering depressions with their associated rainfall around the periphery. Positive temperature anomalies occur within the southerly flow to the west of the block, negative anomalies to the east.

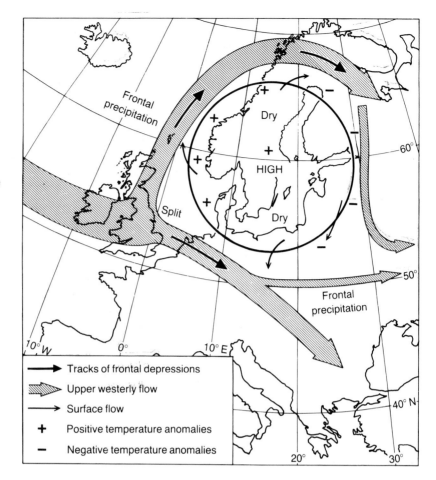

track following the southern jet stream into the Mediterranean lands. These upper flows steer the surface depressions around the periphery of the high. Such a situation may develop with little warning and then persist for one or two weeks.

In a detailed study of blocking in 1950, Rex suggested the following strict criteria for the flow at 500 mb and above:

(1) The westerly current must split into two branches.
(2) Each branch of the current must transport an appreciable mass of air.
(3) The double jet system must extend over at least 45° of longitude.
(4) There is a sharp transition from a zonal-type flow upstream to a more meridional type downstream across the current split.
(5) The pattern must persist with continuity for at least ten days.

The blocking situation is initiated when the first condition occurs, and dissipates when any of the first four is no longer satisfied. While Rex suggests a minimum of ten days' duration is required for a situation to be designated as 'blocked', most other workers are agreed that a minimum of three to five days is sufficient.

The maximum frequency of blocking highs occurs over Scandinavia, Alaska, Greenland and the northwest Pacific in the northern hemisphere, while in the southern hemisphere the main region for blocking is in the Australia-New Zealand area (with other blocking occurring over the Atlantic, east of South America and over the Indian Ocean, southeast of South Africa). The preference for continental locations over the northern hemisphere suggests that perhaps there is some orographic control in the development of blocking; a weak airflow is more easily diverted or contorted by obstacles such as mountain ranges than an oceanic area. But some authors have suggested that sea-temperature anomalies may also be responsible for blocking patterns. In the Atlantic sector, blocking is most frequent in the period January to April; there is a minimum of blocking in late summer; but it can occur in any month of the year. In the Pacific region, most of the days with blocked flow occur around January.

Blocking can have very important repercussions in terms of weather and climate, and is usually significant in producing anomalous months and seasons. The character of the weather depends on the exact location of the blocking anticyclone, the season and the duration of the block: in summer warm conditions with unbroken sunshine may be experienced beneath the quasi-stationary block, while areas some 800 km away may experience a series of depressions moving around its periphery with cool, wet and cloudy conditions.

The cold winter of December 1962 to March 1963 (with only three nights without air frost and maximum temperatures only exceeding 5°C on nine days) was largely due to a blocking high between Iceland and the Baltic producing spells of prolonged easterly winds, severe cold and frequent snowfalls.

Dry summers in the British Isles (such as the anomalous warm summer of 1976 and the drought period of 1975–6) tend to occur when a blocking anticyclone persists near the British Isles. Hot weather in Britain is normally associated with a warm, blocking high over central Europe, with a ridge extending northwestwards towards the British Isles, giving warm, dry, southeasterly winds. Summers tend to be moist and cool, while winters tend to be mild when there is little blocking action, and the westerly zonal flow of maritime air, with embedded frontal depressions, predominates.

The contrast between climatic conditions over Europe during periods of blocking and zonal flow is summarised in Table 11.3. In general,

Table 11.3 A summary of climatic characteristics over Europe during periods of blocking and zonal flow.

Feature	Blocking high	Zonal flow
Precipitation	Rainfall below normal over the continent, Scandinavia and the British Isles; rainfall mainly convective or orographic	Rainfall over the British Isles and Scandinavia above normal; positive anomalies over the Alps; rainfall from fronts and from orography
Temperatures	Winter temperatures above normal over central and northern Scandinavia, but below normal over the continent and the British Isles. Summer temperatures above normal over Scandinavia, the British Isles and west central Europe	Above-average temperatures over continent, Scandinavia and the British Isles during winter; summer temperatures complex but usually below normal
Winds	Light, moderate winds with lack of storminess	Strong westerly winds with stormy weather over northern Europe and Scandinavia; lighter winds and more settled over southern Europe

Source: Rex, D. F. (1950) 'Blocking action in the middle troposphere and its effect upon regional climate' *Tellus* (2) pp. 196–211 and 275–301.

areas south and east of the block, with winds from the north and eastern quadrants, tend to have negative temperature and precipitation anomalies, while areas to the north and west of the high, with winds from the southern and western quadrants, tend to experience positive temperature and precipitation anomalies (see Fig. 11.5).

A case study of blocking action, May 1980

The ten days of 9–18 May 1980 were a period of exceptionally sunny weather over the British Isles, with a circulation pattern dominated by a *blocking anticyclone* which drifted in position around the Scandinavia/North Sea area, as shown in Fig. 11.6. The beginning of this late springtime period of blocking began when an anticyclonic cell developed over England and the Low Countries on 9 May; it drifted eastwards to Denmark by the 10th. The block remained anchored over

Fig. 11.6 Daily synoptic charts for the period of blocking action, 9–18 May 1980. The charts are for 1200 GMT each day. The blocking anticyclone is shaded.

Scandinavia until the 15th, before drifting slowly northwards up the North Sea and its influence had largely disappeared by 18 May.

Over the British Isles, this period was one of warm, dry, southeasterly winds over most of the country, the air was stable (see Fig. 11.3) and the skies were often clear of cloud. Temperatures rose under the clear skies, and on the 13th, a maximum temperature of 27.4°C recorded at Glasgow was the highest May temperature there since records began. Temperatures fell slightly after the 13th, but on the 15th and 16th much of the British Isles was again clear of cloud and the highest temperatures were recorded in western Scotland. By the end of the 16th, central London had registered its second longest continuously sunny spell in 51 years of sunshine records. Figure 11.7 shows daily values of maximum temperature, precipitation and sunshine hours for Manchester Airport and Glasgow Airport, two stations well away from the cooling influence of the North Sea, for the whole of May 1980. During the period under the influence of the blocking anticyclone, the high temperatures, the long hours of sunshine and the almost total lack of precipitation at both stations are very evident.

The photograph on p. 4 shows the situation at 1518 GMT on 17 May, towards the end of the blocking period, viewed from a satellite. The British Isles are largely free of cloud, apart from high cloud over southern England. The cloud associated with frontal systems moving around the block can clearly be seen extending north-south to the west of Eire, and east-west from Iceland to Norway. The infrared image shows the land to be much warmer (darker tones) than the surrounding

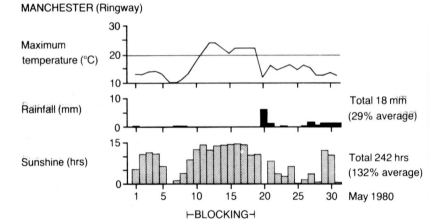

Fig. 11.7 Daily values of maximum temperature, precipitation and sunshine hours for Manchester and Glasgow, May 1980. The period influenced by the blocking anticyclone is indicated.

seas (paler tones); the air temperatures reflected this: northwest England was some 10°C warmer than the east coast, where cool winds were blowing off the North Sea. Figure 11.3 clearly shows the dry air associated with the anticyclone and the subsidence inversion.

For May 1980 as a whole, the lengthy period of easterly and southeasterly winds during the month, with a trajectory over the cool North Sea, chilled temperatures along the east coast of England, so that monthly mean temperatures were below average in east, central and southern England and eastern Scotland. Away from the North Sea, temperatures were above average for the month over much of western Britain, particularly in northwest Scotland where it was the warmest May for sixteen years. The effect of the blocking anticyclone was to steer depressions around its periphery (see for example the chart for 14 May in Fig. 11.6) and away from the British Isles. Rainfall totals for May 1980 were below average almost everywhere, especially in Scotland where in some places less than 25% of the monthly average was received. Sunshine, on the other hand, was generally some 25% above average for the month; Prestwick Airport in southeast Scotland, and Douglas on the Isle of Man, each had its sunniest May on record. With the generally weak circulation and high insolation through clear skies over the land, surrounded by relatively cool sea water, conditions were ideal for the development of sea breezes which were reported from a number of coastal locations during the month.

Weather types

It is clear that much of the character of the British weather and climate is related to the direction, nature (i.e. stability or instability) and persistence of the wind direction. Different wind directions produce different types of weather, which vary in character according to the season. As has been outlined in this chapter, the circulation and weather over the British Isles is frequently governed by the proximity of a persistent anticyclone.

The inadequacies of the airmass concept for classifying weather type have been outlined in Chapter 10. In 1950, Lamb attempted to overcome some of these problems when he introduced a classification of the weather and circulation over the British Isles in terms of seven *airflow* types, based on the location of the major pressure systems and the resultant airflow. Figure 11.8 indicates schematically the circulation responsible for each airflow type, and the seasonal weather associated with each.

It will be seen that with the exception of the cyclonic weather type, the airflow is determined by the location of a major anticyclone or ridge of high pressure. If such an anticyclone persists in that location then the weather type may persist for a period of time; such 'spells' of weather types are common and help shape the character of individual seasons. Over the hundred-year period 1868–1967, the frequency of weather types over the British Isles is as shown in Table 11.4. The westerly and anticyclonic types occur on approximately 50% of days, while some two days in three are either westerly, anticyclonic or cyclonic.

Northerly: In winter the weather is cold, with snow and sleet showers especially along the east coast; blizzards may accompany polar lows. In summer the weather is cool and showery especially along the east coast.

Westerly: Unsettled weather with variable wind directions as depressions cross the country, giving most rain in the northern and western districts with brighter weather in the south and east. Mild in winter with frequent gales; cool, blustery, cloudy weather in the summer.

Easterly: Cold in the winter months, sometimes with severe weather in the south and east with sleet or snow: fine in the west and northwest. In the summer, warm and dry (especially dry in the west), sometimes thundery.

Anticyclonic: Mainly dry with light winds; usually warm in summer, and cold in winter with frosts; mists and fogs are frequent in the autumn months.

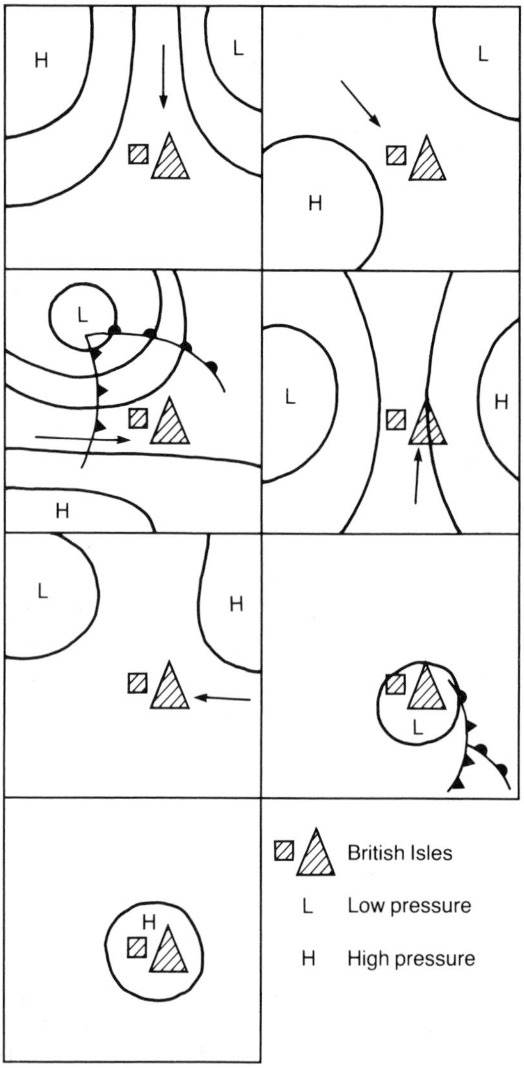

Northwesterly: In winter, cool, showery, changeable conditions with strong winds. In summer the weather is cool, with showers on the windward coasts; southern Britain may have dry, bright weather.

Southerly: Mild and wet in the west in winter; drier and less mild in eastern areas where the airflow has more of a continental trajectory. In summer generally warm and thundery.

Cyclonic: With a depression centred on, or extending over the British Isles, the weather is wet and disturbed in all seasons, with variable wind directions and strengths. Conditions are normally mild in autumn and early winter, cool or cold in spring and summer and cool in late winter. Gales may occur.

☑ △ British Isles

L   Low pressure

H   High pressure

Fig. 11.8 Schematic maps showing circulations associated with Lamb's weather types over the British Isles.

Table 11.4 Average incidence of Lamb's weather types over the British Isles, 1868–1967, percentage days per month/year.

Airflow type	Jan.	Apr.	July	Oct.	Year
Northerly	6	9	7	7	7.4
Northwesterly	4	5	7	4	4.7
Westerly	34	19	26	27	25.7
Southerly	12	8	5	10	8.6
Easterly	6	11	4	8	7.6
Cyclonic	14	17	22	17	17.5
Anticyclonic	22	27	24	24	24.9

Source: Lamb H. H. (1972) 'British Isles weather types and a register of the daily sequence of circulation patterns 1861–1971' *Met. Office Geophysical Memoirs* 116.

12 Upper atmospheric circulations and jet streams

Wind speeds normally increase with height above the surface owing to the decreasing influence of surface friction and the reduced air density. Atmospheric flows in the middle troposphere at 500 mb and above display a much simpler, smoother pattern of circulation than at the surface, both in the long-term mean situation and on a day-to-day basis. Figures 12.1 and 12.2 show the average circulation at 500 mb (approximately 5.5 km) in January and July in the northern and southern hemispheres. All the charts show a single large vortex centred close to each pole, producing westerly winds at this level (these are strongest and most persistent at around 50° latitude), and nearly continuous belts of high pressure in the subtropics. Over the equator there is a weak band of easterly winds which extends halfway round the earth in January and round most of the equatorial belt in July; the easterlies attain maximum speeds of 36 m/sec at 100 mb above India.

The dominating westerly flow aloft is mainly determined by the north-south temperature gradient between the cold polar and warm tropical regions. The *troughs* (regions of locally lower pressure) and *ridges* (regions of locally higher pressure) within the flow pattern are mainly caused by orographic barriers (such as the Rocky Mountains and the Andes, both aligned north-south at right-angles to the flow), and to a lesser extent by land-sea temperature differences. The vortex in the northern hemisphere is asymmetric, with deep troughs in winter over (1) eastern North America at 80°W, (2) eastern Asia at 140°E, and (3) a lesser trough over eastern Europe at 10°–60°E, producing a three-wave pattern (see Fig. 12.1a). These troughs appear to be relatively fixed in location in the mean flow. There are minor ridges west of Europe and over Alaska. In July the intensity of the flow is reduced to about 30% of its January vigour, as can be seen from the wider spacing of the contours in Fig. 12.1b. This reduction is due to the reduction in the temperature gradient between pole and equator in the summer (the temperature difference between the two can be 70°C in January, while in July, with the summer warming of the polar regions, it is normally about half this figure). In the summer the troughs at 500 mb are more variable in location (i.e. that over east North America is further east than in January), while the subtropical highs are located closer to the equator (at 25°N) than their surface positions.

In the southern hemisphere, where 81% of the surface is ocean, conditions are more uniform. The waves in the westerlies are more subdued and the circulation much more zonal (west–east) than in the northern hemisphere (see Fig. 12.2). The mean 500-mb circulation reveals three broad troughs over (1) western Australia at 110°–120°E, (2) 20°–40°W, downstream from the Andes, and (3) the South Pacific at 120°–160°W. Between these mean troughs there are slight ridges over the Andes (equatorwards of 50°S), over the western Pacific (150°E–150°W) and in the longitude of South Africa (40°–60°E). Above 300 mb the trough-and-ridge pattern in the westerly flow is hardly recognisable on the mean charts. In general, the westerlies of the southern

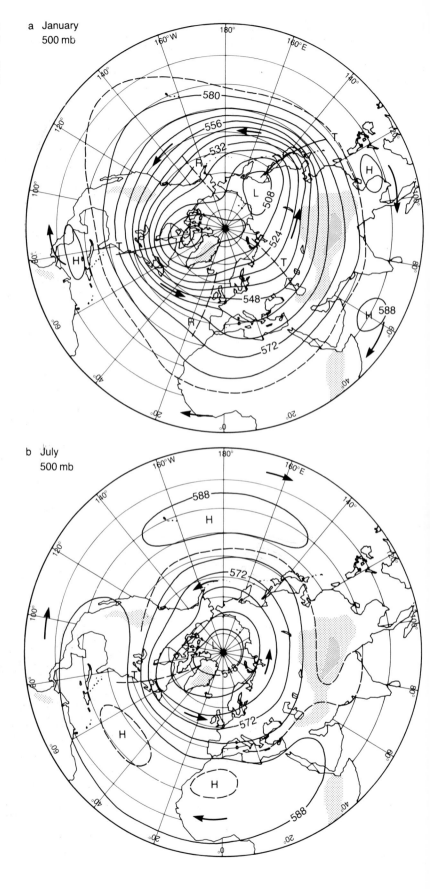

Fig. 12.1 Mean 500-mb contours for (a) January and (b) July over the northern hemisphere, in decametres. (H: high; L: low; T: trough; R: ridge)

a January 500 mb

b July 500 mb

Fig. 12.2 Mean 500-mb contours for (a) January and (b) July over the southern hemisphere, in decametres. (H: high; L: low; T: trough; R: ridge)

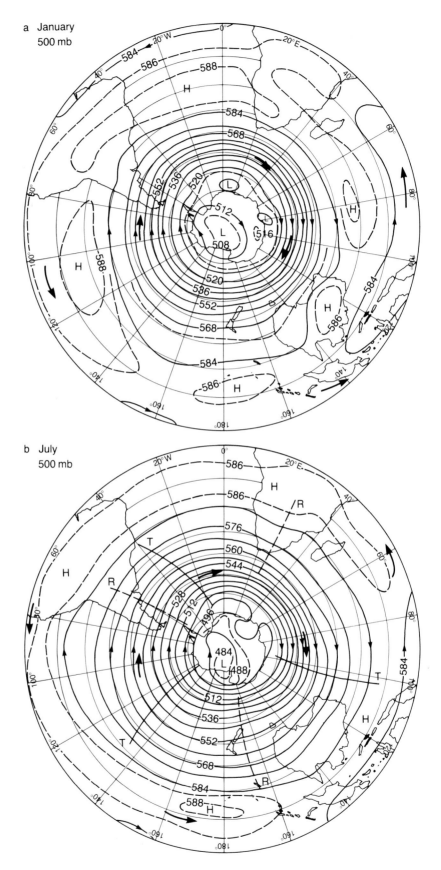

a January
500 mb

b July
500 mb

hemisphere are about 50% more vigorous than those in the northern hemisphere, owing to the larger temperature gradient between the Antarctic and the tropics.

In any particular January or July, and especially on any *daily* 500-mb chart, there may well be a substantial deviation from the long-term mean circulation, for, with the exception of the semi-permanent troughs and ridges already described, the averaging process smooths out the essentially wavy nature of the upper tropospheric flow. The upper westerlies move around both hemispheres in a series of long waves. The waves change only slowly in number and amplitude compared with surface systems, and they travel more slowly than the winds blowing through them. These waves in the westerlies are usually known as *Rossby waves* (after Carl-Gustav Rossby who first outlined their causes in 1939).

The Rossby waves develop in response to the air flowing over orographic barriers and in response to broad-scale thermal patterns. There are normally some three to six long waves around the northern hemisphere on any one day (four to six in summer when thermal patterns are weaker and the waves tend to assume a more meandering pattern, and three in the winter when the circulation is more vigorous) and three to four in the southern hemisphere. The waves are well illustrated by the trajectory of a GHOST balloon (Global Horizontal Sounding Technique) which was launched from New Zealand on 30 March 1966, shown in Fig. 12.3. This balloon reached an altitude of 12 km and drifted with the wind at that constant level around the southern hemisphere for 49 days in the upper westerlies. The movement of the balloon (tracked by satellite) traced out the shape of the Rossby waves at 30°–50°S during this seven-week period. On average there were about four long waves, although the trough positions changed with time.

The position and intensity of the waves help to determine the large-scale atmospheric circulations beneath, for air converges and diverges as it flows through the waves. *Divergence* occurs *ahead* (to the east) of a *trough* in the upper westerlies, inducing convergence at the surface, with *rising motion* in between; the region beneath the eastern side of a trough is therefore a favoured area for depressions, deep cloud development and rainfall (see Fig. 12.4). *Convergence* occurs *ahead* (to the east) of an upper *ridge*, inducing divergence at the surface and *subsidence* between the two levels – this is a region favourable for the development of surface anticyclones (or ridges of high pressure) and relatively dry conditions.

Jet streams

The velocity of the meandering upper westerlies is not uniform everywhere, for in certain regions the flow becomes concentrated in narrow cores of stronger than normal winds known as jet streams. These are regions some hundreds of kilometres wide and some 2–4 km deep in which the wind is typically blowing at speeds of over 40–100 msec^{-1} (80–200 knots) at a height of between 7.5 and 14 km above the surface, just below the tropopause. Jet streams play an important role in the rapid transfer of energy over long distances within the atmosphere, for at latitudes 40°–50°N, the air may well be carried right round the earth in a week.

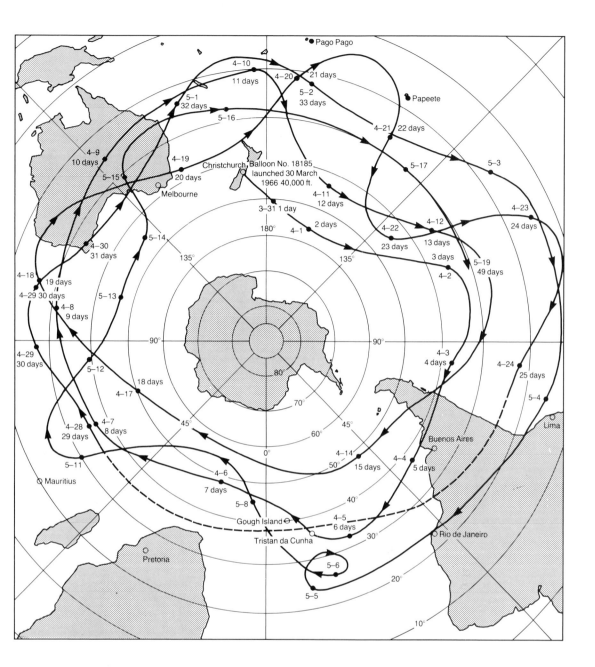

Fig. 12.3 The Rossby waves of the southern hemisphere as determined by the trajectory of a GHOST balloon launched from New Zealand on 30 March 1966. It drifted at an altitude of 12 km with a mean speed of over 110 km/hr for 49 days; its daily position is shown, together with its inferred daily path.

The WMO definition of a jet stream is as follows: 'A strong, narrow current, concentrated along a quasi-horizontal axis in the upper troposphere or in the stratosphere, characterised by strong vertical and lateral wind shears and featuring one or more velocity maxima'. In addition, the following characteristic criteria are recommended: 'Normally a jet stream is thousands of kilometres in length, hundreds of kilometres in width, and some kilometres in depth. The vertical wind shear is of the order of 5–10 m/sec per km [i.e. wind velocity decreases by 5–10 m/sec for every kilometre above or below the jet] and lateral wind shear of the order of 5 m/sec per 100 km. An arbitrary lower limit of 30 m/sec [108 km/hr or 67 knots] is assigned to the speed of the wind along the axis of the jet stream.'

111

Fig. 12.4 A schematic representation of the relationship between the location of surface highs and lows and the position of the troughs and ridges in the Rossby waves at higher levels.

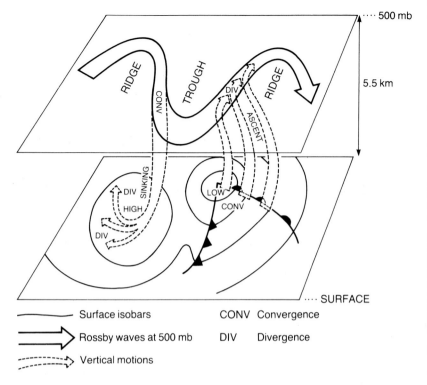

——— Surface isobars	CONV Convergence
⟹ Rossby waves at 500 mb	DIV Divergence
- - -⟩ Vertical motions	

The wind speed decreases rapidly both above and below the jet stream axis and on either side of it (see Figs. 12.5 and 12.6), so the jet stream may be regarded as a core of very strong winds embedded in lighter ones. However, it is important to realise that the axis of the jet stream (the wave in the upper flow) is neither a streamline nor a trajectory, for air rises into the jet in some areas and sinks beneath it in other areas (see Fig. 12.4). Winds blow *through* the system rather than along it, and maps and cross-sections represent slices through part of a three-dimensional flow.

If the WMO definition is used in conjunction with upper air charts, then five types of jet stream can be recognised:
(1) the *polar front jet stream*, which normally reaches a maximum at 200–300 mb between latitudes 40° and 60° in association with polar front depressions at the surface;
(2) the *westerly subtropical jet stream*, which occurs at about 200 mb around latitude 30°, at the poleward limit of the Hadley cell of the tropics;
(3) the *easterly equatorial jet stream*, which occurs at 200 mb and above over certain sectors of the equatorial region, particularly over the Indian subcontinent at the height of the summer monsoon;
(4) the *stratospheric subpolar jet stream*, which develops a maximum velocity above 30 km and varies from being a strong westerly jet in winter to a more moderate easterly jet in summer; and
(5) *local jet streams* which arise in response to local thermal or dynamic circumstances, such as the Somali (or Findlater) jet off the East African coast, particularly in the summer months.
In this chapter most attention will be given to the principal global tropospheric jets, the polar front jet and the subtropical jet.

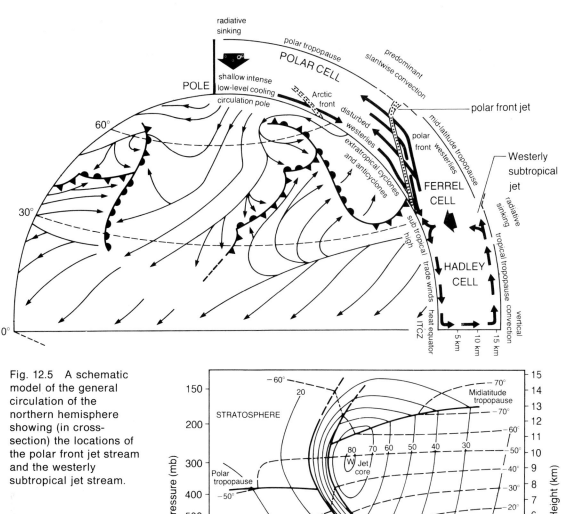

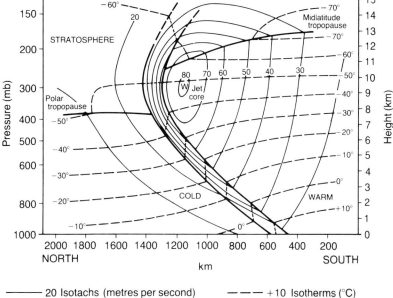

Fig. 12.5 A schematic model of the general circulation of the northern hemisphere showing (in cross-section) the locations of the polar front jet stream and the westerly subtropical jet stream.

Fig. 12.6 A schematic vertical section through a polar front zone showing the location of the polar front jet stream, together with profiles of wind and temperature. The heavy lines represent the tropopause and the boundaries of the cold front zone.

——— 20 Isotachs (metres per second)   ——— +10 Isotherms (°C)

The polar front jet stream

The westerly polar front jet stream meanders around the mid-latitudes beneath the tropopause at or above 300 mb or 9–12 km, as shown in Figs. 12.6 and 15.2. It exhibits areas of speed maxima and minima along its axis, and it may not always be continuous all round the globe. Its maximum speed is usually of the order of 60 ms^{-1} but on occasions it can be much faster than this. The main jet stream cores are associated with the principal troughs of the Rossby long waves; as a consequence, the speed of the jet and its location varies from day to day (as indicated in Fig. 12.3) in conjunction with the development and movement of the Rossby waves. This variability has important repercussions for the patterns of convergence and divergence and associated vertical motions within the mobile mid-latitude weather systems beneath.

In a vertical cross-section through a polar front zone, the jet core is always located within the warm air, above that level of the frontal zone where the horizontal temperature gradient (the baroclinity, represented by the steepness of the isotherms in the frontal zone) has its greatest value, as shown in Fig. 12.6. There is normally a gap or discontinuity in the tropopause at the height of the polar front jet, with the polar tropopause often being some 100 mb lower than the mid-latitude tropopause. This locally reverses the poleward temperature gradient, for instead of cold polar air on the northern side of the frontal zone there is now warmer stratospheric air on the poleward margin of the jet. This reversal partly determines the oval shape of the core in cross-section and the fact that the wind speed maximum occurs some distance below the tropopause, not at it.

The cause of the polar front jet stream is the temperature gradient across the polar front itself. The jet stream develops as a consequence of the poleward temperature gradient being concentrated into a narrow polar frontal zone, where the polar and tropical airflows converge, through what is termed the *thermal wind* mechanism. The thermal wind concept is illustrated in Fig. 12.7. In this diagram it is assumed that atmospheric pressure is uniform at the surface AB, but the air above A is *colder* at every level than the air above B – a temperature structure typical of any north-south cross-section through a frontal zone. The atmospheric pressure is simply a measure of the weight of the column of air above any particular point, so that at the earth's surface the weight above A is the same as the weight above B. Cold air is denser than warm air, and through the action of gravity most of its mass will be concentrated at lower levels compared with the warm air. Thus there will be a larger decrease in pressure with height above A in the cold air than above B in the warm air. This is shown by the slope of the isobars on Fig. 12.7, for the rate of fall of pressure with height is proportional to the density of the air. The higher the level chosen in the atmosphere, the greater the pressure difference over the two sites becomes – a pressure gradient caused simply by a temperature gradient.

There is no wind blowing at the surface AB as the pressure there is uniform, but the pressure gradient aloft arising from the thermal differences sets up a wind which becomes stronger with height – the *thermal wind*. In the diagram a strong westerly wind (blowing into the paper) will develop with low pressure on the left of its direction of motion. However, pressure is rarely uniform at the surface, particularly in the vicinity of a front, and this thermally-induced pressure gradient must be superimposed on, or added to, the pre-existing surface pressure gradient, which will have the effect of accentuating the westerly flow aloft even more.

The strength of the flow is a function of height and a function of the temperature contrast between the two airmasses across the frontal zone (thus the more intense the temperature difference, the more active is the front and the stronger is the jet stream).

Thus a horizontal temperature gradient produces a pressure gradient at higher levels, resulting in a change in the geostrophic wind aloft. This

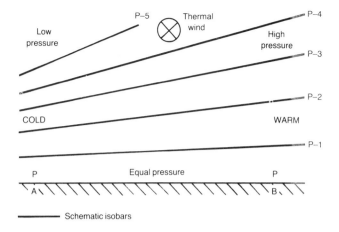

Fig. 12.7   The thermal wind mechanism.

P–5   Thermal wind

Low pressure

High pressure

P–4

P–3

COLD

WARM

P–2

P–1

P   Equal pressure   P

A   B

Schematic isobars

change in geostrophic wind with height due to temperature variation in the horizontal is called the *thermal wind* component. This component of flow 'blows' parallel to the mean isotherms (or mean thickness lines) in the layer, with low temperatures (low thickness values) to the left of the flow in the northern hemisphere (to the right in the southern hemisphere), and its magnitude is proportional to the thermal gradient in the layer. Thus high-level isobars depend not only on the pattern of sea-level isobars, but also on the distribution of temperature in the horizontal.

In the troposphere there is a general equator-to-pole (north-south) temperature gradient of the type illustrated in Fig. 12.7, which will induce a strong westerly component of flow aloft. In the vicinity of the polar front, where the temperature gradient is intensified, the thermal wind component of the upper air flow will be accentuated, producing a strong westerly polar front jet aloft.

At the gap in the tropopause associated with the jet stream, where the horizontal temperature gradient is reversed, the thermal wind component is also reversed – hence the wind velocity does not increase with height right to the tropopause in the warm air, but attains its maximum value some distance below it.

Incidentally, pressure gradients induced by the variation of temperature in the horizontal of the type shown schematically in Fig. 12.7 can also affect the nature of other pressure systems at high levels. If an anticyclone is locally colder than the surrounding air (i.e. a cold anticyclone), then the pressure will decrease more rapidly with height at the centre than around it, and at a sufficient height the pressure at the centre of the high will no longer be higher than the surrounding air. Thus cold highs weaken and dissipate with height, while warm anticyclones surrounded by colder air become more intense with height, as described in Chapter 11 and illustrated in Fig. 11.4.

It has been stated earlier that waves in the upper westerlies may be generated downwind of large-scale mountain barriers. Consider a broad, deep and straight westerly flow meeting a north-south oriented mountain range, such as the Andes or Rockies. As the airflow rises up to the crest of the mountains, its depth must decrease as it becomes 'compressed' between the top of the mountains and the tropopause. Because the air is compressed vertically, it *diverges* or 'spreads out' horizontally as shown schematically in Fig. 12.8. After the airflow has passed over the highest part of the barrier it expands (or stretches)

Fig. 12.8 The development of ridge and trough in a westerly flow as it crosses an orographic barrier.

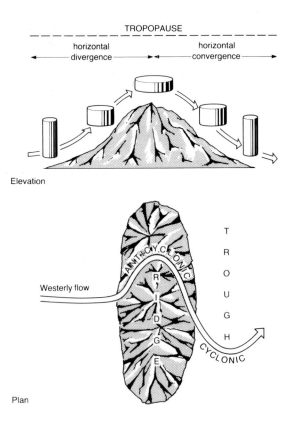

vertically and converges horizontally. The horizontal divergence up to the crest of the mountain results in the flow developing *anticyclonic* curvature, while the horizontal convergence downwind of the crest will generate *cyclonic* curvature in the flow. In this way an anticyclonic ridge develops over the mountain ridge, and a trough develops in the lee of the barrier. Such a configuration is common over the Rocky Mountains and the Andes, which act to anchor waves in the upper westerlies in preferred locations (see Figs. 12.1 and 12.2).

The polar front jet and vertical air motion

In Chapter 4 it was explained that the pressure gradient force and the Coriolis force are *not* in balance for the case of gradient wind flow around curved isobars. The difference between the two produces a centripetal force acting inwards that makes the air turn in a curve. Airflow around high pressure is *supergeostrophic*: the wind is blowing faster than the geostrophic wind value for the same isobar spacing. Airflow around centres of low pressure is *subgeostrophic*: less than the geostrophic wind for the same isobar spacing.

In the Rossby waves aloft containing the polar front jet stream, air is continually flowing through ridges and troughs (i.e. through regions of anticyclonic and cyclonic curvature). Assuming that the pressure gradients (and isobar spacing) aloft are uniform in the ridges and troughs, then air moving through a ridge will be moving faster than air moving through a trough. Between the ridge and the trough the air must therefore be slowing down and *converging* horizontally (just as traffic does on a motorway when it is forced to slow down). The air can move in three dimensions, however; it cannot rise and penetrate the tropopause, so it sinks and diverges at low levels. From the upper trough to the next ridge the air will be speeding up and *diverging*, which encourages air at low levels to converge and rise from beneath the upper flow. The anticyclonic and cyclonic curvature of the flow aloft therefore produces patterns of convergence and divergence which induce the vertical motions.

The westerly subtropical jet stream

The westerly subtropical jet stream occurs in both hemispheres between latitudes 25° and 30° in winter (it is further polewards and less pronounced in summer) at a height of 12–13 km and at a pressure level of 200 mb as indicated in Fig. 12.5. It is one of the most powerful wind systems on earth with a mean speed of 40 ms^{-1} (78 knots), but with winds of up to 135 ms^{-1} (260 knots) over southern Japan in winter. The jet system has the basic form of a standing three-wave pattern (see Fig. 15.2) with troughs over the Pacific and Atlantic subtropical highs and northern India, and speed maxima associated with the ridges over the southern USA, north Africa and south-east Asia.

The jet stream is more geographically permanent than the more mobile and meandering polar front jet (especially in winter). There is little propagation of the waves from west to east, and there are only slight day-to-day deviations of wind speed and geographical position from the seasonal mean situation. This constancy is linked to the relative constancy of the Hadley circulation as a whole (discussed in Chapter 13); furthermore, in the winter season there is a strong latitudinal temperature gradient in the vicinity of the Himalayas which, together with the orographic effect of the east-west oriented mountain barrier, has the effect of anchoring the whole circulation. In general the waves of the subtropical jet stream are not in phase with the high latitude waves, although in certain locations such as southeast Asia they may merge together and reinforce each other. In the summer the core of the jet is located further north (in the Asian sector the jet is located to the north of the Himalayas), but mean speeds are reduced.

In the southern hemisphere the westerly subtropical jet is normally located near 30°S, and is most pronounced in July over eastern Australia, with speeds of 50 ms^{-1} (97 knots), but speeds decrease rapidly towards the equator.

The westerly subtropical jet stream is located at the poleward limit of the Hadley circulation (see Figs. 12.5 and 13.1) above the zone of the subtropical highs. In the vertical cross-section it is located on the tropical side of a break between the tropical tropopause (at 100 mb) and the mid-latitude tropopause (at 250 mb). Its circulation is confined to the upper troposphere where there is only a shallow baroclinic zone (in contrast to the polar frontal situation); thus there is strong vertical wind shear associated with the jet and beneath 400 mb little evidence of the jet above. The jet is generated as a result of the systematic poleward drift of air in the upper branch of the Hadley circulation, a response to the air conserving its absolute angular momentum; see Chapter 4.

Unlike the polar front jet, no large-scale vertical motions are induced in the troposphere in association with the broad troughs and ridges of the subtropical jet.

13 The Hadley circulation of the tropics

The Hadley circulation of the tropics, named after the Englishman George Hadley (who formulated a theory to explain the trade winds in a classic paper in 1735), may be considered to operate between the axes of the subtropical anticyclones of both hemispheres, which have mean positions at approximately 32°N and 32°S, as shown in Fig. 15.2. It therefore covers more than half the earth's surface and it is vitally important in terms of the general circulation and energy exchanges of the atmosphere as a whole. Although the circulation of the tropics is being treated here in a separate chapter, this is purely for the sake of descriptive convenience; it must be emphasised that the atmosphere has no boundaries, it is indivisible and there are many interactions between tropical and mid-latitude circulations, particularly in the zones between the major subtropical anticyclone cells. There are also longitudinal variations in the extent and operation of the Hadley circulations as described here, particularly over the region influenced by the Asian monsoon.

The Hadley circulation consists of four basic elements, as shown in Fig. 13.1:

(1) The *subtropical anticyclones*, providing the subsiding limb of the circulation.
(2) The *trade-wind belt* (northeasterly in the northern hemisphere and southeasterly in the southern hemisphere), blowing around the equatorial flank of the subtropical anticyclones – these are especially dominant over the tropical oceans.
(3) The *intertropical convergence zone* (ITCZ) at the convergence of the two trade-wind systems in the equatorial trough of low pressure.
(4) Weak upper easterlies to the top of the troposphere above the ITCZ which decrease polewards, becoming westerlies which increase in velocity to the core of the westerly subtropical jet stream – the return flows of the Hadley circulation.

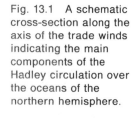

Fig. 13.1 A schematic cross-section along the axis of the trade winds indicating the main components of the Hadley circulation over the oceans of the northern hemisphere.

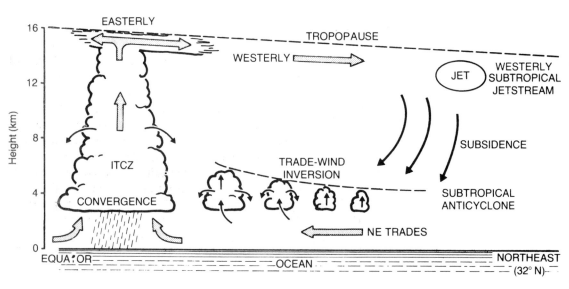

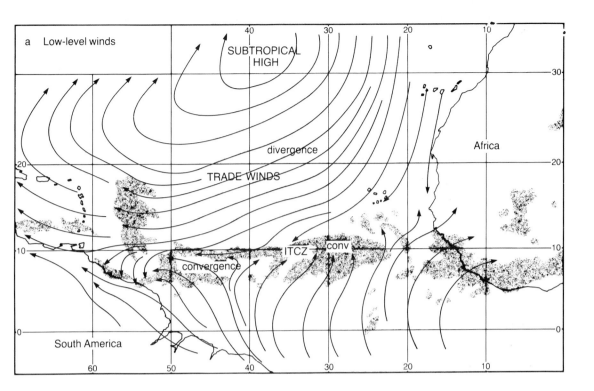

a   Low-level winds

SUBTROPICAL HIGH

divergence

TRADE WINDS

Africa

ITCZ   conv

convergence

South America

Fig. 13.2 (a) The distribution of low-level winds in the vicinity of the intertropical convergence zone at 1500 GCT, 14 July 1969; the main ITCZ cloudiness is shaded.

Superimposed on this mean climatological scene are synoptic-scale disturbances (such as easterly waves and tropical cyclones), developing both from the ITCZ itself and from within the trade winds.

The circulation at low levels and in the upper troposphere in the vicinity of the ITCZ over the tropical Atlantic for 14 July 1969 are shown in Fig. 13.2a and b. The winds at these levels have been derived from analysis of the motion of the clouds (trade-wind cumulus at low levels and cirrus spreading from the tops of cumulonimbus clouds at the higher level) as viewed every 30 minutes by a geosynchronous satellite 'hovering' over the equator at a fixed longitude. The ITCZ, the Azores anticyclone and the trade winds are all evident; to the south of the ITCZ there is a narrow belt of low-level southwesterly winds, arising from the deflection of the southeasterly trades to the right (by the Coriolis force) as they cross the equator. Note how the two trade-wind systems from either hemisphere *converge* in the ITCZ at low levels, with *divergence* from the top of the ITCZ cloudiness at high levels.

The observed tropical circulation on any given day is likely to resemble the seasonal mean circulation to a greater extent than in middle latitudes, but following increased monitoring of tropical circulations by weather satellite and conventional means, the assumed simplicity of tropical weather which was current before World War II has now been largely disproved. Knowledge has also been greatly increased from observations made during an intensive study of the circulation of the tropical Atlantic known as GATE (the *GARP Atlantic Tropical Experiment* – GARP being the Global Atmospheric Research Programme). This was an international research project lasting 100 days during the summer of 1974 in the vicinity of the ITCZ

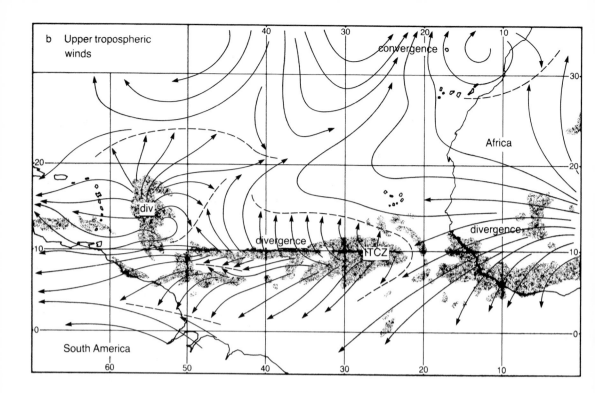

b Upper tropospheric winds

40 30 20 10

convergence

Africa

div

divergence

ITCZ

divergence

20

10

0

South America

60 50 40 30 20 10

Fig. 13.2 (b) The distribution of upper tropospheric winds (derived from cloud motions, radiosonde and aircraft observations) at 1500 GCT, 14 July 1969.

off the west African coast, in which detailed observations were made of the structure of the atmospheric and oceanic circulation in that region, with particular attention given to the structure and evolution of convective cloud systems.

The Hadley circulation is essentially a thermally-direct cell (i.e. one that owes its origin to thermal causes). It is maintained by the release of latent heat of condensation in the ITCZ, where it has been transported by the moisture-laden trade winds. The release of heat produces potential energy which is transferred back to middle latitudes in this form, and in the form of kinetic energy within the high-level waves which help to maintain the powerful subtropical westerly jet stream.

The tropical atmosphere itself has six important meteorological characteristics:

(1) It is a region of net radiation surplus (see Chapter 3).
(2) It is dominated by surface easterly flow (unlike middle latitudes where westerlies prevail).
(3) It has low values of the Coriolis parameter f, which aids the direct circulation; from the geostrophic wind equation (see Chapter 4) it follows that a small pressure gradient in the tropics will produce a larger geostrophic wind than in middle latitudes.
(4) In general there are small temperature and pressure gradients in the tropics (there are no fronts, unlike in middle latitudes).
(5) It has a high humidity content.
(6) The release of latent heat of condensation, and its transport, are much more important than in middle latitudes (this also follows from the higher temperature and humidities which prevail).

The tropics are thus an important source area for heat energy which is transferred polewards.

Subtropical anticyclones

There are generally two belts of quasi-permanent anticyclonic cells around the globe at approximately 32° N and 32° S, with central sea-level pressures averaging some 1,015–1,020 mb. In the northern hemisphere there are the North Pacific, Atlantic and North African highs, while in the southern hemisphere there are the South Pacific, South Atlantic and South Indian Ocean highs (see Fig. 15.3). These are usually separated by cols, which form important corridors for meridional (north-south) interaction and energy exchange between tropical and middle latitudes; these are common positions in which to find frontal troughs penetrating into the heart of the tropics on weather satellite imagery.

These are warm anticyclones resulting from convergence and subsidence beneath the westerly subtropical jet stream at the poleward limit of the Hadley circulation (see Chapter 11). The subsidence is most pronounced on the eastern side of the anticyclonic cells. The air does not sink right to the surface, but normally spreads out above a cooler surface layer. The warming induced by the subsidence creates a marked temperature inversion and very stable conditions. Under such conditions, and with the low relative humidities which result, it is impossible for extensive cloud to form, and such regions are climatologically almost rainless, providing the world's greatest desert regions, such as the Sahara and Kalahari deserts. In these areas the sun shines from generally cloudless skies, leading to high surface temperatures. Temperatures of over 37.8°C are common in the deserts, and the hotter part of the Sahara commonly experiences mean monthly maximum temperatures of 45°C in the shade (at Al'Azizyah in Libya, 58.0°C was recorded in 1922, the highest shade temperature ever recorded).

In regions adjacent to cool sea currents offshore (e.g. the coast of Chile and Peru), temperatures will not be as high, as the surface air is chilled; despite the moist surface air the chances of rain are slight, as the surface cooling accentuates the atmospheric stability.

Divergence out of the subtropical anticyclones gives rise to the equatorward flow of the trade winds, representing the main surface flow of the Hadley circulation.

The trade winds

The trade winds play a very dominant role in the Hadley circulation, and therefore in the whole general circulation of the atmosphere. They blow over nearly half the surface of the earth. The trade winds originate over the eastern side of the major oceans, on the eastern margins of the subtropical high pressure systems, and flow towards the equatorial trough of low pressure as northeasterly winds in the northern hemisphere and southeasterly winds in the southern hemisphere (see Figs. 13.3 and 15.2). They exhibit great steadiness both in speed and direction; hence their name which originates from the era of sailing ships. In some areas the winds exhibit a relative constancy of 80–90% (see Fig. 13.3), and this constancy extends up to 700 mb. This steadiness reflects the permanence of the subtropical anticyclones. The trades are strongest in winter when the subtropical highs are most intense, and weakest in summer.

Fig. 13.3   The spatial
extent of the trade winds
in January and July. The
isopleths indicate the
relative constancy of the
wind direction, and
enclose shaded areas
where 50%, 70% or 90%
of all winds blow from
the predominant
quadrant with speeds
greater than 3.4m/sec.
(Beaufort force 3 or
more).

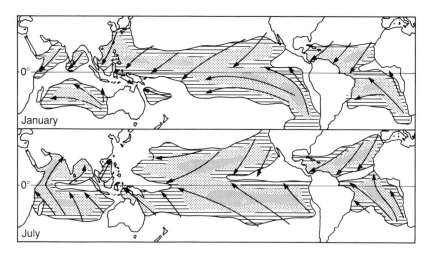

It has been known for over a century that the trade winds have a
marked two-tier structure in the vertical, but it is only since the 1950s
that this structure has been more precisely determined. The essential
features of this vertical structure are shown schematically in Fig. 13.4,
which represents conditions along the trajectory of the trades over an
oceanic environment. There are two main layers: a lower moist layer of
unstable air where ascent is dominant; and an upper dry, stable layer
where the dominant motion is one of subsidence. The two are separated
by the trade wind inversion, which normally exhibits an increase in
temperature and a decrease in humidity upwards.

Fig. 13.4   A schematic
cross-section through
the trades over the
northern Pacific Ocean,
showing the main
features of the vertical
structure.

Within the sub-cloud layer (i.e. the layer above the ocean and below
the clouds), the air near the surface is normally slightly cooler than the
water temperature; hence it is unstable. Vertical mixing in the unstable
air, together with turbulence, helps to maintain the relative humidity at
about 80–90%. Thus over a large area of the tropics the atmosphere is
continually being fed with both heat and water vapour from the

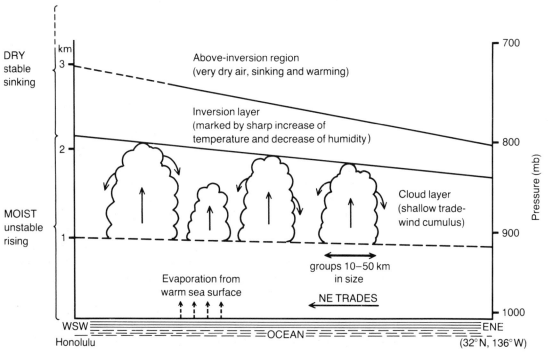

surface. An unstable lapse rate is maintained within this layer, and buoyant eddies, some 50–150 metres in diameter, transfer considerable amounts of both latent and sensible heat upwards. In this layer the winds are strong and steady, with a maximum velocity at a height of about 0.5 km. The latent heat and sensible heat are transferred equatorwards by the trades. Sea temperatures and wind speeds within the trades are both important controls in determining the size of the latent and sensible heat transfers (or fluxes) which occur. The sea temperatures locally control the degree of instability (or stability) of the overlying air and hence the potential for cloud development, while both sea temperature and wind speed govern the local rate of evaporation from the sea surface. This affects the humidity of the overlying air, the amount of latent heat being transferred within the trades, and ultimately the intensity of the whole Hadley circulation itself.

The clouds within the unstable layer are normally shallow cumulus (or stratocumulus), whose vertical extent is limited by the trade wind inversion, which forms an almost impenetrable lid on cloud development and is too shallow to allow much precipitation from the clouds. The cloud base normally occurs at a height of some 600 metres or more, with tops at a height of 1–2.5 km (see Fig. 13.4). The clouds normally occur in groups or cloud 'streets', they are usually of small horizontal extent and have a typical lifetime of some 30 minutes before evaporating. A large amount of water vapour is therefore being continually pumped into a shallow layer of atmosphere and transferred equatorwards. For example, the humidity mixing ratio of trade wind air over the Pacific in July changes downwind from 10 g/kg in California to values of 18 g/kg in the Philippines.

The moist, unstable layer is separated from the dry, stable layer aloft by a layer of pronounced temperature inversion, the trade wind inversion (see Fig. 13.4). This is a region of rapid drying and stabilisation of the lapse rate, which may exhibit a temperature increase of 8°–15°C in 1 km through the layer. In general the height of the trade wind inversion increases equatorwards (as shown in Fig. 13.5), its thickness increases downwind, while the intensity of the inversion decreases, implying a weakening of the subsidence away from the core of the anticyclone.

One explanation for the increase in height of the trade wind inversion downwind along the trades is that towards the equator, ocean temperatures in general tend to increase, accentuating the instability and allowing the convective clouds to penetrate higher into the atmosphere. They occasionally overshoot into the warm, dry air above, whereupon evaporation of the cloud droplets occurs leading to local cooling of the air and an increase in its humidity, both processes changing its character. If this continues, the inversion layer will become eroded towards the equator. This can be seen in Fig. 13.5, demonstrating that the height of the inversion layer over the tropical Atlantic increases downwind towards the equator. Air near to the equator, where the inversion is high and weak, will thus be in a more favourable environment for the development of deep convection (often within disturbances). Investigations over the Pacific Ocean have revealed a similar structure.

Above the inversion, conditions are warm and very dry, with relative humidities often less than 1%, owing to the subsidence from aloft. This occurs at a rate of some 50 metres per day and originates in the vicinity

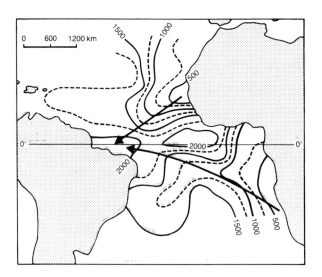

Fig. 13.5   The height of the base of the trade wind inversion (in metres) over the tropical Atlantic; the arrows indicate the mean trajectories of the trades in the two hemispheres.

of the 400–300 mb level. This sinking air is slowly and continually being incorporated from above into the inversion layer, and in turn from the inversion layer into the cloud layer. The height of the inversion is thus a function of the height to which convection can penetrate from below and the upper flow can subside from above. Both the airstreams above and below the inversion are flowing in the same general direction, and there is usually no discontinuity in either wind speed or direction across the inversion.

There are two interesting consequences of the trade wind inversion. On tropical islands, such as Hawaii, where mountains penetrate the inversion, rainfall may not simply increase with height as is common in temperate latitudes. The mountain tops may be dry, while below the inversion, on the lower mountain slopes, there is a region of high rainfall. In the centre of Hawaii, for example, at 3,000 metres the annual rainfall is approximately 250 mm, whereas below the inversion at 1,000 metres the annual rainfall is 7,500 mm or more. The trade wind inversion also acts as a lid on the vertical diffusion of atmospheric pollution, which has unfortunate consequences for urban areas near to trade wind source regions, such as Los Angeles. In summer a low-level inversion spreads over the city, trapping pollution from industrial and domestic sources, together with the exhaust fumes from over 2 million cars. In conditions of strong sunlight (common in such anticyclonic situations), photochemical reactions occur within these pollutants producing a brown haze over the city – the Los Angeles 'smog'.

The intertropical convergence zone

The intertropical convergence zone (ITCZ) represents the region of convergence of the two moisture-laden trade wind systems. It is a region of relatively low pressure and great instability, containing clusters of deep, convective cloud which produce heavy precipitation. The ITCZ occurs in general in a compromise location, where low-level convergence is at a maximum and in the vicinity of the latitude of maximum surface temperature. Over the oceans the zone of maximum temperature (and thus maximum instability) does not normally exhibit much variability in location except where ocean currents are influential, but over land areas conditions are usually more complex, and there is more of a seasonal migration in its position in conjunction with the migration of the latitude of maximum insolation. The locations of the ITCZ in January and July are shown in Figs. 15.2 and 15.3.

Weather satellite imagery of the tropics has demonstrated the complexity of the ITCZ, showing it to be a dynamic entity made up of convective cloud clusters which are continually evolving. The old view of a simple linear form (like a line of frontal cloud), widely held in the 1950s, has now largely been negated. The ITCZ cloudiness is very evident on satellite imagery, generally taking the form of an incomplete necklace, with the cloud clusters representing the 'beads', separated by areas which are cloudfree. Over the Atlantic Ocean the ITCZ cloud clusters are relatively linear, but over the Pacific Ocean they often appear as a double feature with two lines of convergence separated by a cloudfree area over a region of cool sea surface temperatures along the equator (especially over the eastern Pacific where a double ITCZ is quite common). Over the Indian Ocean multiple lines of convergence have even been observed.

The ITCZ cloudiness can be considered as a zone of clusters of towering cumulonimbus clouds, formed where the weak trade wind inversion is broken through, and there is deep convection to great heights. The violent upcurrents within the convection in this zone are the powerhouse of the whole general circulation, converting the latent heat acquired by the trade winds into sensible heat, which in turn is transformed into potential energy within the rising air, which is then exported to high latitudes in the upper atmosphere. In 1958 Riehl and Malkus suggested that the necessary upward transport of energy and mass in this region is accomplished by some 1,500–3,000 giant 'hot tower' cumulonimbus clouds, in which ascent takes place in protected central cores without entrainment from the surrounding cooler air and organised within some 30 disturbances or clusters around the globe. The cloud clusters themselves may be some 100–1,000 km across; these are composed of meso-scale convective cells some 10–100 km across, which in turn are built up from individual cumulonimbus clouds some 1–10 km across. The organisation of the meso-scale structure of the ITCZ cloudiness is shown schematically in Fig. 13.6. The internal structure of the clusters cannot normally be distinguished on satellite imagery because the cirrus shields from the various convective components often appear to merge aloft giving a fairly uniform cirrus canopy over the whole ensemble.

The cloud clusters represent areas of local convergence, with divergence in the outflow layer aloft at 200 mb (see Fig. 13.2), and strong vertical motions at middle levels. During GATE in 1974, vertical velocities of 2–18 cm/sec were measured within the clusters. Subsidence occurs between the clusters giving rise to the cloudfree areas. The clusters usually propagate slowly westwards as disturbances producing locally heavy precipitation.

Upper atmospheric flows

As mentioned in Chapter 12, weak upper easterlies occur above the ITCZ at tropopause level, and extend over a latitudinal band of some 15°–30° in the mean situation. The velocity decreases to near zero at the

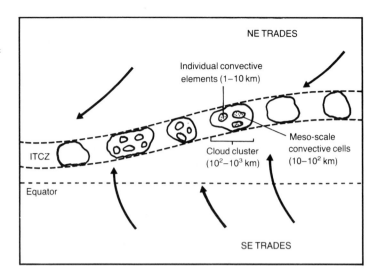

Fig. 13.6 A schematic representation of the meso-scale and synoptic scale structure of the intertropical convergence zone cloudiness.

outer limit of this band, beyond which westerlies occur at high levels, increasing in velocity to the cores of the subtropical jet streams in each hemisphere.

The westerly subtropical jet stream occurs just below the tropopause at the poleward limit of the Hadley circulation. It is best developed in winter and may extend around the globe at 200 mb. It occurs as a quasi-stationary three-wave pattern, exhibiting great steadiness in wind direction and geographical location from day to day. Its steadiness is related to the constancy of the whole Hadley circulation, but in the northern hemisphere in winter it is also anchored in position by the Himalayan massif, which has a length approximating to the wavelength of the jet stream. The subtropical jet stream is one of the most powerful wind systems of the globe, and it is an important mechanism for transporting kinetic energy in the general circulation. Winds of up to 130 m/sec (260 knots) have been recorded over Japan, with monthly mean speeds of 70 m/sec (140 knots).

During the northern summer it is replaced over Asia and Africa at a latitude of about 10°N by a strong upper easterly jet, which forms part of the monsoon circulation in these regions.

Recent tropical circulation anomalies

According to Kraus, about 90% of the water vapour accumulated in the trades is precipitated in the tropics, of which 60% falls in a belt between the equator and 10°N – a belt which largely coincides with the axis of the ITCZ. The ITCZ, together with disturbances which develop within its vicinity, are therefore responsible for the majority of tropical rainfall. Subtle shifts in the location and intensity of the ITCZ, or in any of the other components of the normally reliable Hadley circulation, can produce serious climatic repercussions. Two examples of recent circulation changes which have resulted in significant local rainfall anomalies will be presented in outline to demonstrate this point.

The Sahel

The Sahel region of West Africa lies astride the 15°N parallel, between the Sahara Desert to the north and tropical rain forest to the south. It extends from Ethiopia in the east to Senegal in the west (see Fig. 13.7). In this climatically marginal region some 700 km wide, there has been a marked decline in rainfall since the 1950s. The period 1950–8 was wetter than normal, encouraging nomadic herdsmen to move into the Sahel grasslands, which could sustain this population growth at the time. From 1959 to 1967 the area received near-average rainfall, but since 1968 the drought has been severe, with the worst conditions in 1972, 1977 and 1981, as shown in Fig. 13.7. Between 1968 and 1972 the Sahel rainfall was generally only 40–60% of the 1931–60 mean; the drought of the 1970s still persists and the region has not experienced 'average' rainfall since 1969. This has led to overgrazing and destruction of the land which can no longer support the numbers of livestock and people present. Food shortages have resulted and less seed is available for the following year's sowing. In 1975 about 725,000 and 348,500 people migrated from Upper Volta and Mali respectively to the Ivory Coast. Hundreds of thousands of people and 80% of the former cattle stock in the Sahel have died as a result of the failure of the rains. The human misery caused by the drought was – and is – enormous.

Some climatologists consider that such runs of dry or wet years are an integral part of the natural variability of the Sahel climate, and are to be expected. Similar dry periods have occurred in the past (1913, 1921, 1926 and 1941 were particularly dry years) and will occur again in the future. Others suggest that the region is undergoing a climatic change involving changes in the general circulation, leading to the southward spread of desert conditions (desertification).

In an 'average' year the Sahel receives some 100–500 mm rain, concentrated in the rainy season from July to September. The major rain-producing weather systems (such as the West African disturbance lines) lie within the warm, humid, unstable equatorial southwesterly flow which pushes northwards across West Africa from March to July (see Fig. 15.3). This airstream is deepest over the Gulf of Guinea/Atlantic coast, but is shallow further north where it is overlain by dry, continental northeasterly air coming southwestwards from the Sahara. The ITCZ, or the intertropical discontinuity (ITD) as it is more

Fig. 13.7 Annual rainfall for the Sahel, 1941–84, based on data for 14–20 stations, expressed in terms of standard deviations from the 1941–74 mean (the zero anomaly line represents average conditions). The shaded area on the map of Africa indicates the approximate limit of the Sahel.

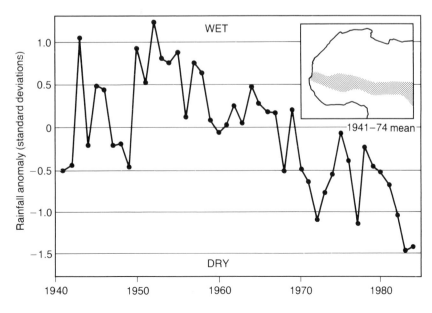

127

commonly referred to in this area, forms the leading edge of this wedge of the southwesterlies. The annual cycle of rainfall in the region is the result of the seasonal northward advance and subsequent retreat of the warm, humid, unstable air from the southwest; any deviation in the northward advance of the ITD or in the southwesterly airflow produces serious climatic consequences.

There is no current agreement on the cause of the present Sahel drought. During the drought years there has been an equatorward shift in the main components of the large-scale circulation. In particular: (1) the average northward migration of the ITD and its associated rainfall has been some 200–300 km south of normal – even a 1° latitudinal difference in the July location of the ITD can produce a reduction of 175 mm in rainfall over northern Nigeria, and shifts of up to 4° latitude have occurred in places; (2) there has been a 2° southward shift of the Atlantic subtropical high between 1961/5 and 1969/73 (stabilising the air over the region), and a stronger dry northeasterly flow north of the ITD; and (3) the tropical easterly jet has been further south than normal, accentuating subsidence over the Sahel.

One theory to explain this change suggests that the shift in circulation is related to the observed cooling of 0.3°C in the annual average surface temperature in the extratropical latitudes of the northern hemisphere since 1945. This increases the pole-equator temperature gradient producing an equatorward expansion of the upper westerly flow of middle latitudes (analagous to the southward shift of wind belts from summer to winter for the same reasons). This should, though, produce an effect which is hemispheric in extent and not limited to Africa. In the Sahel it is suggested that the drought may be perpetuated by the effects of overgrazing in dry areas; this reduces the vegetation cover and increases the albedo of the land surface. Less heat is absorbed (an effect further accentuated by the dust in the dry atmosphere), rendering the overlying air less unstable and reducing the convection responsible for the rain, inducing further drying.

The El Niño

One of the world's major climatic anomalies is the dry zone which straddles the equator for some 11,000 km across the Pacific Ocean. Here, *between* the two Hadley cells of the northern and southern hemispheres, there is a zonally organised (east-west) circulation, called the Walker circulation. A northern ITCZ occurs around 5°–12°N for most of the year, and a more ephemeral southern ITCZ at around 6°S in a 'normal' year (see Fig. 13.8). The dry zone is a region of sinking air over the equator, marked by cloudfree conditions; here divergent easterly winds occur at the surface with a westerly return flow aloft, between the clusters of deep convective clouds of the double ITCZ. Rainfall totals are low, but these increase westwards across the oceanic desert and are variable from year to year. On either side of the dry zone, rainfall totals are high beneath the two limbs of the double ITCZ.

The atmospheric circulation is largely influenced by the Peru Current which moves up the South American coast – where equatorial sea temperatures are 8°C below the latitudinal mean in summer – with upwelling bringing cool water to the surface. It then extends westwards as a tongue of relatively cool water across the equatorial Pacific, where further upwelling increases its relative coolness. The overlying air in the dry zone is chilled and stabilised, suppressing cloud development. The double ITCZ represents the locations of highest sea surface temperatures and thus greatest instability, on either side of the cool tongue.

Occasionally, however, there is a phenomenal reversal of the circulation and weather over the area, known as 'El Niño'. Such changes usually begin around December (hence El Niño: 'the Christ child'), when warm water extends unusually far south along the coast of Ecuador and Peru, over-riding the denser cool water and causing sea temperatures to rise from 16°C to 27°C, and resulting in heavy rainfall along the normally arid coast. The warming gradually extends westwards across the equatorial Pacific, where the overlying air becomes unstable, resulting in heavy rain along the normally dry zone. Such events are infrequent (the last three occasions were in 1965, 1972 and 1982/3) but they may persist for a year or more.

The atmospheric circulation changes dramatically during an El Niño episode: over the Pacific the trades are weaker than normal, the northern ITCZ shifts much closer to the equator (bringing wet conditions to the dry zone), and the southern ITCZ disappears (see Fig. 13.8). Instead of the normal double ITCZ, extending in the shape of a tuning-fork on either side of the Walker circulation, a single ITCZ in the vicinity of the equator (the 'classical' Hadley circulation) occurs during an El Niño episode. Over the western Pacific, conditions are much drier than usual resulting from the South Pacific convergence zone (a persistent cloud feature in this region) moving northeastwards and weakening. Over Ecuador and Peru the ITCZ tends to move south of the equator, bringing wet conditions and northerly winds instead of the usual very dry conditions and southerly winds.

The 1982/3 El Niño was one of the most pronounced and anomalous on record. The warming of sea temperatures began in April 1982 in the central and western Pacific. The effects extended eastwards and reached the coast of Peru in November, raising the sea-level by 15–20 cm and sea temperatures to 32°C (5°C more than normal El Niño events). The resultant torrential rains and floods destroyed crops and caused

Fig. 13.8 El Niño. A schematic representation of the surface atmospheric circulation over the tropical Pacific in the normal situation with the Walker circulation along the equator (top) and during an El Niño episode (bottom).

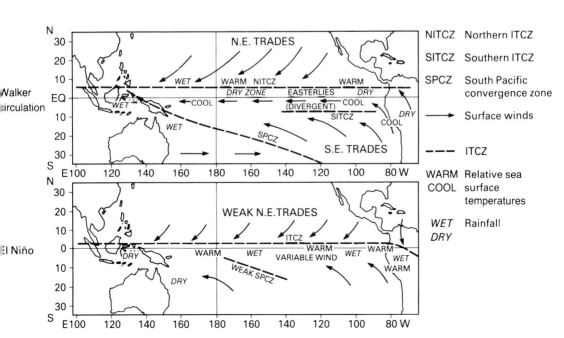

Fig. 13.9 Monthly rainfall totals for Guayaquil during the 1982/3 El Niño episode; monthly totals are shown by the grey-toned columns, the long-term mean values by the hatched columns.

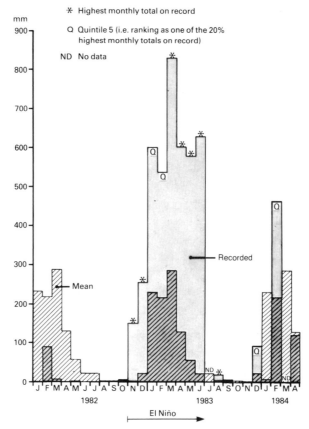

Guayaquil (Ecuador)
02°09'S 79°53'W
(annual mean rainfall 843 mm)

✳ Highest monthly total on record

Q Quintile 5 (i.e. ranking as one of the 20% highest monthly totals on record)

ND No data

widespread damage, and a state of emergency was declared in most of northwest Peru. In Ecuador flooding was widespread; Guayaquil received fifteen times its normal May rainfall (three times its previous record) and 4,195 mm of rain fell between November 1982 and June 1983 compared with the *annual* mean of 843 mm (see Fig. 13.9).

A normal El Niño tends to be preceded by a period of strong trade winds over the northern Pacific. This causes an accumulation of water ahead of them in the western Pacific, where sea-level rises. When the trades eventually weaken, the accumulated warm water tends to 'slosh back' across the Pacific, intensifying warm eastward-flowing currents (particularly at 10°N beneath the northern ITCZ) and eventually leading to the development of an area of warm water off the coast of Peru. This warm water over-rides the cooler, denser Peru Current, so that anomalous warmth is first experienced off the coast and gradually the warming effect expands across the equatorial Pacific (the reverse of the 1982 event). A secondary cause may be the weakening of the South Pacific anticyclone which weakens the southerly winds along the South American coast and thus the wind-driven Peru Current.

Indonesia and eastern Australia both suffered anomalous droughts during the 1982/3 episode, resulting in the change in the circulation across the Pacific, but the climatic repercussions of an El Niño may be felt beyond the Pacific shores (e.g. the drought in southern India and South Africa) owing to changes in the whole tropical circulation; such 'teleconnections', as they are called, are still being investigated.

14 Tropical disturbances

It has been suggested that organised synoptic-scale disturbances produce more than 90% of the rainfall in the tropics. These disturbances may take a variety of forms, but the commonest types of disturbance are varieties of the easterly wave within the trade winds and the tropical cyclone.

Easterly waves

The classical model and description of the easterly wave was developed by Riehl and his fellow workers in the Caribbean area after World War II. An easterly wave is a wave, or trough of low pressure, within the trade-wind easterlies; the trough extends polewards and is oriented northeast-southwest in the northern hemisphere, and with a vertical tilt to the east (see Fig. 14.1). These move westwards between latitudes 5° and 20° at some 5–8 m/sec (half the speed of the trades at the height of their maximum windspeed), undergoing little change over time.

Easterly waves occur mainly in western oceanic areas after the period of high sun, when the trade wind inversion is weak or absent and the trades extend up to 400 mb in depth. Some 50 waves cross the central tropical Atlantic each year during the summer and autumn months; a wave is normally present over some part of the Caribbean almost daily between June and September (see Fig. 13.2). Waves which originate over Africa can often be tracked westwards across the Atlantic, across the Caribbean, across central America and even into the Pacific; two-thirds of the waves leaving the west African coast will reach the Windward Islands six or seven days later; about one-half are detectable over central America, the majority of which will reach the Pacific. It is considered that one-quarter of easterly waves intensify into tropical depressions, and 10% eventually become named tropical storms.

Such a wave is illustrated schematically in Fig. 14.1, which shows typical surface and mid-tropospheric flows associated with an easterly wave over the Caribbean. The wave is present on the surface chart, but typically reaches its greatest intensity around 700–500 mb (about 4 km), and then decreases upwards. *Ahead* of the trough, according to Riehl, low-level divergence and subsidence with fine weather is characteristic; the moist layer is relatively low (1,200–1,800 metres) owing to the low altitude of the trade-wind inversion. Scattered cumulus builds up in cloud 'streets' to the height of the inversion, with little or no precipitation resulting. *At* the trough line the trade-wind inversion rises and weakens considerably; deep convection occurs within cumulus clouds, producing the occasional shower. *Behind* the trough line (i.e. to the east), there is a veer in wind direction, and low-level convergence with strong ascent is dominant. Deep cumulonimbus clouds develop, producing heavy, thundery showers and a general cooling of surface temperatures; divergence occurs aloft. The inversion is pierced by thunder clouds which may rise to 9 or 10 km or more; line squalls are a common form of assemblage for the storms, and may be locally intensified by relief or land/sea temperature contrasts at coasts. Rainfall rates are typically 2.5 cm per day (or more in land areas of marked relief and these may be locally intensified).

Fig. 14.1 The structure of an easterly wave over the Caribbean:
(a) surface streamlines of wave moving westwards (in the direction of the heavy arrow) at a speed less than that of the trade winds – the barbs on the wind arrows indicate speed, with each small barb representing 2.5m/sec.; (b) 500-mb streamline pattern – the wave amplitude is greater (i.e. more pronounced) than at the surface, and the axis is further east;
(c) vertical cross-section from west to east, indicating the limited convection ahead of the trough and deep cloud behind the trough – the arrows indicate horizontal wind speeds and directions.

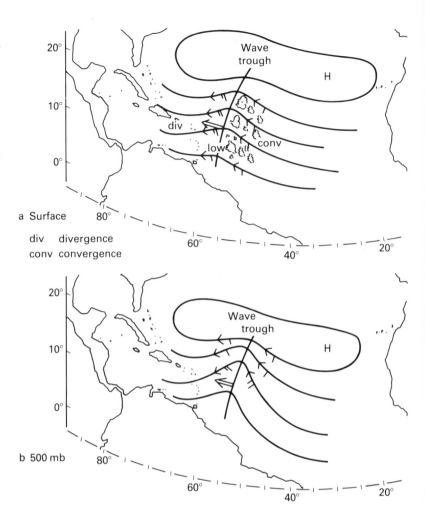

a Surface

div divergence
conv convergence

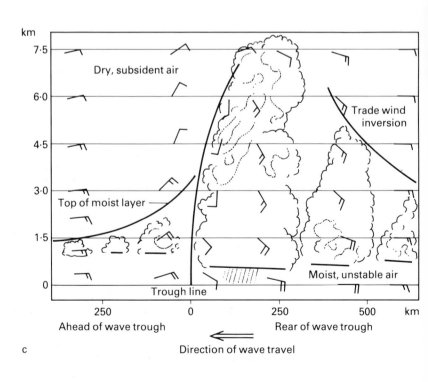

On satellite photographs, an easterly wave resembles a cloud cluster, with a cover of cirrus at high levels above the lines of cumulonimbus cloud (only 1–2% of the area of the wave may be occupied by deep convection). The spatial organisation of easterly waves is more variable than Riehl's classical Caribbean model may indicate. In fact in 1967 he presented evidence of easterly waves over the eastern Caribbean which moved faster than the trade-wind current which contained them. As a result, convergence (with the associated convective activity) developed ahead (to the west) of the trough. Similar results were obtained in studies of waves coming off the coast of Africa during GATE in 1974, when the main vertical motion occurred ahead of the trough. In general it is fair to say that the classical easterly wave model has been over-used, and it may not fit all wave configurations. It is now known that the easterly wave has a variety of subtypes, including waves which have cloud forms in the shape of an inverted V which have been observed over the eastern Atlantic and the Pacific. Under favourable conditions easterly waves may develop into tropical cyclones.

Tropical cyclones

Tropical cyclones, or hurricanes, are violent tropical maritime storms, often of an approximately circular shape when fully developed, with very low central sea-level pressures, and wind speeds in excess of 33 m/sec (115 km/hr or 64 knots). Frequently the wind speed is over 50 m/sec, and they are one of the most devastating and frightening of all natural phenomena. Forecasting the development and movement of these systems remains one of the major unsolved problems of meteorology today.

Travelling tropical disturbances within the Hadley circulation are known as *tropical depressions* if the wind speed averaged over one minute does not exceed 17 m/sec (33 knots); they are *tropical storms* if the winds average between 17 and 33 m/sec; and they are designated *tropical cyclones* only if the winds exceed 33 m/sec (64 knots) measured over one minute.

Tropical cyclones are known as *hurricanes* around the coast of North America and the Caribbean, as *typhoons* in the western North Pacific and as *cyclones* in the Bay of Bengal and around Australia. Since 1953 they have been given individual names (in alphabetical sequence through the season) when they have attained tropical storm intensity, in order to aid communications and description on weather charts.

Tropical cyclones are regions of intensely low pressure (often below 950 mb at the surface, and 900 mb or less is not unknown), but they are very different in character and intensity from mid-latitude cyclones or depressions:

(1) They are strictly oceanic phenomena, and tend to die out over land.
(2) They form only in those ocean areas where sea temperatures are at least 26°–27°C (see Fig. 14.2), and where there is a reasonably deep layer of warm water down to 60–70 metres or more. If the latter condition is not met, the stirring of the sea water by the winds will quickly bring cool water to the surface, killing the system; as Maury stated in 1858, 'Hurricanes prefer to place their feet in warm water'.
(3) They only occur in certain seasons (mainly late summer and early autumn, as shown in Table 14.1).

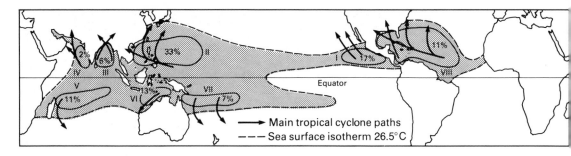

Fig. 14.2 Areas of tropical cyclone formation, showing the percentage of tropical cyclones occurring in each area as a percentage of the global total, the usual paths taken by the tropical cyclones, and the location of the 26.5°C sea-surface isotherm for August in the northern hemisphere and January in the southern hemisphere.

(4) They only occur in certain regions of the tropics (many more occur in the northern hemisphere than in the southern hemisphere, and none occurs in the South Atlantic and the southeast Pacific Oceans, owing to the presence of the cool Benguela and Peruvian sea currents respectively).

(5) Given the appropriate region and the appropriate season, however, they still do not develop with any regularity from year to year, despite the reliability of the Hadley circulation, and the numbers recorded vary greatly from year to year.

(6) They only form in barotropic atmospheric conditions (where temperature, pressure, lapse rate and humidity are fairly uniform over large areas), unlike the baroclinic atmosphere associated with frontal depressions.

(7) They tend to develop symmetric shapes about the centre of circulation, with circular isobars when fully developed, and no associated fronts.

(8) They derive their kinetic energy from latent heat of condensation released within the clouds, rather than from airmass temperature contrasts.

(9) They are only about one-third the size of extra-tropical cyclones (averaging some 650 km in diameter), but are much more intense.

Tropical cyclones are hardly ever found within 5° of the equator, where the latitudinal value of the Coriolis parameter f is of insufficient magnitude to allow balanced geostrophic flow to develop (80–85% of tropical cyclones originate in, or just poleward of the ITCZ, in latitudes 5°–15°, most of the remainder forming within the trades). They are

Table 14.1 Frequency of tropical cyclone occurrence by area, 1958–77.

Area	Mean no. per year	Range[a]	Season[b]	Maximum/month
West Atlantic Ocean	8.8	4–14	Aug.–Oct.	September
East North Pacific Ocean	13.4	6–20	June–Oct.	August
West North Pacific Ocean	26.3	17–39	May–Dec.	September
North Indian Ocean	6.1	4–9	Oct.–Nov.	November
Northern hemisphere	54.6 (69% total)			
South Indian Ocean	8.4	4–13	Dec.–March	January
Australian Coast	10.3	5–17	Jan.–March	February
South Pacific Ocean	5.9	2–10	Jan.–March	January
Southern hemisphere	24.6 (31% total)			
Global total	79.2	67–97		

[a]the highest and lowest annual totals recorded during 1958–77
[b]defined here as the period of the year when there is a long-term average of at least one tropical cyclone per month

Source: Gray, W. M. (1979) 'Hurricanes: their formation, structure and likely role in the tropical circulation' in Shaw, D. B. (ed.) *Meteorology Over Tropical Oceans* (Royal Meteorological Society) pp. 155–218.

134

A photograph of Hurricane Gladys over the Gulf of Mexico, taken by astronauts aboard the Apollo 7 space mission on 17 October 1968.
Kindly supplied by NASA

unusual in that when fully developed they have a central core of calm or very light winds. This core – known as the *eye* – averages some 20 km in diameter and is largely free of cloud.

The photograph above is of Hurricane Gladys taken by astronauts during the Apollo 7 space flight, from a height of 185 km over the Gulf of Mexico on 17 October 1968; the hurricane was centred 200 km west of Florida. The lines of convective cloud spiralling in towards the main vortex can clearly be seen; the top of the main cloudmass is covered by a veil of cirrostratus cloud – this wispy cloud marks the area of outflow from the top of the storm. Hurricane Gladys had formed two days earlier over the Caribbean; it had crossed Cuba (with winds exceeding 35 m/sec and heavy rain producing flash floods) and Florida Keys by the time it had reached the situation shown. It then curved eastwards and passed inland, causing damage to property and to the Florida citrus industry estimated at about \$6 million.

An examination of Table 14.1 and Fig. 14.2 will reveal that the climatology of tropical cyclone occurrence is more than a little curious. There are large variations in the numbers experienced per year over each of the tropical oceans; they are most frequent over the western North Pacific Ocean (off the coast of East Asia), while one-half of the world's total occurs over the Pacific Ocean as a whole. Despite the larger expanse of tropical oceans in the southern hemisphere, some 69% of the tropical cyclones occur in the northern hemisphere. Explanations for these figures must be linked with explanations for the formation of tropical cyclones, which will be considered later.

Enormous amounts of destruction and damage can be caused by one tropical cyclone, particularly in coastal areas. For example, on 12 November 1970 a tropical cyclone moving up the Bay of Bengal hit the coast of Bangladesh, sending a 6-metre surge of water ahead of it, which moved into a low-lying convergent coastline at a time of high tide. The resultant hurricane storm tide destroyed the island of Bhola; over 300,000 people died and some 4.7 million people were affected by the disaster. A similar cyclone hit the unprotected mud-flat islands of the Ganges in May 1985 killing up to 15,000 people. In America in 1965, Hurricane Betsy caused $1\frac{1}{2}$ billion worth of property damage in Florida and the Gulf states.

There are three main causes of hurricane damage:

(1) *Winds* These can blow at over 50 m/sec (180 km/hr), with gusting in excess of this. The highest sustained winds ever recorded were 88 m/sec (317 km/hr) in Hurricane Inez of 1966, and maximum gusts have exceeded 100 m/sec (360 km/hr). The damage arises from the winds themselves, from the objects which are blown along by the wind (e.g. signs, roofing), and from pressure differentials which are set up between the upwind and downwind sides of buildings causing oscillations and ultimately building collapse.

(2) *Storm surges* These inundate coastal areas, with wind-driven seawater 'piled up' ahead of the storm (especially in constricted coastal configurations). Sea-level will be locally increased beneath the cyclone because of the drop in surface pressure; if this coincides with a normal high tide, and a storm surge of water is superimposed on this abnormally high sea-level (with waves up to 10 metres high arising from the winds), the danger of severe coastal flooding is very serious.

(3) *Flooding* This results from the storm surge and coastal inundation, and from the very heavy rainfall associated with the tropical cyclone. In 1972 Hurricane Agnes produced 30 cm of rain in twelve hours, killing 117 people and causing $3 billion worth of damage.

Such heavy rainfall may cause river flooding and landslides inland. Frequently this damage is experienced most by countries where disaster preparedness (radio warnings, storm shelters, reinforced structures, for example) are not well developed. During the period 1947–73, Asia suffered 96% of the known deaths caused by tropical cyclones (according to the United Nations). In the United States, hurricane warning systems (using satellites, aircraft and radar) have been developed this century. As a consequence, the numbers of human deaths resulting from hurricanes has decreased since 1900 (see Fig. 14.3), but the numbers of buildings constructed in the hurricane-prone areas (mainly the Gulf states and along the southeast coast) has increased dramatically (particularly holiday and retirement homes), and the amount of property damage has increased with time.

The structure of tropical cyclones

It is difficult and dangerous to obtain good-quality measurements of the structure of tropical cyclones using conventional methods, for these are oceanic phenomena producing violent weather. Knowledge has been considerably improved in recent years, using three new tools for their investigation:

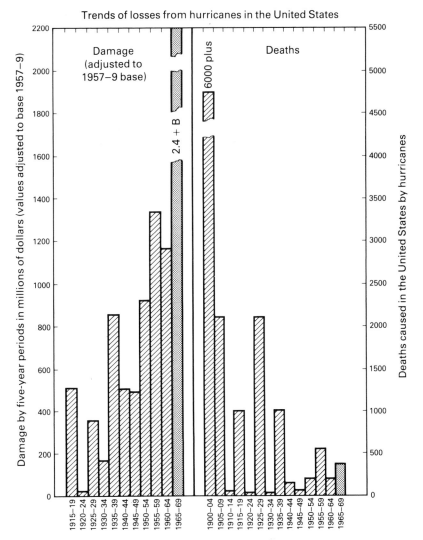

Fig. 14.3 Trends in property damage and deaths in the United States caused by tropical cyclones, 1915–69.

(1) Reconnaissance aircraft flights locate, fly through and fly over the systems (using reinforced aircraft fitted with instruments); these have been used systematically in the USA since 1944.

(2) Meteorological satellites have been used to locate and track tropical cyclones since the launching of TIROS I (nicknamed the 'hurricane hunter') in April 1960; the availability of geostationary satellite imagery and data (e.g. that from Meteosat) every 30 minutes by day and night, enables storm warnings and forecasts of expected conditions to be issued and updated at regular intervals.

(3) *Weather radar* has been used during the last 30 years to locate storms within 100–300 km of the radar station (particularly on the eastern seaboard of the southern USA), and to investigate the internal structure of the storms (especially their cloud and rainband structure on the meso-scale).

By combining the information from these sources with the conventional surface and upper air information where it is available, a reasonably clear picture of the structure of the mature tropical cyclone has emerged. Horizontal and vertical sections through the circulation are shown in Figs. 14.4 and 14.5.

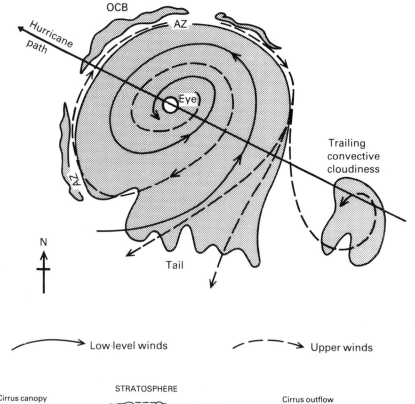

Fig. 14.4 A plan view of a mature tropical cyclone, showing the wind directions and main cloud features. (OCB: outer convective band; AZ: annular zone)

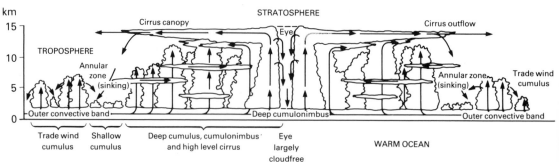

Fig. 14.5 A vertical cross-section through a mature tropical cyclone.

Horizontally, the tropical cyclone is characterised by *strong convergence* and *cyclonic inflow* towards the low-pressure centre at low levels, with *divergence* and *anticyclonic outflow* aloft. It can be considered to consist of six regions (in a transect from the outside of the storm to the central eye):

(1) Away from the main cloudmass there is limited cloud and limited depth of convection within the trade-wind regime; subsidence from the outflow of the tropical cyclone appears to lower the trade-wind inversion locally, intensify it and suppress cloud. Here wind-speeds increase towards the storm and become increasingly cyclonic.

(2) The outer convective band consists of an outer fringe of deep convective cloud around the edge of the main cloudmass; it is often fragmented (i.e. it may not extend around the periphery of the main cloudmass as a continuous cloud feature), and it occurs where the subsident outflow from the edge of the storm aloft converges with the main surface inflow, triggering off localised instability.

(3) The annular zone (discovered from satellite imagery) is a region of suppressed cloudiness, relatively high temperatures and low

humidities associated with subsidence from aloft around the outer limits of the tropical cyclone (it is sometimes referred to in the USA as the 'moat').

(4) A region of intense convective cloud provides the main cloudmass of the storm; here winds increase to hurricane force towards the centre and very heavy rainfall occurs from rainbands (or 'feeder bands') which spiral towards the storm centre in a cyclonic sense; typically there may be six of these meso-scale features within a hurricane.

(5) Everything attains its greatest intensity in a more-or-less circular inner rain region, the 'throat' of the storm, some 10–20 km wide. The convection occurs in towering cumulonimbus clouds with violent vertical motion (sometimes spawning tornadoes beneath their cloud-bases, which may add to the damage potential), violent winds with speeds gusting to over 50 m/sec are not uncommon (see Fig. 14.6), and the rainfall is torrential (often driven sideways by the winds).

(6) The 'eye', in the heart of the storm, is some 5–50 km in diameter. Here there is a rapid decrease of windspeed to low values (see Fig. 14.6), there are comparatively clear skies (or scattered low-level stratocumulus), subsidence occurs (in contrast to the intense vertical motions surrounding the eye), the sun may be shining, and the temperature is warmer than in the body of the storm, particularly at middle and high tropospheric levels.

Vertically, the tropical cyclone can be divided into three layers:

(1) The lowest layer is the *inflow layer* from the ocean surface up to 3 km. This layer is the basic engine for the storm, generating the storm's circulation; water vapour evaporated into the air in large quantities from the warm ocean surface subsequently condenses in the convective clouds, liberating latent heat. This potential energy is converted into the kinetic energy of motion of the storm. In this layer the motion of the inflow is essentially radial towards the low pressure centre.

(2) The *middle layer* is from 3 to 7 km; this is the main cyclonic circulation of the storm, within the cloudiness; the airflow is here more tangential (i.e. circular in form) than radial.

Fig. 14.6 The wind speed during the approach and passage of Hurricane Celia, 3 August 1970 at Gregory, Texas. The eye passed directly over the station.

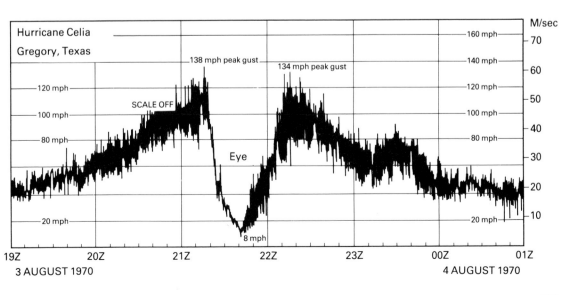

(3) The *outflow layer* is from 7 km upwards to the tropopause, with maximum outflow at 12 km and above. The air motion here is anticyclonic, and air which has passed through the storm is evacuated to higher latitudes, via the upper westerly flow.

There is much recycling of air within the tropical cyclone; the air does not simply flow into the storm, up through the throat and out in the outflow; it may be recycled several times in updraughts and downdraughts before reaching the core of the storm.

The basic mechanism of the tropical cyclone is essentially the transfer of the latent heat of condensation within the convective clouds from its form of potential energy, into kinetic energy of motion to maintain the violent circulation. It has been estimated that a tropical cyclone converts an equivalent amount of energy per day to that released in half a million bombs of the size that fell on Hiroshima. Intense convection is achieved by some 100–200 deep cumulonimbus towers with protected cores (i.e. 'hot towers') which are the essential link in the process, but these towers may only cover 1–10% of the total area. The heat and moisture transfer from the underlying warm ocean surface is all-important in maintaining the temperature and humidity structure of the inflow layer. Evaporation rates are anomalously high beneath the storm owing to the high sea temperatures and the very strong winds.

The eye of the tropical cyclone only develops when the storm has reached it most intense state, at maturity. It is a circular region of quiescence, characterised by abnormal warmth, limited cloud and active subsidence, which contrasts markedly with the violent thunderstorm activity to tropopause levels on all sides of it. The warm core of the storm is important in maintaining the central low pressure (a deep column of warm air exerts a lower pressure on the surface than the surrounding columns of cooler air, because of their differing densities), and in maintaining the high-level outflow. Within Typhoon Ida in 1958, a record central sea-level pressure of 877 mb was recorded in which warm dry air within the eye reached sea-level with a temperature of 33°C and a relative humidity of only 50%.

The air within the eye comes from two separate sources: most comes from mixing and subsidence from the surrounding cloud walls, the remainder from subsidence from the stratosphere through the break in the tropopause often evident above the eye. Air within the eye is therefore warmed as it sinks at the dry adiabatic lapse rate, producing the anomalous warm core of the tropical cyclone. It is thought that the physical size of the eye is determined by the rate of inflow of the storm. At a critical radius (the radius of the eye) the pressure gradient force which causes the air to accelerate inwards towards the storm centre cannot overcome the outward centrifugal force arising from the cyclonic rotation about a small radius. The air cannot therefore penetrate beyond this radius, is forced upwards, to be eventually thrown outwards at high levels, in a manner analogous to the action of a centrifuge. The manner in which the warm core of the eye is first developed within an initial disturbance is still far from being fully understood, however.

The formation of tropical cyclones

Explanation of the formation of tropical cyclones is still one of the most uncertain areas of knowledge of this weather system. Disturbances (such as easterly waves) are common in the tropics and many develop into tropical storms. A trigger mechanism is then required to transform these frequent storms into the rarer tropical cyclone with winds of over 33 m/sec, a well-developed cyclonic organisation, intensely violent weather and a central warm core. The necessary trigger is the result of several necessary conditions being 'right' at the same time; when all the necessary atmospheric conditions have been met, there is a good chance of tropical cyclone formation, but no more than that. There are essentially seven of these conditions which are considered important, and the sequence in which these work together to produce a tropical cyclone is summarised in Fig. 14.7 and discussed below.

(1) The basic requirement is a suitable source of sensible and latent heat. This is derived from a warm tropical ocean with surface temperatures above 26°C, and warm conditions extending through the top 60–70 metres of the water. This allows deep convection to occur, unaffected by any cooler water being brought to the surface by the churning and mixing of the disturbed water beneath the tropical cyclone. The main reason for the lack of tropical cyclones in the South Atlantic and eastern South Pacific Oceans is that these are regions affected by cool sea currents, and sea temperatures do not reach the critical 26°C temperature required.

(2) A pre-existing low-level disturbance is necessary. This can be in the form of an easterly wave or an organised disturbance in the ITCZ cloudiness. Within the disturbance convergence will be present in the boundary layer above the ocean providing the initial organisation required, but on 87% of occasions cloud clusters will develop; these will propagate westwards across the ocean, but will not develop further.

Fig. 14.7 The set of necessary conditions for tropical cyclone formation.

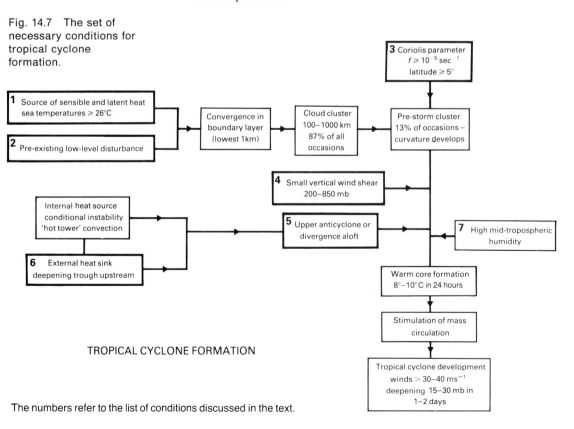

The numbers refer to the list of conditions discussed in the text.

(3) The Coriolis parameter f (a function of latitude) must exceed a certain critical value. From case studies it is evident that f must exceed 10^{-5}/sec in magnitude, which means that tropical cyclones do not form within 5° of the equator. Maximum development occurs around 15° latitude (with 65% of the global total developing between latitudes 10° and 20° according to Gray).

(4) There must be minimal vertical wind shear between the upper and lower troposphere (i.e. the layer 850 mb to 200 mb); this is needed to establish the development of the circulation around a vertical axis, and means that the optimum conditions occur where high-level easterlies overlie the surface trade-wind easterlies.

(5) There must be divergence in the upper troposphere, for the large pressure fall at the surface will only develop if the outflow from the system aloft exceeds the surface inflow. This allows the removal of the mass of air which flows through the convective cloudmass.

(6) This flow must be linked to a deepening trough in the upper westerlies in higher latitudes which transports excess energy away from the storm, acting as an external heat sink. The internal heat source which generates the warm core and provides potential energy for the system is provided by the hot tower convection within protected cumulonimbus cores.

(7) Humidity levels in the mid-troposphere need to be high, for entrainment of moist air into updraughts does not inhibit their growth within cumulonimbus clouds as much as the entrainment of dry air. Cumulonimbus convection tends not to occur over oceanic areas where the relative humidity of mid-tropospheric air is less than 50–60%.

If *all* of these necessary conditions are met, then there is a chance that warm core formation may develop. This will stimulate the generation and maintenance of the cyclonic circulation, with closed isobars, the feature may deepen by 15–30 mb in up to 48 hours and a tropical cyclone may form (if the conditions continue to be met during this two-day period). The problem of predicting tropical cyclone formation is that it occurs in data-sparse areas of the tropical oceans, and data are not easy to acquire. The development of the warm core, critical to the whole process, is particularly difficult to monitor.

Once developed, tropical cyclones tend to move northwestwards and then northeastwards, recurving around the periphery of the subtropical anticyclones (see Fig. 14.2) before entering the circulation of the mid-latitude westerlies where they either die out or regenerate into extratropical depressions. The tropical cyclone will dissipate when any of the conditions discussed is no longer met. Two common causes of dissipation are: (a) the removal of the heat source when the storm moves over colder sea water away from the equator, or moves over land where heat and especially moisture fluxes are much smaller than those over the oceans; and (b) the effect of friction on the circulation, either over land or in mid-latitudes where vertical wind shear (from the upper westerlies) distorts the organisation of the flow. Dissipation may be slow, and movement of the storm is often erratic (frequently following local warm patches of water over the oceans) before it dies. Even in its death throes the tropical cyclone may still produce excessive amounts of precipitation.

15 The general circulation of the atmosphere

The general circulation of the atmosphere manifests itself in the persistent easterly wind belt of the trade winds in the tropics and the prevailing westerly wind belt of temperate latitudes. Apart from long-term fluctuations, this is a constant arrangement, indicating an underlying order in the general pattern of the circulation of the global atmosphere, or the general circulation. The general circulation can be considered as the long-period average circulation of the atmosphere, free from all but the largest-scale seasonal trends of airflow. It is this which determines the patterns of world climate and their main characteristics.

The mean global circulation

Figure 12.5 on page 113 shows that in the mean situation there are three main interconnected units or *cells* of the general circulation of the troposphere in each hemisphere: the Hadley cell in tropical latitudes; the Ferrel cell of middle latitudes; and the less well organised and defined Polar cell. The limits of each cell are marked at the surface by the subtropical anticyclones, the polar front and the less well defined Arctic front respectively. At high levels, the poleward limit of the Hadley cell is marked by the westerly subtropical jet stream, while the polar front jet marks the poleward limit of the Ferrel cell.

These three cells vary from place to place and from season to season, but over the year as a whole their respective intensities are in the ratio of approximately 20:4:1. In the winter the total mass circulated within the Hadley cell is some 230×10^6 tonnes/sec (according to Palmen and Newton 1969), while that in the Ferrel cell is some 30×10^6 tonnes/sec. In summer both cells circulate some 30×10^6 tonnes/sec. Figure 15.1 shows the intensity of the meridional circulation within these cells in the period March–May, derived from observational studies.

The spatial and seasonal variability of these cells over the globe is shown in Figs. 15.2 and 15.3. These maps show how the mean sea-level isobars, together with the mean surface and upper tropospheric winds, integrate into the three-dimensional general circulation in January and July. The main surface circulation features include the following:

(1) A belt of *high latitude easterlies* diverge from the surface anticyclone over the poles – these are best developed in the winter hemisphere.

(2) A belt of *disturbed westerlies* extend from approximately 35° to 70°N within which are embedded mobile depressions and anticyclones, making the circulation generally more complex than that at lower latitudes. The main circulation features within this zone in the northern hemisphere in January are the regions of low pressure which persist in the vicinity of Iceland and the North Pacific (the Aleutian low), with high pressure in northern USSR (Siberia). In the summer weak low pressure exists over Iceland and northern Canada. In the southern hemisphere, a zonal westerly flow exists over this broad expanse of ocean in both seasons (strongest in July), between the edge of Antarctica and the subtropical

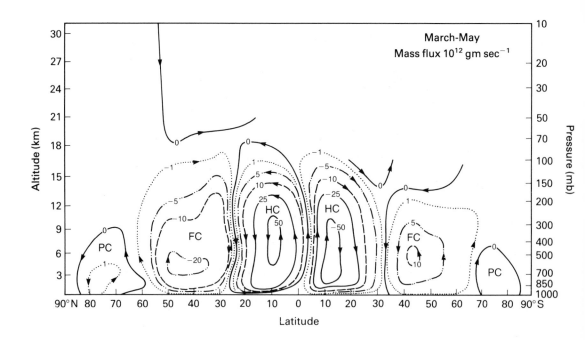

Fig. 15.1 Mean meridional circulation for March to May. (PC: Polar cell; FC: Ferrel cell; HC: Hadley cell)

anticyclones – hence the term 'Roaring Forties' applied to the latitudes 40°–50°S.

(3) The *subtropical anticyclones*, with centres around 30° latitude, lie over the main subtropical oceans. These are more intense in the winter months and some 5° nearer the equator.

(4) The *trade winds* (northeasterly in the northern hemisphere and southeasterly in the southern hemisphere) extend over latitudes 10°–25°N and 5°–20°S; these are particularly well developed in the winter months over the eastern sides of the major oceans.

(5) The *intertropical convergence zone* is a region of relatively low pressure between 10°N and 5°S, where the two trade wind systems converge from either hemisphere. The axis of the ITCZ cloudiness is shown in Figs. 15.2 and 15.3; it will be seen that it undergoes much greater seasonal migration over the major continents (especially Africa and South America) than over the oceans.

The mean locations of the major jet streams are also indicated on the maps. It will be seen that the upper circulation is westerly almost everywhere, except over the tropics in July, where a high-level tropical easterly jet extends from the western Pacific to west Africa, with maximum velocity over India – this is a response to the change in high-level temperature gradients which occurs during the summer monsoon over India.

Causes of the general circulation

Aristotle was the first to attribute the global winds to the heating of the sun, some 2,000 years ago in his *Meteorologica*. There is general agreement that the basic driving force for the global wind patterns is drawn from the differential distribution of solar radiation over the earth. Because there are only very small year-to-year changes in the mean global temperature, then the energy received from the sun must

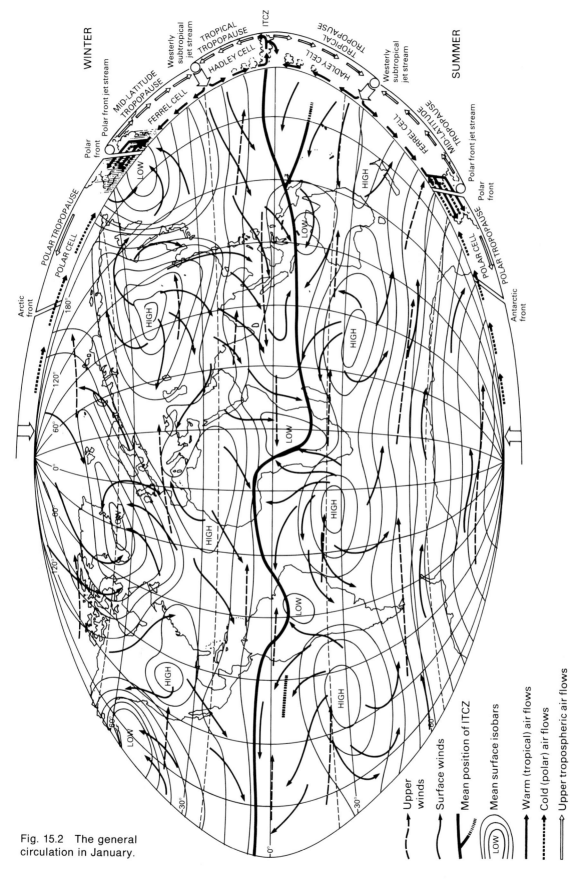

Fig. 15.2 The general circulation in January.

145

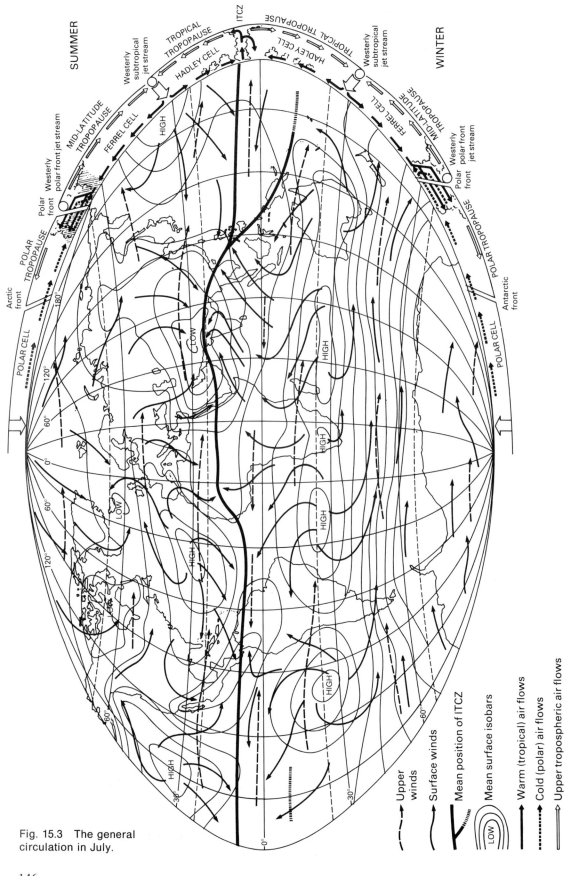

Fig. 15.3 The general circulation in July.

146

be balanced by that lost from the earth and the outer margins of its atmosphere as long-wave radiation. This balance does not exist for individual parts of the system, however.

Figure 3.4 on p. 23 shows that there is a surplus of net radiation for the earth-atmosphere system in low latitudes and a net deficit in latitudes polewards of approximately latitude 35°. Sixty per cent of the earth's surface experiences a net surplus, while 40% experiences a deficit. If the tropics are not to get warmer and warmer, and the high latitudes not to get colder and colder with time, there must be a continuous transfer of energy (with a magnitude shown in Fig. 3.4) from the tropics to polar latitudes. The general circulation of the atmosphere (and oceans) acts to effect this transfer to remedy this overall net radiation imbalance. The transfer is effected in several ways, each of which varies in importance with latitude: (1) sensible heat exchange within the atmosphere; (2) latent heat transfer; and (3) ocean currents transferring heat energy polewards. The maximum transfer of some 5×10^{27} kW occurs in latitudes 30°–40°.

The atmosphere uses the solar radiation in various ways, but in general the relationship can be expressed thus:

Energy from sun =
    potential energy + kinetic energy + latent heat exchanges
    (temperature)   (motion)
    + long-wave radiation to space + 'friction' (see Fig. 3.3)
The aim of general circulation theory is to explain how this is effected.

General circulation theory

As well as an atmospheric imbalance of energy, there are also imbalances of water, mass and momentum with latitude. The general circulation acts to redress these imbalances. Any sound model or theory of the general circulation must therefore incorporate the following:

(1) It must fit the observed wind directions throughout the depth of the troposphere.
(2) It must maintain the hemispheric heat balance. Any model must incorporate a mechanism whereby heat is transferred polewards from the regions of net radiation surplus to the regions of deficit. Transfers of sensible heat (by movement of warm airmasses), latent heat (water vapour transfers) and transfers by ocean currents act to redress this imbalance, while maintaining the temperature gradient between tropical and mid-latitude regions, as shown in Fig. 15.4. The most important flux is the transfer of sensible heat, where the maximum at latitudes 50°–60°N is related to the presence of travelling disturbances within the mid-latitude westerlies transferring energy polewards. The latent heat flux is closely linked to the transfer of water vapour within the atmosphere and reflects in particular the presence of the trade winds on either side of the equator. Ocean currents, such as the Gulf Stream of the Atlantic and the Kuro Shio of the Pacific, play a significant role in transferring heat energy polewards.
(3) It must maintain the global moisture balance. Over the globe as a whole there must be a close balance between the amount of precipitation (P) which occurs and the amount of evaporation (E). There are large imbalances in certain areas: E greatly exceeds P

Fig. 15.4 The mean annual distribution of the components of the poleward energy transfer in the earth-atmosphere system.

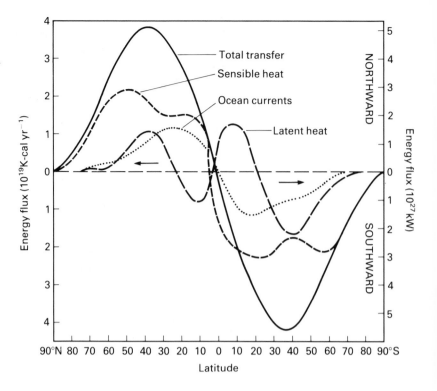

Fig. 15.5 The average annual evaporation (solid line) and precipitation (pecked line) per unit area. The arrows represent the direction of the required water vapour flux in the atmosphere.

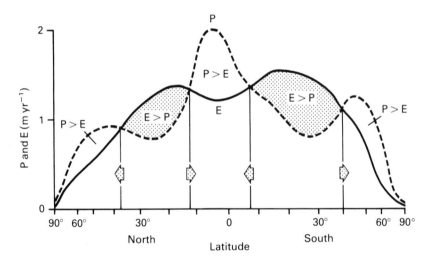

within the subtropical anticyclones which cover much of the subtropical oceans; within the ITCZ P is greater than E, as it is over most of the continents. Thus there are differences in the atmospheric input of moisture (E) and output (P) as shown in Fig. 15.5; a flow of water vapour is therefore required from sources to sinks. In general the trade winds produce an equatorward water vapour transport in low latitudes, while there is a general transfer polewards beyond latitude 20°, with a maximum transfer at latitudes 35°–40°. At these latitudes, poleward-moving air usually contains more moisture than air moving equatorwards; the transfer in the southern hemisphere is some 40% greater than in the northern hemisphere owing to the differing land-sea distributions in the two hemispheres. It should be noted that the meridional flux of water vapour is only about half of the zonal (east-west) flux, owing to the predominantly zonal nature of the major wind belts.

(4) It must maintain the earth's angular momentum balance. There must be no overall slowing down or speeding up of the earth's rotation due to friction at the earth-atmosphere interface. Easterly winds will end to slow down the rotation, while westerlies increase the earth's speed of rotation. As the 24-hour-day is constant, there must therefore be a long-term equivalence of the torques from easterly and westerly winds.

(5) It must obey the principle of continuity, such that the net transport of air across a latitudinal circle must be zero, otherwise a vacuum will result. In the vertical plane, convergence at the surface must be compensated by divergence aloft, and vice versa.

(6) The troposphere is a very thin shell of air whose vertical dimensions are of the order of 1/1,000 of the radius of the earth. This has two consequences: all diagrams of the general circulation contain much vertical exaggeration; and in the large-scale motion of the atmosphere, the vertical velocities are on average 1/1,000 of the horizontal velocities.

The fundamental problem that arises is that some of these transfers are produced by the long-term mean circulation, while some are produced by the eddies and disturbances which are superimposed on the mean circulation. Which is more important: the mean flow pattern of the atmosphere arranged in the vertical plane, or the day-to-day disturbances (depressions, anticyclones, etc.) in the horizontal plane?

There are basically two types of general circulation model which have been developed arising from two fundamentally different approaches to the problem.

Classical three-cell models

The classical approach to modelling and explaining the general circulation is based on the analysis of average flow patterns observed in the atmosphere and represents a climatological approach to the problem. It assumes that the *average* structure of the general circulation is of the greatest importance for the necessary transfers of energy, and represents the circulation as three meridional cells, arranged in the vertical plane.

The first model (of part of the circulation) was that of Edmund Halley, who in 1686 outlined a thermal circulation with warm air rising in the zone of maximum heating in low latitudes, producing a simple equatorward flow in the trades and a poleward flow aloft. This was improved by George Hadley, who in 1735 incorporated the effects of the earth's rotation, deflecting flows to the right in the northern hemisphere and to the left in the southern hemisphere, with northeasterly and southeasterly trades resulting (see Fig. 15.6a) at the surface. He envisaged a compensating southwesterly flow aloft in the northern hemisphere. This circulation is today referred to as the Hadley cell (but limited to tropical latitudes). This model did not deal with the mid-latitude westerlies.

Such early models simply assumed that warm air rises over the equator and cold air sinks over the poles. Hadley's paper remained

Fig. 15.6 Some early
models of the general
circulation: (a) Hadley's
thermally direct cell on a
rotating earth (1735);
(b) three-cell model
according to Ferrel
(1856); (c) three-cell
model including the
polar front, according to
Bergeron (1928).

unnoticed (in the doldrums!) for many years. His ideas were based on a
single thermally direct cell and required high pressure over the poles
and low pressure over the equator, with a uniform pressure gradient
between them. In the nineteenth century, new observations of surface
pressures contradicted this, for belts of high pressure were observed in
the subtropics as well as at the poles, with low pressure in middle
latitudes as well as at the equator; such a distribution required the
existence of *three* cells, not one.

In 1856, Ferrel improved on Hadley's model, producing the first
reasonably complete model of the major wind systems – the first three-
cell model. Ferrel included a belt of southwesterly winds in middle
latitudes, between the easterlies of high and low latitudes, with
subsidence in the subtropical highs and ascent in higher latitudes (see
Fig. 15.6b) at the limits of what is now known as the Ferrel cell. A
three-cell model was again suggested by Bergeron in 1928 (Fig. 15.6c)

and Rossby in 1941. Amendments included the incorporation of the polar front and upper level westerlies in middle latitudes.

In such three-cell models, the trade winds converge in the ITCZ in clusters of cumulonimbus clouds, reaching to the tropopause. The air diverges aloft and flows polewards. As it does so it acquires a westerly component of motion, as it conserves its angular momentum (see Chapter 4), becoming a westerly flow in both hemispheres. The air cools by radiational cooling at some 1°–2°C per day, and eventually subsides around latitude 30° in the subtropical anticyclones, where the air diverges, some flowing equatorwards as the trade winds and some polewards as mid-latitude southwesterlies.

Air at the poles sinks owing to radiational cooling; the cold, dense air flows out from the polar anticyclones, eventually converging with the mid-latitude southwesterlies along the polar front. Here warm air ascends at the fronts and flows polewards at high levels, while the cold air moves equatorwards.

This approach successfully explains the ITCZ, the trade winds, the subtropical anticyclones, the polar anticyclones and the polar easterlies. It fails, however, to explain the mid-latitude westerlies which increase with height aloft.

The energetics of three-cell models are shown in diagrammatic form in Fig. 15.7. Differential heating of the earth-atmosphere system provides the potential energy for the general circulation, which is converted into kinetic energy of motion via the mean meridional (north-south) cells; the flows are deflected by the earth's rotation producing the mean zonal westerlies and easterlies, embedded within which there are disturbances. The Hadley cell and Polar cell can be explained on the principle that warm air rises and cold air sinks – these are known as *thermally direct* cells. The mid-latitude Ferrel cell is dynamically driven by the two bordering cells and is *thermally indirect*.

Fig. 15.7 The energetics of three-cell and wave theory models of the general circulation.

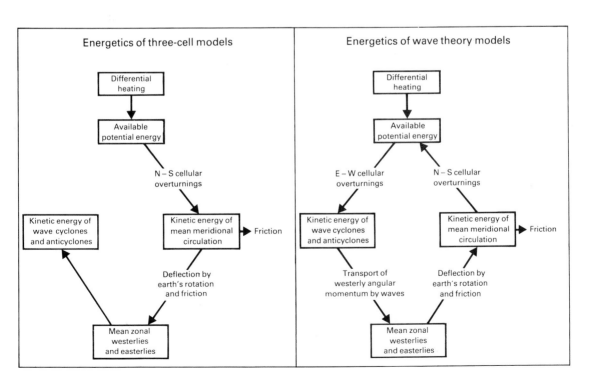

There are a number of problems with this approach: (1) it neglects longitudinal variations of the general circulation (such as the Indian monsoon) and land-sea differences – it emphasises latitudinal variations, but most of the major components have an important zonal (west-east) component; (2) it assumes that the disturbances producing the day-to-day weather (such as depressions and anticyclones) play a negligible role in the general circulation; (3) there should be a return flow above the mid-latitude westerlies with an easterly component – this does not happen as the westerlies increase with height; (4) the reality of the polar cell is doubtful; and (5) it cannot explain the existence and maintenance of the mid-latitude westerlies.

The wave theory approach

In 1951 Palmen had incorporated the presence of the mid-latitude westerlies and their disturbances, together with the upper westerly flow, into the three-cell model by modifying the configuration of the Ferrel cell. This provides a useful descriptive model of the general circulation, but it is not really successful in elucidating the basic mechanisms of the Ferrel cell.

An alternative approach to general circulation studies is provided by the 'modern' wave theory approach; this represents a *meteorological* approach. It assumes that the fundamental features of the atmospheric circulation of importance for energy transfers are the eddies and disturbances appearing on the daily weather charts. These are not extraneous 'noise' superimposed on the mean steady state, but important and integral parts of the general circulation. The emphasis within this approach is therefore on energy transfers (and momentum transfers) due to cyclones and anticyclones in the horizontal plane, rather than meridional cells in the vertical plane. This approach is much more successful in explaining the presence of the mid-latitude westerlies and the energy transfers within them than the three-cell approach.

In the mean state, there are belts of easterly winds in the tropics and polar regions – these are blowing against the direction of the earth's rotation in space and are acting, through surface friction, to slow down the earth's rate of rotation over time. In middle latitudes the prevailing westerlies are moving across the earth's surface in the same direction that the earth is rotating, and are therefore exerting a force (called a torque) to speed up the rate of rotation (see Fig. 15.8).

In order to understand how the mid-latitude westerlies are maintained, the angular momentum balance of the earth-atmosphere system must be considered. The absolute angular momentum of the earth and atmosphere remains constant over time. Since the rotation rate of the earth does not change, the atmosphere must also conserve its angular momentum.

In the *tropics*, where surface winds are easterly, the atmosphere is constantly gaining westerly angular momentum from the earth: friction at the surface tends to slow down the easterly winds over time, which can be considered as adding a westerly component to their motion. In *middle latitudes*, where the winds are westerly, the atmosphere must transfer westerly angular momentum to the earth (that is, through the action of surface friction the westerly winds exert a force or torque to speed up the earth in a westerly sense), as shown in Fig. 15.8. The contribution of the polar easterlies is minor, because the distance from

Fig. 15.8 A schematic diagram showing the transfers of westerly angular momentum within the atmosphere.

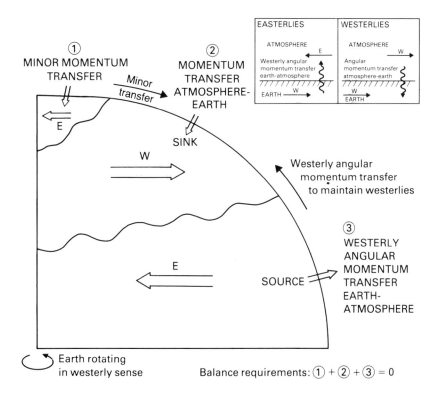

Earth rotating
in westerly sense

Balance requirements: ① + ② + ③ = 0

the earth's surface to the axis of rotation is only small in polar latitudes, the torques produced are only small, and thus they can be largely neglected. If friction is not to act to slow down the westerlies over time and bring them to a halt, and if the mid-latitude westerlies are continually to add westerly angular momentum to the earth, there must be a net transfer of westerly angular momentum within the atmosphere from the zones of easterlies to the zone of westerlies (see Fig. 15.8). Furthermore, the angular momentum transferred to the atmosphere from the earth in the easterlies must balance the angular momentum given to the earth by the westerlies if the angular momentum of the atmosphere is to remain constant.

The maximum transfer of westerly angular momentum occurs at the latitude separating the easterlies and westerlies at approximately 30°. The transfer across latitude 30° is performed by the flow within the large-scale horizontal waves and eddies in the atmospheric flow. Here both troughs and ridges in the upper flow, and the anticyclones at the surface, are tilted with a NE-SW axis. Figure 15.9 shows typical configurations of streamlines within a wave in the upper westerlies and within the surface circulation at 30°N, both having an axis tilted NE-SW (axes aligned NW-SE are extremely rare). Air moving north has a largely westerly component and therefore is transferring a large amount of westerly (angular) momentum; air moving south either has a weak westerly component (in the upper wave) or a weak easterly component (around the anticyclone). The sum of all the momentum transfers within the flow across the latitudinal circle is clearly a large westerly momentum transfer. It is this transfer which maintains the mid-latitude westerlies; such a transfer cannot possibly be achieved by the traditional three-cell model with circulations in the north-south (meridional) plane.

Fig. 15.9 Schematic horizontal streamlines within a typical wave in the upper westerlies and within the surface flow at 30° latitude around a subtropical anticyclone. Note the net transfer of westerly angular momentum northwards.

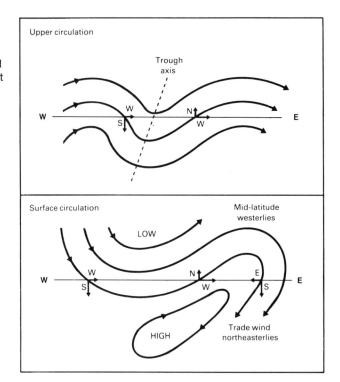

The emphasis in this approach is thus away from purely thermal mechanisms to explain the major winds, to dynamic considerations. The significant new concept here is that the energy source of the westerlies is the eddies – the cyclones and anticyclones; the meridional circulation gets its kinetic energy from the kinetic energy within the disturbances, rather than the reverse (as shown in Fig. 15.7). This is exactly the reverse to the energy cycle invoked for the three-cell approach.

In order to examine the relative importance of the transfer of energy polewards in the general circulation via the mean meridional overturnings in the vertical plane (the three-cell models) and the flux of energy in the horizontal plane arising from horizontal eddies within the atmosphere (the wave theory), three main approaches have been used.

1 Observational studies

Observational studies of the behaviour of the global circulation of the atmosphere using real surface and upper air data allowed detailed calculations to be made of the energy transfers, moisture fluxes and angular momentum transfers within the real atmosphere.

One of the most intensive studies ever made of the general circulation occurred during the Global Weather Experiment, which took place from December 1978 to November 1979 and involved all the member countries of the WMO. This period of intensive surveillance of the global atmosphere utilised all available data sources: the network of surface, upper air and ocean weather stations was extended; extra reports from ships, aircraft, drifting buoys and high-level balloons were used, together with data from five geostationary satellites (including Meteosat) and four polar orbiting weather satellites, with a view to collecting as much global data as possible for one year. The entire atmosphere of the earth and its oceans were observed in detail for the first time and a vast data set has been produced. This is still being analysed, but three interesting findings have already emerged from the project: (1) much lower pressures were observed in the southern hemisphere low pressure belt at 40°–60°S than had previously been estimated, with a stronger than normal westerly flow in the middle and upper troposphere; (2) the variability of synoptic-scale weather systems in time and space in the tropics was greater than expected; and (3) there are indications that the tropics may influence middle and high latitudes much faster and more substantially than had been assumed previously.

2 Laboratory models of the atmosphere (dishpan experiments)

If it is assumed that the two primary controls of the general circulation are the equator-to-pole temperature gradient and the rate of rotation of the earth, then it should be possible to gain insights into certain aspects of the behaviour of the atmosphere with experiments on rotating fluids under controlled laboratory conditions. In such experiments a circular dishpan of water (a fluid used to simulate the atmosphere), or an annulus (a deep column of water contained between two concentric cylinders of differing radii) is heated at its outer rim (representing the heat source at the equator) and cooled by ice in the centre (the pole). The container, with a typical diameter of some 30 cm, is rotated to simulate the rotation of the earth, and the resulting fluid motion is observed by putting aluminium powder on the surface of the water and monitoring its motion using time-lapse photography. A camera is mounted above the apparatus and rotates in synchronisation with the dishpan; when its shutter is opened for one second, the moving particles of white powder appear as streaks on the resultant photograph. If the temperature gradient across the dishpan is held constant, while varying the rate of rotation, it is possible to simulate the behaviour of the atmosphere at different latitudes.

With a constant temperature gradient across the fluid a range of different flow patterns is observed at different rotation rates, as shown in the examples of Fig. 15.10. At low rotations, a single convection centre is observed with the fluid flowing towards the warm rim, rising at the heat source and sinking in the centre – such a flow is analogous to the Hadley cell of low latitudes (where the Coriolis parameter is small). If the rotation rate is increased (1.21 radians/sec in Fig. 15.10) the flow develops three long waves, through which a flow similar to the westerly subtropical meanders. At high rotation rates, five long waves develop, which progress around the central axis (analogous to the polar front jet of middle latitudes) and if the rate is increased still further the wave forms break down and become chaotic. It would seem that the waves and the jet phenomena arise as an essential and natural feature for transferring thermal energy in such a rotating system – the influence of topography in stimulating such wave development may have been overstressed.

Among the features which have been simulated in such laboratory experiments are depressions, anticyclones, jet streams, mid-latitude westerlies, low-latitude easterlies and even frontal features. Measurements show that angular momentum is indeed transported by the waves from the easterlies to the westerlies and that the energy cycle proceeds as it does in the real atmosphere. The analogues occur despite

Fig. 15.10 Streak photographs revealing the flow in a series of rotating dishpan (annulus) experiments in which the rate of rotation was increased while the temperature gradient was held constant. Waves developed at higher rotation rates which became irregular for the highest rotation rates.

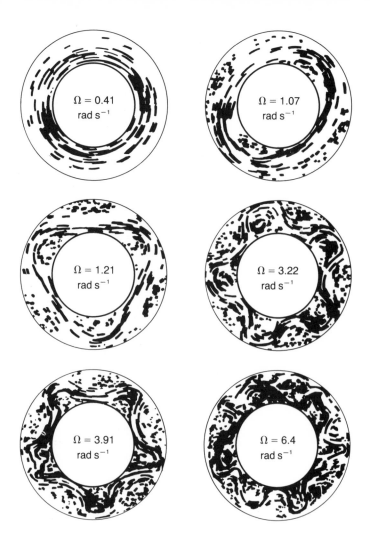

$\Omega = 0.41$ rad s^{-1}

$\Omega = 1.07$ rad s^{-1}

$\Omega = 1.21$ rad s^{-1}

$\Omega = 3.22$ rad s^{-1}

$\Omega = 3.91$ rad s^{-1}

$\Omega = 6.4$ rad s^{-1}

the fact that the experimental conditions differ from the real ones on earth in several respects: the fluid chosen is water (which is incompressible) rather than air (highly compressible); the dishpan is uniform and flat, whereas the earth's surface is curved and has land/sea contrasts; there are side walls at the rim of the dishpan, but none exist on earth; and there are no latent heat exchanges in the dishpan and no tropopause.

3 Numerical modelling of the atmosphere

As well as simulating the behaviour of the atmosphere using models in the laboratory, it is also possible to simulate the general circulation using numerical models with a computer. Such numerical models are a set of mathematical equations that represent the laws governing the behaviour of the atmosphere, arranged in a form suitable for solution by numerical methods. Such models have developed in recent years from the advances made in numerical weather forecasting by computer.

In simplified terms, if the state of the atmosphere (in terms of pressure, temperature, humidity, wind direction) is known both at the surface and at a number of other levels within the atmosphere for a given moment in time, then applying the laws which are known to govern atmospheric motion and behaviour, it should be possible to predict the state of the atmosphere for some future time (perhaps a minute or an hour ahead). Such laws include the laws of motion, the laws of thermodynamics, the hydrostatic equation and the principle of continuity within the atmosphere, expressed as equations capable of solution by numerical methods. Using the predicted state of the atmosphere as a base, one can then apply the laws again to predict the future state after another interval of time, then another, and so on. This is the basis of numerical weather forecasting which has developed since the 1950s.

Larger computers can now handle more data and solve the equations more quickly, so that circulation features at smaller and smaller levels of spatial and temporal resolution can be incorporated. Improvements in satellite technology have allowed temperatures and other parameters to be measured in remote areas of the globe from space, so that there are fewer data gaps in the global observing network. The development of numerical weather forecasting techniques has allowed a greater understanding of the physical processes governing weather and climate.

The long-term mean general circulation can be derived as the average state of the atmosphere derived from these numerical forecasts when run over sufficiently lengthy time periods. The mathematical models cannot yet treat all the relevant processes (particularly those operating at the meso-scale) in a satisfactory way, but progress is encouraging. The earth-atmosphere system is complex and full of interacting feedback processes. These processes act at a variety of scales in time and space. Mathematical models will never be able to include every process operating in the system; their main use is to try to simplify reality, and in particular to examine the contribution of particuar factors and processes. For example, such models have been used to assess the possible consequences of a doubling of CO_2 concentrations on the global circulation and global climate.

Conclusion

The earth-atmosphere system is complex; the behaviour of the global atmosphere is also complex. A full understanding of all the processes involved is beyond the scope of this book. Various approaches to the problem of the general circulation have been outlined. The main conclusion to be drawn from the enormous amount of research on the subject is summarised in Fig. 15.11 on page 158. This represents the contribution of the mean meridional circulation and eddy circulations to the mean annual poleward heat flux over the northern hemisphere. The mean meridional circulation (through the operation of the Hadley cell) makes the dominant contribution to the heat flux in the tropics (although the presence of disturbances within the mean flow is important). In middle latitudes the contribution of eddies (waves and disturbances within the zonal flow) is dominant both in terms of energy transfer (shown here) and angular momentum transfer. The three-cell approach is appropriate for the tropics, but the wave theory explains the basic features of the circulation in middle latitudes.

Fig. 15.11 Contributions of the mean meridional circulation and eddy circulations to the mean annual poleward heat flux.

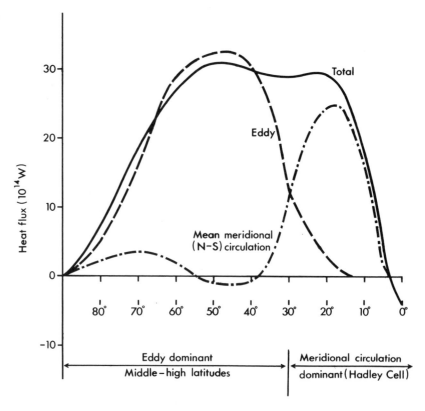

Further reading

Barrett, E.C. (1974) *Climatology from Satellites* (Methuen, London).
Barry, R.G. and Chorley, R.J. (1982) *Atmosphere, Weather and Climate* (Methuen, London).
Battan, L.J. (1984) *Fundamentals of Meteorology* (Prentice-Hall, London).
Boucher, K. (1974) *Global Climate* (English University Press, London).
Chandler, T.J. (1981) *Modern Meteorology and Climatology* (Nelson, Walton-on-Thames).
Day, J.A. and Sternes, G.L. (1970) *Climate and Weather* (Addison-Wesley, Reading, Mass., USA).
Fotheringham, R.R. (1979) *The Earth's Atmosphere Viewed from Space* (University of Dundee, Dundee).
Gribbin, J. (ed.) (1986) *The Breathing Planet* (Basil Blackwell, Oxford).
Lockwood, J.G. (1974) *World Climatology, an Environmental Approach* (Arnold, London).
McIlveen, J.F.R. (1986) *Basic Meteorology, A Physical Outline* (Van Nostrand Reinhold (UK), Wokingham).
McIntosh, D.H. and Thom, A.S. (1972) *Essentials of Meteorology* (Wykeham Publications, London).
Mason, B.J. (1975) *Clouds, Rain and Rainmaking* (Cambridge University Press, Cambridge).
Meteorological Office (1981) *Looking at the Weather, the Work of the Meteorological Office* (HMSO, London).
Neiburger, M., Edinger, J.G. and Bonner, W.D. (1982) *Understanding our Atmospheric Environment* (W.H. Freeman, San Francisco).
Pedgley, D.E. (1978) *A Course in Elementary Meteorology* (HMSO, London).
Riehl, H. (1979) *Climate and Weather in the Tropics* (Academic Press, London).
Riley, D. and Spolton, L. (1974) *World Weather and Climate* (Cambridge University Press, Cambridge).
Taylor, J.A. and Yates, R.A. (1967) *British Weather in Maps*, Macmillan, London.
Wallace, J.M. and Hobbs, P.V. (1977) *Atmospheric Science – An Introductory Survey* (Academic Press, London).

Index